THE TACTICAL TEACHER

PROVEN STRATEGIES TO
POSITIVELY INFLUENCE
STUDENT LEARNING &
CLASSROOM BEHAVIOR

DALE RIPLEY

Solution Tree | Press

a division of
Solution Tree

Copyright © 2022 by Solution Tree Press

Materials appearing here are copyrighted. With one exception, all rights are reserved. Readers may reproduce only those pages marked "Reproducible." Otherwise, no part of this book may be reproduced or transmitted in any form or by any means (electronic, photocopying, recording, or otherwise) without prior written permission of the publisher.

555 North Morton Street
Bloomington, IN 47404
800.733.6786 (toll free) / 812.336.7700
FAX: 812.336.7790

email: info@SolutionTree.com
SolutionTree.com

Visit **go.SolutionTree.com/behavior** to download the free reproducibles in this book.

Printed in the United States of America

Library of Congress Cataloging-in-Publication Data

Names: Ripley, Dale, 1948- author.
Title: The tactical teacher : proven strategies to positively influence
    student learning and classroom behavior / Dale Ripley.
Description: Bloomington : Solution Tree Press, [2021] | Includes
    bibliographical references and index.
Identifiers: LCCN 2021047294 (print) | LCCN 2021047295 (ebook) | ISBN
    9781952812590 (Paperback) | ISBN 9781952812606 (ebook)
Subjects: LCSH: School psychology--Methodology. | Influence (Psychology) |
    Behavior modification. | Classroom management.
Classification: LCC LB1027.55 .R57 2021 (print) | LCC LB1027.55 (ebook) |
    DDC 370.15--dc23/eng/20211106
LC record available at https://lccn.loc.gov/2021047294
LC ebook record available at https://lccn.loc.gov/2021047295

Solution Tree

Jeffrey C. Jones, CEO
Edmund M. Ackerman, President

Solution Tree Press

President and Publisher: Douglas M. Rife
Associate Publisher: Sarah Payne-Mills
Managing Production Editor: Kendra Slayton
Editorial Director: Todd Brakke
Art Director: Rian Anderson
Copy Chief: Jessi Finn
Content Development Specialist: Amy Rubenstein
Acquisitions Editor: Sarah Jubar
Proofreader: Elisabeth Abrams
Text and Cover Designer: Laura Cox
Editorial Assistants: Charlotte Jones, Sarah Ludwig, and Elijah Oates

This book is dedicated to you, the teacher who chooses to pick up the heavy burden of working with your school's most challenging students; the teacher who works hard at establishing a relationship with even the most challenging students; the teacher who is prepared to help those students who need help the most; the teacher who strives to have a positive impact on the lives of every student.

I honor you and your work with this book.

ACKNOWLEDGMENTS

I would be unable to write a book such as this without the assistance and guidance of the many friends, colleagues, and students who led me to this place in my thinking.

First, I would like to thank my friend and partner Rae Gajadhar for her comprehensive edit of this book's first draft.

I would also like to thank Dan Ripley, who provided a response to each chapter's first draft and, thus, saved me from embarrassing myself when I gave subsequent drafts to other educators to review.

My thanks to the master teachers who reviewed the first draft of the book in its entirety: Garrick Burron, Tara Crouter, Bob Gagnon, Kathy Higgins, Heather Jamieson, Larry Rankin, Ron Schlender, and Robyn Shewchuk. They graciously shared many stories and strategies that they used throughout their careers, and many of these are included in this book. The stories, opinions, and insights of these educators have served to make this work so much better than anything I could have written on my own.

I would also like to acknowledge the assistance of the University of Alberta library services. Their online databases allowed me access to the primary sources of much of the research contained in this book.

My thanks to Amy Rubenstein, content development specialist with Solution Tree. Her competence and positivity made the hard work of the initial restructuring of this book all the more pleasant. I would also like to thank Todd Brakke, editorial director with Solution Tree, who saw the potential of this book to positively impact the lives of so many teachers and their students. Thank you for your enthusiasm, your editorial expertise, and your great taste in music and movies.

Last, I would like to acknowledge the thousands of students whom I have taught since the 1970s. I believe that I learned the most about teaching from you. You showed me what worked, what didn't, and what worked some of the time but not all of the time. You were patient and supportive, and you taught me what it means to have the heart of a teacher.

Herein lies a lesson for all teachers who strive to be excellent and continually improve their teaching practice so as to better serve their students. You cannot be masterful at teaching if you try to go it alone. *Great teaching is a team sport!*

Solution Tree Press would like to thank the following reviewers:

Jenna Fanshier
Sixth-Grade Teacher
Hesston Middle School
Hesston, Kansas

Charles Ames Fischer
Education Consultant
Decatur, Tennessee

Caitlin Fox
Instructor
Red Deer College
Red Deer, Alberta, Canada

Whitney Freije
Instructional Coach and Mathematics Teacher
Windsor Central School District
Windsor, New York

Kelly Hilliard
Mathematics Teacher
McQueen High School
Reno, Nevada

Alex Kajitani
Mathematics Teacher
MultiplicationNation.com
San Diego, California

Neil Plotnick
Special Education and Computer Science Teacher
Everett High School
Everett, Massachusetts

Joshua Ray
Principal
East Pointe Elementary School
Greenwood, Arkansas

Jenna Sage
Author and Coach
Tampa, Florida

Neil Wrona
Social Studies Teacher and Technology Facilitator
Youth in Transition School
Baltimore, Maryland

Visit **go.SolutionTree.com/behavior** to
download the free reproducibles in this book.

TABLE OF CONTENTS

Reproducible pages are in italics.

ABOUT THE AUTHOR

 **Dale Ripley, PhD,** teaches in the Departments of Elementary and Secondary Education at the University of Alberta. Dale has taught at the elementary, junior high and middle school, high school, and college and university levels since 1972. Additionally, he served as a principal at the elementary and secondary school levels and as the superintendent for a small rural school district near Edmonton, Alberta, Canada, as well as a large urban school district in Edmonton.

Although Dale has worked in high-performing schools located in affluent areas, his first love has always been working in schools where many of the students were considered "at risk" or "challenging." For this reason, he chose to spend most of his teaching career working in inner-city schools, or what many refer to as high-needs or priority schools. In 2009, Dale asked to establish a high school on a First Nations Reserve, where he then taught for six years, taking high school graduation rates to an unprecedented level, with many of his students going on to graduate with post-secondary degrees.

In 2019, Dale wrote *The Successful Teacher's Survival Kit: 83 Simple Things That Successful Teachers Do to Thrive in the Classroom* in response to the myriad questions that his pre-service teacher-education students posed in regard to how to deal with the day-to-day practical problems and issues novice teachers face.

Dale received his bachelor's and master's degrees in education from the University of Alberta and then returned to attain his doctorate in curriculum design and educational leadership.

To book Dale Ripley for professional development, contact pd@SolutionTree.com.

INTRODUCTION

The central premise of this book is that you *can* change the negative behaviors of many of the most challenging students you will ever teach. I do not promise that this will be easy, nor do I promise this will happen 100 percent of the time, and I do not promise that it will happen quickly. I do, however, promise that it is possible—in fact, it is very likely—and this book will show you how.

In *To Sell Is Human*, Daniel Pink (2012) tells a story about Rosser Reeves, an American advertising executive who was one of the first advertisers to create television ads for presidential candidates in the 1950s. The story Pink (2012) relates is a powerful example of how the tools of persuasion, properly applied, can work so effectively to change human behaviors:

> One afternoon, Reeves and a colleague were having lunch in Central Park. On the way back to their Madison Avenue office, they encountered a man sitting in the park, begging for money. He had a cup for donations and beside it was a sign, handwritten on cardboard, that read: I am blind. Unfortunately for the man, the cup contained only a few coins. His attempts to move others to donate money were coming up short.
>
> Reeves thought he knew why. He told his colleague something to the effect of: "I bet I can dramatically increase the amount of money that guy is raising simply by adding four words to his sign."

> Reeves's skeptical friend took him up on the wager. Reeves then introduced himself to the beleaguered man, explained that he knew something about advertising, and offered to change the sign ever so slightly to increase donations. The man agreed. Reeves took a marker and added his four words, and he and his friend stepped back to watch.
>
> Almost immediately, a few people dropped coins into the man's cup. Other people soon stopped, talked to the man, and plucked dollar bills from their wallets. Before long, the cup was running over with cash, and the once sad-looking blind man, feeling his bounty, beamed.
>
> What four words did Reeves add? *It is springtime and.* The sign now read:
>
> It is springtime, and I am blind. (pp. 133–134)

This is an example of how subtle strategies, which I call *soft tactics*, can have an enormous impact on perceptions and behaviors.

As educators, many of us have faced situations where no matter what we try, we simply cannot seem to change these students' behaviors. Students who fit this description often don't *seem* to care much about their own learning, and their behaviors in the classroom often have a profoundly negative effect on teaching and learning. I've been a teacher since 1972, much of that time in circumstances where educators described many students as being "challenging" or, in more extreme cases, "at risk" of dropping out of school. Even when I was teaching in more mainstream schools, there were typically one or two students in my classes who were not interested in school; as a result, their behaviors were often disruptive. I found that in most such instances, there were ways to connect with these students and to have a positive impact on their attitudes and their behaviors.

This book is based on extensive research in the fields of influence and persuasion as well as my decades of experience in K–12 education, much of it working with students considered at risk. It presents a range of influence and persuasion strategies and illustrates how K–12 teachers and administrators can use specific strategies as tools to positively impact the attitudes and behaviors of all students, even the most challenging ones. You will learn how to be tactical in your approach to students by exploring what psychology teaches about effective influence tactics, how game designers use payoff strategies to get people to keep playing, the techniques highly successful sales and advertising people use to persuade others to do what they want them to do, and even how professional hostage negotiators ensure peaceful outcomes. In the following sections, I explore the importance of influence tactics and how I've crafted my approach to applying them to students' benefit. I then outline how I've structured and organized this book to help you do the same.

TACTICS AND INFLUENCE

I've dedicated most of this book to the exploration of soft tactics and how teachers and administrators can effectively use them in a classroom. In *Influence: Mastering Life's Most Powerful Skill*, Kenneth Brown (2013) defines *soft tactics* as those that support a target's autonomy:

> They attempt to get someone to think or act in a certain way by making that alternative more appealing than others. These tactics include attempting to persuade with reason or with

emotion, complimenting the target (ingratiation), and offering an exchange. (p. 76)

In other words, soft tactics work to get the student to cooperate with you *willingly*. Soft tactics are very effective in positively influencing student behavior and attitudes over an extended period of time, and they're quite different from *hard tactics*, which Brown (2013) describes as an "attempt to get someone to think or do something specific by metaphorically pushing them in that direction. These tactics include making reference to formal authority, building a coalition, and applying pressure" (p. 76). A teacher who announces to a student, "You should do what I tell you because I'm the teacher," or a teacher who threatens to send a student to the principal's office or to call home is using hard tactics. As you will discover in chapter 14 (page 171), these strategies can sometimes be effective in getting students to comply in the short term, but they seldom have any positive long-term effect.

Although I use examples from a variety of contexts and sources, I examine the tactics and techniques in this book primarily through the lens of classroom teachers. You will see how effective these tactics are in a school context, with students from elementary to high school, even with those students who are the most challenging. Through real-life examples and the application of a wide range of research, you will learn various strategies to effectively influence the students in your classes to become cooperative and successful in school.

Teachers and administrators who read this book and utilize even a fraction of the tactics described herein will see a significant improvement in their ability to positively impact student behaviors and achievement. To be clear, this is not a book about *classroom management* but one about behavior and influence. While there are certainly some strategies included that can work for an entire class, I mean for you to use most of the strategies I describe with an individual student or with a small group of students.

As well, when you read this book's strategies, you will likely find some that immediately attract you; you will see a natural fit with both your teaching style and the students you teach. There will be other strategies that you may instinctively dismiss as unworkable for you and your teaching situation. Some beginning teachers may look at a number of these tactics and find gems, while a teacher with extensive experience may see these same strategies as being somewhat obvious. This is understandable and expected. Teaching is contextual, and every teacher and every situation are unique. You will find the ideas in this book range from relatively simple and low risk to much more sophisticated and complex (and sometimes high risk), and you should implement only those tactics that you feel comfortable with—the tactics that you believe have a high chance of success in your particular teaching situation. My goal is to give you a smorgasbord of persuasion and influence tactics that can work with students—when used appropriately. Only you know which of these tactics is most likely to work with a particular student in your unique teaching context. *The choice is yours.*

At this point, you might ask, "Why should I take on the burden of trying to work with some of the most challenging students in my classroom?" Certainly, it is much easier to write them off or throw them out of class when their behaviors go too far. Teaching students who come to school well-fed, clean, and eager to learn is certainly a lot of fun. But it is akin to a doctor telling their patients to only visit when they are feeling healthy. Just as it's the sickest patients who need a doctor the most, it is the challenging students who need you the most. I argue it is one of the highest possible goals for teachers to assume the responsibility for teaching the most difficult students in their classes. And while doing this work can certainly be a heavy burden to carry, please don't dismiss doing it because it is difficult. As teachers, we all need something heavy to carry. It not only makes us stronger, but there is solace to be found here as well. You may say to yourself, "I may not teach the most engaging classes, and I may not make the most creative assessments, but at least I refuse to give up on the most difficult students. That alone gives me value as a teacher."

Inspiration is an important motivator for all teachers. For example, I keep a starfish hanging on the wall beside my desk. I do this because it reminds me of the following story—a popular adaptation of "The Star Thrower" by Loren Eiseley (1969):

> A man was walking along a deserted beach at sunset. As he walked, he could see a young boy in the distance. As he drew nearer, he noticed that the boy kept bending down, picking something up and throwing it into the water. Time and again, the boy kept hurling things into the ocean. As the man approached even closer, he was able to see that the boy was picking up starfish that had been washed up on the beach and, one at a time, he was throwing them back into the water.
>
> The man asked the boy what he was doing. The young boy paused, looked up, and replied, "Throwing starfish into the ocean. The tide has washed them up onto the beach, and they can't return to the sea by themselves. When the sun gets high, they will die unless I throw them back into the water."
>
> "But," said the man, "you can't possibly save them all. There are thousands of starfish on this beach, and this must be happening on hundreds of beaches along the coast. You can't possibly make a difference."
>
> The boy smiled, bent down and picked up another starfish, and as he threw it back into the sea, he replied, "I made a difference to that one."

In *Beyond Order: Twelve More Rules for Life*, psychology professor Jordan B. Peterson (2021) states, "Work as hard as you possibly can on at least one thing and see what happens" (p. 181). I would paraphrase this, work as hard as you possibly can with at least one challenging student, and see what happens. If you choose to pick up the heavy burden of working with one (perhaps two?) of the more difficult students in your classes, in doing so, you will have established a close relationship with one of the most fundamental virtues of the teaching profession: to help those most in need of your help. I invite the teacher in you to call on your better angels and ask them to help you accept the responsibility for showing some of your most difficult students that there is a different path they can choose. It is in accepting responsibilities such as this that teachers realize their greatest potential for engaging in rewarding work—making a difference to that one student.

ABOUT THIS BOOK

I have structured this book into seventeen short chapters, each one focusing on a particular motivational or influence strategy or the background information necessary to understand why these strategies work. I did this so that teachers and administrators can easily return to the specific chapter or chapters that focus on the influence strategies they want to utilize in their practice. Please also note that because family structures vary in significant and critical ways, I use the term *caregivers* throughout to refer to any adult person acting in a parental capacity for a student.

I've organized this book into three parts: (1) Natural Selection and Student Behavior, (2) Soft and Hard Tactics, and (3) Ethics and Unseen Motivators. You cannot make effective use of this book's soft and hard tactics without understanding why your students behave the way they do, which is why chapter 1 kicks off the first part of the book by exploring student behavior through the lens of natural selection and how it impacts the way people view their world and how they respond to a variety of motivators. Chapter 2 helps develop an understanding of student behavior by taking a close look at how the hardwiring of natural selection plays out in the way students behave and react to their peers and to their teachers in schools. You will understand more deeply why students behave the way they do and how you can use the hardwiring of natural selection to influence more positive student behaviors.

In part 2, you begin your exploration of tactics that enable you to use your understanding of students to positively influence their classroom behavior. This part includes chapters 3–15, with each of the following chapters highlighting a specific group of influence tactics.

- Chapter 3 looks at the ways in which a student's self-image governs their behaviors. We then look at soft tactics that influence your ability to positively impact a student's self-image.

- Chapter 4 examines how all people are hardwired to want to return favors to people who have done something for them. It shows how to utilize the rule of reciprocity in your classroom to establish effective working relationships with students.

- Chapter 5 demonstrates clearly how much better students learn and how much more cooperative they are when they like their teacher. This chapter shows you how to get your students to like *and* respect you and how student achievement improves in the process.

- Chapter 6 shows you how important it is that your students know you are committed to them and their learning. It also explores the substantial power of commitment over the long haul in getting students to change their negative behaviors into positive ones.

- Chapter 7 takes a look at common classroom dynamics that most often go unnoticed by teachers and students alike. It highlights how, by becoming aware of these dynamics and utilizing their hidden power, teachers can subtly but effectively improve student behaviors and achievement.

- Chapter 8 explores strategies for persuasion, using models and approaches the FBI developed over many decades to successfully negotiate a positive end to high-stakes confrontations; it describes how you can effectively use these same tactics to positively influence students.

- Chapter 9 examines the subtle but powerful ways in which the physical environment of the classroom—what students see, hear, and smell—can move them in the direction you want them to go.

- Chapter 10 looks at the basic desire of all people to avoid losing something they already possess, which is called *loss aversion*. This chapter flips loss aversion on its head in the classroom and shows how you can use this to effectively motivate your students.

- Chapter 11 explores the power of words to move students in the direction you want. From the power of rhyme and repetition to enhanced recall to the contrast principle that we looked at earlier in this introduction with the story of the blind man and his sign, this chapter shows you powerful ways to use words to achieve your goals in the classroom.

- Chapter 12 investigates the upsides and downsides of using rewards in the classroom to influence students. You will see what kinds of rewards work and which types don't, when to use rewards and when to avoid them, and in what kinds of teaching situations rewards work best.

- Chapter 13 emphasizes the power and importance of first impressions. It shows how to make a great first impression on students through the conscious presentation of yourself as a teacher and the intentional staging of the physical environment of your classroom. By implementing the practices discussed here, you will positively influence your students the moment they enter your classroom for the first time.

- Chapter 14 looks at the hard tactics teachers sometimes resort to in order to change student behaviors. While there are certainly situations that call for the use of hard tactics, this chapter shows the downside of using them as your default strategies on a continuing basis.

- Chapter 15 delves into the question of when you should attempt to influence a student. You will learn that a great strategy that's poorly timed will likely fail. It also shows you under what circumstances it is best to attempt to change a student's attitude or behaviors and what you need to consider in making decisions around when you will try to influence a student.

Part 3 wraps up the book with two chapters that explore the ethics of influence and hidden factors that influence teacher motivation with regard to students. Chapter 16 looks at the power of the persuasive tools you have learned and asks you to reflect on how you intend to use them. Like all tools, you can use the tactics of influence and persuasion that this book explores to help both students and yourself, but it's also possible to use them for purely self-serving ends. This chapter will help you conduct your own personal ethics check to ensure you are on the right path. Chapter 17 examines the impact teacher preconceptions can have on student achievement as well as the effect that physical appearance can have on your teaching and assessment practices. By highlighting and confronting some common ways students can subconsciously influence their teachers, you empower yourself to be more fair-minded with your students, making your use of the influence tactics in this book that much more powerful.

At the end of each chapter, there is a "Reflective Practice" reproducible to help you think about and apply the ideas and strategies explored in each chapter. Use this to engage with critical questions and try out new practices with your students. A closing epilogue offers some final guidance as you reflect on what you've learned in this book. While I strongly recommend that you start this book by reading chapters 1 and 2, you can read chapters 3–13, which all discuss soft tactics, in any order. Finally, I've included an appendix with information about two ways to help you in your tactical approach to students: the Newspaper of the Self and the Adopt-a-Kid program.

As you begin your adventure of reading this book and implementing some of these strategies with your students, know that you will unquestionably make a positive difference in the learning and the behaviors that occur in your classroom. Both you and your students will benefit from your efforts!

NATURAL SELECTION AND STUDENT BEHAVIOR

WHY YOUR STUDENTS BEHAVE THE WAY THEY DO

The internal and external factors that motivate our behavior as human beings are complex and often mysterious to us. About this, Pink (2009a) writes:

> As humans formed more complex societies, bumping up against strangers and needing to cooperate in order to get things done, an operating system based purely on biological drive was inadequate. In fact, sometimes we needed ways to restrain this drive—to prevent me from swiping your dinner and you from stealing my spouse. (p. 16)

Imagine you are in a large room. There is one door through which you can exit this room. Between you and the exit, there are approximately thirty predators. They are all staring at you. How do you feel? Seriously, before you continue reading, please answer the question: How do you feel?

We will revisit this question later in the chapter, but I am going to surmise that it doesn't feel very good. And why should it? I also suspect that you felt threatened because, if you are like any normal human being, you would prefer to survive.

This chapter lays a foundation for the rest of this book by establishing perspective about why students behave the way they do. We'll first consider just who your students are in the classroom and then use that necessary perspective to examine the impact of natural selection on human behavior generally. We'll then reflect on how natural selection specifically influences student behavior.

A NATURAL HISTORY IN YOUR CLASSROOM

To date, I have taught approximately ten thousand students, and, like most teachers, I have described them using numerous adjectives. For many years, I used descriptors such as *little kids*, *my babies*, *teenagers*, *young men and women*, and the like to describe students at various grade levels. However, that changed when I first read Ralph Waldo Emerson's (1844/1903) phrase, "First be a good animal" (p. 124). Was Emerson correct? Should people (and students) properly be thought of as a kind of animal? What did that say about my students? Then it struck me: What did that say about *me* as their teacher? If we all were *a kind of animal*, just what kind of animal were we?

Poet and naturalist Diane Ackerman offered an answer to that question, albeit quite an unsettling one. In *A Natural History of the Senses*, Ackerman (1990) describes the evolutionary development of human senses. In describing the evolution of our eyes, Ackerman (1990) tells us to take a good look at ourselves in a mirror, describing what we see looking back at us:

> The face that pins you with its double gaze reveals a chastening secret: *you are looking into a predator's eyes.* Most predators have eyes set right on the front of their heads, so they can use binocular vision to sight and track their prey. . . .Prey, on the other hand, have eyes at the sides of their heads, because what they really need is peripheral vision, so they can tell when something is sneaking up behind them. Something like us. If it's "a jungle out there" in the wilds of the city, it may be partly because the streets are jammed with devout predators. (p. 229; emphasis added)

This view can apply—at least to some degree—to our classrooms and our schools. Given our evolutionary heritage and genetic hardwiring, I find myself surprised at times that there isn't *more* bullying and violence in schools than there actually is.

All of us have violent instincts within us because all of us have evolved from predators. While we don't often like to think of ourselves and our ancestors this way, this is indeed the case. As religious scholar Reza Aslan (2017) reminds us:

> We need to remember that for nearly two and a half million years of our evolution—more than 90 percent of our existence as hominids— we foraged the earth for our food. We were predators, stalking through forests and plains, competing for prey with beasts far more adept than we were—though not nearly as clever. This experience as hunter-gatherers shaped and defined us. (p. 58)

The question for teachers in modern classrooms thus becomes: How might those predator instincts manifest themselves? While students do not hunt one another for food, violence does show itself in many other forms, and students do prey on one another. Face-to-face bullying, cyberbullying, behaving passive-aggressively, and gossiping are all more socially acceptable than stalking and killing, but all of these behaviors are nonetheless forms of predatory violence that take place in schools.

Please pause now and think about the question I asked you at the beginning of this chapter: How did you feel when you imagined yourself in a room filled with predators that were all staring at you? This is not the only, or usual, way of looking at a classroom, but it's a valid perspective nonetheless. Can we view people— in this instance, students—as animals? And not only as animals but as *predators*? Let's take a closer look at what such a perspective may reveal to us and how this new view may help us understand and more successfully work with our student predators.

THE IMPACT OF NATURAL SELECTION ON HUMAN BEHAVIOR

On December 27, 1831, a twenty-one-year-old naturalist by the name of Charles Darwin boarded a ship called the *HMS Beagle* (Desmond, n.d.). Its planned two-year voyage lasted for almost five years. As the *Beagle* traveled around the world, mapping various places, Darwin gathered an astonishing collection of plant and animal specimens from the various sites the *Beagle* visited. When he left on that voyage, young Charles was still planning to be a clergyman. When he returned, he was an established naturalist who had in his mind the genesis of a theory that would forever change the way people thought about themselves and their world. He called his theory *natural selection*.

Darwin's (1958) *On the Origin of Species by Means of Natural Selection, or the Preservation of Favoured Races in the Struggle for Life* was first published in 1859. In the introduction to his book, Darwin (1958) describes his theory:

> As many more individuals of each species are born than can possibly survive; and as, consequently, there is a frequently recurring struggle for existence, it follows that any being, if it vary however slightly in any manner profitable to itself, under the complex and sometimes varying conditions of life, will have a better chance of surviving, and thus be *naturally selected.* From the strong principle of inheritance, any selected variety will tend to propagate its new and modified form. (p. 29; emphasis added)

In *The Moral Animal: Why We Are the Way We Are*, journalist Robert Wright (1995) describes natural selection in simpler terms:

> All the theory of natural selection says is the following: If within a species there is variation among individuals in their hereditary traits, and some traits are more conducive to survival and reproduction than others, then those traits will become more widespread with the population. The result is that the species' aggregate pools of hereditary traits changes. (p. 23)

Not that long ago, many thought that evolution would have to remain an unprovable theory because the changes in organisms that natural selection proposed simply took so long to occur as to be well beyond the scope of scientific experimentation. That has changed. We have direct observations of species that have evolved quickly over extremely short periods of time. For example, author Brendan Koerner (2019) tells us:

> During the second half of the 19th century, the predominant color of England's peppered moths had steadily shifted from mostly white to almost entirely black. . . . Darwin's disciples came to suspect that natural selection was at play. As England had become more urban, moths who possessed the rare mutation for black pigmentation appeared to enjoy a fitness advantage over their white peers. (p. 77)

Koerner (2019) writes that experiments conducted by Oxford University's Bernard Kettlewell in the 1950s showed *why* these black-colored moths had adapted so quickly. Kettlewell released hundreds of white and black moths and tracked their fate, finding that species under intense environmental pressures can evolve quickly, in years rather than millennia (as cited in Koerner, 2019).

Evolutionary biologists are investigating how many different species are evolving quickly in order to adapt to changes in their urban environment brought about by cars, garbage, construction, and so on. What they have discovered are rapid evolutionary changes taking place in urban-dwelling lizards, ants, spiders, mosquitos,

pigeons, snails, swans, and more (Koerner, 2019). Writing for *National Geographic*, Dina Fine Maron (2018) finds that a large percentage of African elephants is now born without tusks, an evolutionary defense against poachers. Clearly, Darwin was on to something.

It doesn't stop with these examples. In *Origin Story: A Big History of Everything*, historian David Christian (2018) looks even deeper than individual species, at *individual cells*, for what motivates our behaviors:

> The spooky thing about life is that, though the inside of each cell looks like pandemonium—a sort of mud-wrestling contest involving a million molecules—whole cells give the impression of acting with purpose. Something inside each cell seems to drive it, as if it were working its way through a to-do list. The to-do list is simple: (1) stay alive despite entropy and unpredictable surroundings; and (2) make copies of myself that can do the same thing. And so on from cell to cell, and generation to generation. Here, in the seeking out of some outcomes and the avoidance of others, are the origins of desire, caring, purpose, ethics, even love. (p. 76)

The significance of all this, as biologist Bill Sullivan (2019) argues, is that we, as teachers, would be foolish to underestimate the power that genes play in shaping student behaviors. Sullivan (2019) explains how hidden biological forces impact our behaviors both at a predetermined genetic level and from lived environmental factors that affect our genes, concluding:

> Evolutionary psychologists remind us that at our core, virtually everything we do emerges from a subconscious urge to survive and reproduce our genes, or lend support to others (such as family) who carry genes like our own. . . . The truth is, every human behavior—from addiction to attraction to anxiety—is tethered to a genetic anchor. (p. 20)

Knowing that many of your students' feelings, thoughts, and actions are tied to their *genetic anchors* enables you to devise ways to structure your classrooms and your interactions with students to nudge them in the directions you want them to go.

HOW NATURAL SELECTION INFLUENCES STUDENT BEHAVIOR

For teachers, it's vital to understand how natural selection can provide us with insight into students' fundamental nature (not to mention our own). Since students, like all of us, are a product of natural selection, and since the traits they possess and exhibit are a result of these traits being conducive to survival and reproduction as natural selection claims, it makes sense that you need to understand the nature of these characteristics if you want to know how to successfully influence your students. By understanding their nature more completely, you will be able to understand more fully and more deeply why your students think, feel, and act the way they do. And, if you find their behaviors to be undesirable or disruptive, you will be much better able to determine effective ways to change them.

An important component of understanding natural selection's role in student behavior starts with your own thinking. Once you start looking at students' actions and feelings through the lens of natural selection, they begin to look different, and you will discover useful insights into what lies behind these actions and feelings—insights that will help you understand what is really going on and insights that will help you change behaviors you see as undesirable.

For example, we know human beings are social animals who normally live in groups. Living in a cooperative group (terms such as *tribe*, *band*, or *clan* apply here) greatly enhanced one's chances of survival on the ancient plains of Africa. The value that we place on the opinions of others has its genesis from this past. Rolf Dobelli (2013), a Swiss author and entrepreneur, reminds us of the critical importance of belonging to a group:

> Belonging to a group was necessary for survival. Reproduction, defense, and hunting large animals—all these were impossible tasks for individuals to achieve alone. . . . In short, *our lives depended on and revolved around others, which*

explains why we are so obsessed with our fellow humans today. (p. 109; emphasis added)

In *Origin Story*, Christian (2018) makes the argument that cooperation in a group and the size of our brains went hand-in-hand:

> To live successfully with other members of your species, you have to keep track of the constantly changing relationships among family, friends, and enemies. Who's up and who's down? Who's friendly and who's not? Who owes me favors, and who am I in debt to? These are computational tasks whose complexity increases exponentially as groups get larger. . . . Close observation of primate societies shows that if you get these social calculations wrong, you'll probably eat less well, be less well protected, get bullied or beaten up more often, and lower your chances of being healthy and having healthy children. So sociability, cooperation, and brainpower seem to have evolved together in the history of primates. (p. 160)

If we look at what Christian (2018) wrote and apply it to our students, this statement might read:

> *To work successfully with other students in your class, you have to keep track of the constantly changing relationships among your classmates. Who's up, and who's down? Who's friendly, and who's not? Who owes me favors, and whom am I in debt to? If you get these social calculations wrong, you'll probably be less well protected, get bullied or victimized more often, and lower your chances of feeling safe and welcome in your class.*

With the advent of modern brain imaging, we have very specific measures of just how powerful this need to be connected with other people is. Jean M. Twenge (2017), a psychologist who specializes in generational differences, describes how ancient hunter-gatherers exiled from their tribe often died from lack of food and how that experience lives on even now in how we respond to social acceptance and rejection, noting,

"Neuroscientists have found that when people are left out of a game by other players, the brain region involved in *physical pain* is activated" (p. 89; emphasis added).

To survive, early humans had to live in a group, know their place within the group, learn how to navigate the complexities of other group members' wants and emotions, and contribute in such a way that the group chose to keep them as one of its members. Why? Because living in a group—and being seen as someone who mattered to the group—greatly enhanced one's chances of survival. To be banished was almost certain death. There were predators out there who wanted to kill you—some walked on four legs, others on two.

While survival in those times often meant actual physical survival, in today's classrooms, social survival is almost as important. Your students are hardwired to need and desire the approval and acceptance of their group. Why? Because their distant ancestors needed this same approval and acceptance in order to survive, and those ancestors passed this trait on to you and to the students who inhabit your classroom. Belonging to a group is an essential part of what constitutes being a normal human being.

As teachers, when we look at student behaviors, one of the things we learn very early in our careers is that students generally behave quite differently when they are alone than when they are with their friends. For example, *National Geographic*'s David Dobbs (2011) penned an article stating that teenagers generally do *not* take more risks than adults. Rather, *teenagers weigh risks and rewards differently than adults do*, and the major variable in their calculations is whether they are with friends—members of *their group*. In the article, Dobbs (2011) describes a study in which teenage boys are tasked with using a driving simulator to drive across town in as little time as possible while still obeying the traffic laws. The simulation added time for infractions such as speeding or running a red light. When placed in the driving simulators *by themselves*, teenage boys took risks at about the same rate as the adults did. However, when the teenagers' friends were brought into the room to watch, these young drivers took *twice as many risks*

getting across town as they had when driving unobserved by their friends (Dobbs, 2011).

Why? Because for the students, the payoff had changed. The reward of obtaining their friends' approval for risky behaviors far outweighed the risk of losing time and driving dangerously. They hadn't suddenly become poor drivers. Rather, they now weighed risk and reward differently, *just as natural selection had encouraged them to do*. They wanted the approval of their group members.

Natural selection teaches us that our ancestors, the ones who sought and obtained the approval of the group, had a much greater chance to survive and reproduce. This trait—wanting to belong to a group and have the approval of the group—was passed along via those who survived and reproduced for hundreds of thousands of years. The poet John Donne (1624) expressed it this way, "No [person] is an island entire of itself; every [person] is a piece of the continent."

In 1943, Abraham Maslow published his now-famous theory on the hierarchy of human needs in which our need to belong came just after physical and safety needs were met. This is one of the reasons why in-school suspensions, in which a student is placed in some form of isolation to do their work, can be so effective. When this happens, the student is no longer a member of their class community, and that feeling of being disconnected, of being alone, can be very unpleasant.

While many people like to think that we as a species have evolved in very significant ways since moving out of caves thousands of years ago, many of these changes have been external—the veneer of modern civilization. As Stephen Hawking (2018) reminds us, "There has been relatively little change in human DNA in the last 10,000 years" (pp. 160–161). One such remnant from our distant past we can see in modern classrooms is what psychologist and economist Daniel Kahneman (2011a) terms the *focusing illusion*. Kahneman (2011a) posits that when people focus intently on something, the object of their focus takes on a disproportionate degree of importance in their lives. Think about how important it would have been for our ancestors to be aware of what was going on around them as they hunted and gathered on the savanna (a mixed woodland-grass-land ecosystem) hundreds of thousands of years ago. If they weren't focused, if they let their attention wander, they might quickly turn from hunter to hunted.

Present-day examples abound. Think about the last time you watched a movie that you found really engrossing—you were *in* the film; you had left your daily world behind. Or, think about avid sports fans watching the clock run down in the final minutes of an extremely close hockey or football game. There is nothing else in their world during those moments except the desire to see their team win. Time remaining, their team's performance, the score—these are all that exist during those final moments of the big game. Essentially, what Kahneman (2011a) is saying is that nothing in life is quite as important as the thing you are thinking about *while you are thinking about it*. This is the focusing illusion.

And it goes deeper. Kahneman (2011b) describes in great detail the two systems which we use to think, which he calls *System 1* and *System 2*. For now, all that is necessary to know is that System 1 involves what Kahneman calls *thinking fast*, situations in which your students react by reflex and instinct alone. For example, when people unexpectedly hear a loud, strange noise behind them, they turn around immediately. They don't think, "Hmmm, I wonder what is causing that sound. Should I turn around to see, or should I stay focused on what I was doing before I heard that noise?" As humans, we don't think; we react. Similarly, if someone sees a heavy object hurtling toward their face, they duck—quickly and automatically. There is no thinking, only instinct and response. This is System 1 in action. Some of the behaviors teachers see in students result from System 1 thinking, the realm of intuition, instinct, and automatic reaction. There is a long evolutionary history of instinct for survival that is the basis of System 1 thinking, and it is alive and thriving in the classrooms in some of the ways students behave.

Daniel Kahneman, Alan B. Krueger, David Schkade, Norbert Schwarz, and Arthur A. Stone (2006) describe a study in which college students were asked how happy they were in general, followed by a question about how many dates they had the previous month. There was no correlation between their responses to these two questions. However, when asked these questions *in the reverse order*, there was a significant correlation between how happy or unhappy the students felt and the number of dates they had the previous month. "The dating question evidently caused that aspect of life to become salient and its importance to be exaggerated when the respondents encountered the more general question about their happiness" (Kahneman et al., 2006, p. 3).

Think about the myriad applications of this in your classroom to subconsciously influence how to make your students feel better. By simply getting them to focus on something that makes them happy—for example, saying, "Think about the best thing that happened to you at school this week," or, "List three things that make you feel really happy"—their mood will most likely become more positive. Why? Because the question makes them think about something positive, and the thinking-fast unconscious system kicks in automatically.

Let's think about this System 1 thinking from the perspective of natural selection:

> Charles Darwin understood that the emotions are decision-makers that have evolved through natural selection to help organisms survive. The antelope that wants to hug lions is unlikely to pass on its genes to any offspring. The most basic emotions, those least amenable to conscious control, seem to bubble up inside us. They include fear and anger, surprise and disgust, and also, perhaps, a sense of joy. They predispose us to react in certain ways and send the chemical signals that prepare our bodies to run or focus, to attack or hug. (Christian, 2018, p. 145)

That is an excellent description of what is happening inside the students in your classroom at a subconscious level much of the time. That is also an excellent explanation as to why students behave the way they sometimes do.

In *Pre-suasion: A Revolutionary Way to Influence and Persuade*, psychologist, author, and one of the world's foremost experts on influence Robert B. Cialdini (2016) believes that one reason people think what they focus on in the moment is especially important is because it *is* especially important *in the moment*: "It's only reasonable to give heightened attention to those factors that have the most significance and utility for us in a particular situation: a strange noise in the dark, the smell of smoke in a theater" (p. 35).

In an evolutionary sense, this focusing on the immediate helped our ancestors enjoy dinner rather than end up as dinner. However, Cialdini (2016) notes:

This sensible system of focusing our limited attentional resources on what does indeed possess special import has an imperfection. We can be brought to the mistaken belief that something is important merely because we have been led by some irrelevant factor to give it our narrowed attention. All too often, people believe that if they have paid attention to an idea or event or group, it must be important enough to warrant the consideration. (pp. 35–36)

In schools, teachers and students are both susceptible to the focusing illusion—just one among many remnants of evolution and natural selection that we all possess but that can cause errors in judgment and understanding. Perhaps our students (and we as their teachers) are not quite as sophisticated, not quite as evolved, not quite as civilized as we would like to think.

SUMMARY

Knowing that your evolutionary brain can deceive you allows you to be on alert and spot such deceptions. It also gives you the ability to use tactics, such as those in this book, to nudge your students' savanna brains in the direction you want them to go. As you reflect on this chapter, make sure to remember the following.

- Students and teachers are both the product of natural selection. Much of what drives human thinking, behaviors, and interactions is a result of these being successful in helping our hunter-gatherer ancestors survive and reproduce.

- Students are a product of natural selection. Thus, they have innate, even predatory, instincts and drives that—while frequently operating at a subconscious level—are often the main motivators for their behaviors with other students and in regard to their teachers. As a predator species, humans (and that includes students in classrooms) can be prone to violence. This violence can manifest itself physically or psychologically through digital bullying via social media, peer pressure, physical abuse, and so on.

- Students have a strong need to belong to various peer groups and know where they fit within these groups. Teachers can use this desire to belong to both motivate students and to set appropriate boundaries for their students' in-school behaviors.

- We give disproportionate importance to what we are focused on at any given moment. This focusing illusion can cause us to misjudge the relative importance of things or to arrive at faulty conclusions about information we have been given.

- Teachers can use the focusing illusion to change the feelings and behaviors of their students.

- Humans have two systems they use to think. The thinking-fast system works quickly and involves reflexes and instincts. The thinking-slow system takes much more time and involves analytical and rational thinking. Both systems are evident in student behaviors.

REPRODUCIBLE

Reflective Practice

You may choose to use the following questions and activities to reflect on and make improvements to your current practice.

1. Describe one example of each of the following behaviors that you see in your students that the ideas described in this chapter explain.

   a. Where a student chose to act in a fashion that was out of character in order to gain the approval of a group of their classmates

   b. Where a student chose to do something they knew you would not approve of in order to gain the approval of some of their peers

   c. Where you saw a student's behavior change dramatically because now, instead of being alone, their peers entered the scene

   d. Where a student acted in an irrational way because of the focusing illusion

2. Describe two ways in which the ideas explored in this chapter have helped you understand your students' behaviors more deeply.

   a.

   b.

CHAPTER 2

STUDENT BEHAVIOR THROUGH THE LENS OF NATURAL SELECTION

Understanding human behavior requires understanding what motivates us to behave as we do, and filtering that through the lens of natural selection. As renowned historian and author Yuval N. Harari (2018) writes:

> In the last few decades, research in areas such as neuroscience and behavioral economics allowed scientists to hack humans, and in particular to gain a much better understanding of how humans make decisions. It turns out that our choices of everything from food to mates result not from some mysterious free will but rather from billions of neurons calculating probabilities within a split second. Vaulted "human intuition" is in reality "pattern recognition." Good drivers, bankers, and lawyers don't have magical intuitions about traffic, investment, or negotiation; rather, by recognizing recurring patterns, they spot and try to avoid careless pedestrians, inept borrowers, and sly crooks. It also turns out that the biochemical algorithms of the human brain are far from perfect. They rely on heuristics, shortcuts, and outdated circuits adapted to the African savanna rather than to the urban jungle. No wonder that even good drivers, bankers, and lawyers sometimes make stupid mistakes. (p. 20)

From the preceding quote, let's take Harari's idea about the impact of pattern recognition and see what happens when we apply it to your ability to manage student behavior in the classroom. Good teachers rely heavily on their ability to recognize recurring patterns, which enables them to spot trouble when it is just beginning, discern which students need help, know when to reprimand a student, and know when to ignore certain behaviors. However, teachers—like the drivers, bankers, and lawyers in Harari's example—rely on those same circuits that are often best suited to life on the savanna, as you read about in chapter 1 (page 9), than to the modern classroom. This causes educators to occasionally make some truly poor decisions and take actions that are detrimental to both themselves and students—all while being certain they did the right thing based on the inherent defaults of a savanna brain.

This chapter examines student behavior through that lens of natural selection by reflecting on how students respond to teacher behavior, how a brain's conditioning ("wiring") focuses on being part of an in-group and not outside of it, and how our own human nature influences our choices.

HOW STUDENTS RESPOND TO TEACHER BEHAVIOR

Your students are not alone in responding quickly to the reactions of their savanna brains. Teachers do so as well, and when that happens, the results are usually negative. The film *The Emperor's Club* (Hoffman, 2002) provides us with a poignant example of a teacher confronting a student in a classroom. You can see the clip by visiting https://youtu.be/_neu5UcGU3I or searching *The Emperor's Club Stupid Lasts Forever* on YouTube.

In the scene, Mr. Hundert teaches English language classics at an elite boarding school for boys. One day a new student named Sedgewick Bell comes to class. Sedgewick is the son of a U.S. senator. He is a brash and disruptive student. Mr. Hundert calls Sedgewick to the front of the room and asks him to write the names of a series of Roman emperors on the board. Sedgewick is well aware that his classmates are looking at him. He wants *their* approval and acceptance, not his teacher's. Sedgewick replies that he knows seven emperors, and responds, "Grumpy, Happy, Sleepy, Sneezy, Dopey . . ." Mr. Hundert asks him to answer the question seriously, to which Sedgewick then replies, "I only know four—John, Paul, Ringo, and George," counting down on extended fingers until only his middle finger remains.

Hundert glares at Sedgewick and recites a quote that ends with, "Ignorance can be educated, and drunkenness can be sobered, but *stupid* lasts forever" (Hoffman, 2002). Sedgewick glares back at Mr. Hundert, saying nothing but obviously humiliated. Yet, when watching the clip, the viewer gets the feeling that this is not the end of things. Sedgewick will fight back—albeit not at that moment—and he will find a way to extract his revenge. As the movie plays out, this eventually comes to pass.

Situations similar to this happen in thousands of classrooms every day. For our purposes, let's explore how our view of situations like this changes when we put on the glasses of natural selection and look at student behavior through those lenses. How do students—we'll stick to older students (junior high or middle school and high school) for this example—generally react when confronted by their teachers in front of their peers? Natural selection would say that, when confronted, an animal has essentially two choices: (1) fight or (2) flight (Harvard Health Publishing, 2020). The following sections look at an example of what happens when teachers trigger this response and then reflect on such responses through the lens of natural selection.

How Students Respond to Fight or Flight

Confronting students when you are alone with them is one thing. Confronting them in the presence of their peers—like Hundert did—is quite another matter. Why? Because now you are no longer simply confronting the one student. You are confronting one student who now has to consider *how the group will judge them based on how they respond to your challenge.* The student may or may not be consciously considering how their reactions will be judged by their peers. Nonetheless, and as you read about in chapter 1 (page 9), this consideration will be a significant factor in determining how they respond. For many students, it will be the predominant factor.

Let's look at another example of a teacher choosing to confront a student in the presence of their classmates, this time over an issue that can be very common in schools—students' use of cell phones during class. This particular instance occurred in a tenth-grade classroom. The teacher, Ms. Powell (I've changed all teacher and student names throughout this book), was busy lecturing the class, having worked hard preparing what she believed to be a good lesson. The majority of her students were engaged in the material and attentive to what she was talking about. However, at the back of the class, Jon was busy texting on his phone.

Already having reached her limit with regard to student cell phone use, Ms. Powell stopped talking to the class and yelled from the front of the room, "Jon, put your phone away. You're disrupting the class!"

Jon, already on the defensive for a variety of reasons, immediately shot back, "*You're* the one disrupting this class by screaming at me and not even teaching."

Ms. Powell yelled back, "*Get out*! Get to the principal's office *now*!"

Jon gathered up his things, stormed out of the classroom, and slammed the door. A few minutes later, Ms. Powell met Jon in the principal's office. She told the principal about the incident and said, "This kid is supposed to do what I tell him to do. He's supposed to pay attention in class and not be so disrespectful. I want him punished, and I want you to confiscate his phone."

Both Mr. Hundert and Ms. Powell are attempting to influence student behavior through their power and authority (what I call *hard tactics* in this book). They believe their teaching credentials and the accompanying knowledge give them a privileged place in the classroom, a place where they have more power and authority than do their students. Therefore, students should automatically cooperate and do what they are told. If students fail to do this, there should be consequences for this lack of cooperation, compliance, and respect.

The Lens of Natural Selection

Let's look at the examples of both the fictional Sedgewick and very real Jon through the lens of natural selection to see if we can shed a *different* light—perhaps a more informative light—on what happened in these two classrooms and on the reactions of each of these students.

In the first instance, Sedgewick's teacher brought him up to the front of the classroom. He was *on display in front of his group*. This was a boys' boarding school; thus, he spent most of his waking hours with this peer group, which entirely determined his social status. They could elevate or lower his status, or worst of all, ostracize him. Do you remember what happened to our ancient ancestors when they were ostracized by their groups? There were predators waiting for them.

The group's opinion matters to Sedgewick much more than his teacher's. And why should we be surprised at this? It was an innate part of Sedgewick's nature—and the nature of every other student in that classroom (and in yours)—to want to belong and have some status with

their group. It mattered to Sedgewick's ancestors, and it mattered to Sedgewick—at a very primordial level. Mr. Hundert threatened that status publicly, and from Sedgewick's perspective, Mr. Hundert should have to pay a price for doing that.

Viewed from the perspective of primal tribes, Mr. Hundert may have thought that *he* was the alpha male in the room, that by the nature of his size, age, and credentials, he was the de facto leader of the class. In a certain sense, this view is correct. However, Hundert was *not* a part of the tribe called *students*. Cialdini (2007) reminds us of the power of tribe when he quotes Isaac Asimov: "All things being equal, you root for your own sex, your own culture, your own locality" (pp. 197–198). In other words, *your own tribe*—not someone else's. Hundert was *not* a member of the student tribe but of the teacher tribe, and so are you. It helps to remember this, because your opinion of many students will rarely be as important to them as the opinion of their peers.

Hundert's bullying behavior isn't something new in human groups. The dominance hierarchy has been around for about half a billion years. As Peterson (2018) tells us:

> The part of our brain that keeps track of our position in the dominance hierarchy is therefore exceptionally ancient and fundamental. It is a master control system, modulating our perceptions, values, emotions, thoughts and actions. It powerfully affects every aspect of our being, conscious and unconscious alike. This is why, when we are defeated, we act very much like lobsters that have lost a fight. Our posture droops. We face the ground. We feel threatened, hurt, anxious and weak. . . . Under such conditions, we can't easily put up the kind of fight that life demands, and we become easy targets for harder-shelled bullies. (pp. 14–15)

Hundert dominated, and Sedgewick felt helpless in that situation, not wanting to be put down even further. Psychology professor and expert on behavior economics Dan Ariely (2016), in his study of what motivates human beings, argues that overcoming feelings of helplessness is a very powerful motivator for human action. "I realized how many of our motivations spring from trying to conquer a sense of helplessness and reclaim even a tiny modicum of control over our lives" (p. 13).

Let's consider this in the case of Ms. Powell and student Jon. Jon was *instantly* angry. He didn't *choose anger* as the preferred response after carefully considering a range of alternative responses. He was simply instantly angry, and he let his teacher know it by snapping back at her immediately after she confronted him. In *Emotional Contagion*, Elaine Hatfield, John T. Cacioppo, and Richard L. Rapson (1994) explore Darwin's work and conclude that when humans express what they are feeling through physical actions—actions such as yelling back at someone, as Jon did—the feelings intensify. Our emotions are on an elevator going up. Perhaps that is why the playwright Arthur Miller (2017) believed, "All real arguments are murderous. There's a killing instinct in there that I feared." Miller was an astute student of humans and the human condition, and he had great respect for the vestiges of our distant past that drive human emotions to this very day.

Not only was Jon instantly angry and defensive, but Ms. Powell—by stopping the class and confronting Jon so aggressively and publicly—put Jon's status in the group on the line. As you progress into this chapter, consider situations you've experienced (as a teacher or as a student) that are similar to the two examples I describe here, and reflect on this question: Why does the opinion of their group matter so much to so many people?

THE WIRING OF NATURAL SELECTION

Using techniques like mini-plays with puppets and measuring nonverbal responses such as the amount of time an infant looks at an event, psychologists are able to glimpse inside the minds of toddlers as young as three months old (McIntyre & Blanchard, 2012). Using these techniques, psychologists can theorize what babies are thinking long before they learn to talk.

Renée Baillargeon is an Alumni Distinguished Professor of Psychology at the University of Illinois who specializes in infant cognition. In the documentary film *Born to Be Good?* (McIntyre & Blanchard, 2012), Baillargeon states that she believes "babies are born with sort of an exquisite sensitivity to social groups." They quickly recognize in-group members—people like them—and out-group members, people who are different. They then begin to explore the question of how they should behave toward in-group and out-group members.

Alison Gopnik from the Department of Psychology at the University of California, Berkeley supports Baillargeon's view. Gopnik observes that children learn to discriminate against others at a very young age: "These people are like me, and these people are not like me" (as cited in McIntyre & Blanchard, 2012). She further observes that babies' moral sense might be more likely to extend to the people who are like them than to the people who are not like them. In other words, *we favor those who are like us.*

In the same documentary, zoologist and geneticist David Suzuki tells us:

> Research shows that babies prefer not only people who look like them, speak the same language, like the same food, and wear the same clothes, they even think they are better people. A T-shirt is enough to define a group. From there, it's just a short step to thinking my group is superior to yours. (as cited in McIntyre & Blanchard, 2012)

To determine the power of in-group identification, Baillargeon conducted an experiment where children around three years old received a red sticker on their shirt, while across from them, two puppets also had stickers on their shirts—one a red sticker like the child, the other one a blue sticker (as cited in McIntyre & Blanchard, 2012). When these children received two toys and were asked to distribute them to the puppets, they would, in most instances, give one to *each* of the puppets. However, when a third toy was introduced, invariably, the extra toy went to the puppet that had the *same* color sticker as the child. Just by the color of a sticker on a shirt, an in-group was created in the child's eyes, and the in-group member always got more. After all, they were on the same team.

In-group and out-group boundaries are not fixed, however. They can be very fluid. As teachers and parents have observed for centuries, students change friends fairly often as they grow, and their interests, preferences, and values change. Nonetheless, when we have an in-group (teachers sometimes refer to these as *cliques* or, more critically, as *gangs*), they matter to us, and we want to ensure that we matter to them. We stand together, we help one another, and we support one another—especially when confronted by those who are *not* part of our group, people we see as outsiders. As Greg Lukianoff and Jonathan Haidt (2018) put it in *The Coddling of the American Mind*, "We just don't feel as much empathy for those we see as others" (p. 58). After all, they're not us.

Students can be incredibly callous and cruel to other students who they see as not being members of their in-group. Why? Partly because, as Lukianoff and Haidt (2018) note:

> The human mind is prepared for tribalism. Human evolution is not just the story of individuals competing with other individuals within each group; it's also the story of groups competing with other groups—sometimes violently. We are all descended from people who belonged to groups that were consistently better at winning that competition. Tribalism is our evolutionary endowment for banding together to prepare for intergroup conflict. (p. 58)

Thus, in-group versus out-group conflict is something that you should understand and expect to be a part of daily life in most schools. In classrooms, especially as students get older and the opinion of their peers begins to matter more and more, you need to recognize and understand that *social survival* becomes increasingly important to your students.

Returning to the examples of Sedgewick and Jon, understand that their teachers are part of an out-group. While these two students may have wanted to do well in class and achieve, they did not want to do so at the cost of losing status with their in-groups. In-group approval mattered to them. In-group approval matters to students everywhere, including your students. Wise teachers are mindful of this, and it is a significant factor in the decisions they make in regard to how they motivate, influence, and correct student behaviors.

As Ackerman (1990) reminds us, "Nature rarely wastes a winning strategy" (p. 22). Your students—and you—are thinking and acting and feeling in ways that work—well, at least they worked for the most part for your very ancient ancestors. Whether or not these strategies are working now in your classroom is a very different question. Remember, "We may sing in choirs or park our rages behind a desk, but we patrol the world with many a hunter-gatherer's drives, motives, and skills" (Ackerman, 1990, p. 129).

Part of that world for students is your classroom. The following sections examine this effect of internal wiring on student behavior by detailing the physiology of fight-or-flight responses and how being part of a pack influences behavior.

The Physiology of Fight or Flight

Blade Runner (Scott, 2007) is a 1982 science fiction film that tells a story about how a special kind of detective—called a *blade runner*—hunts and detects androids who pose a threat to humans. At the beginning of the film, Rick Deckard (a blade runner) is asked to determine whether Rachael is a human being or a replicant android. He administers the Voight-Kampff test, a series of questions designed to evoke an emotional response in the subject. Why this kind of test?

Because humans have limited control over their emotions, we typically feel *no control whatsoever* over our autonomic responses to these emotions; emotional responses often result in involuntary reactions such as pupil dilation and increased heart rate. Deckard looks through a lens to see if Rachael's pupils dilate, something that would happen automatically in any normal human being. The sequel film, *Blade Runner 2049* (Villeneuve, 2017), continues in this vein by asking Officer K (a replicant designed to hunt and kill other replicants) questions such as: "What's it like to hold the hand of someone you love?" "What's it like to hold your child in your arms?" and "What's it like to be filled with dread?" All normal human beings respond emotionally to these kinds of questions. Why? Because to be a *normal human being* is to be an *emotional human being*. When our emotions kick in, there is a great deal in our bodies that turns on quickly and automatically without us being in control of any of these processes. When confronted abruptly, our body automatically kicks into fight-or-flight mode with all of the accompanying physiological changes.

In "Understanding the Stress Response," Harvard Health Publishing (2020) describes what happens when the fight-or-flight response kicks in:

1. The amygdala sends a distress signal to the hypothalamus, which then activates the adrenal glands.

2. The adrenal glands immediately begin pumping epinephrine (adrenaline) into the bloodstream, causing the heart rate to increase, which in turn causes blood pressure to go up.

3. Breathing rate increases, and small airways in the lungs open, enabling more oxygen to get into the bloodstream for the ensuing fight or flight.

4. Some of the extra oxygen is sent to the brain to increase alertness.

5. The pupils dilate, and the face becomes red and warm as a result of the increased blood flow.

All of these changes happen so fast that we are rarely conscious of them. Also note that these same physiological responses typically happen to teachers when students confront or aggressively challenge them and vice versa. When Mr. Hundert embarrassed Sedgewick

in front of his friends, and Ms. Powell yelled at Jon in front of his peers, specific physiological reactions immediately and automatically began to cascade through their bodies, the same way they do when you confront one of your students. Astute teachers are aware they are just as susceptible to this reaction and make a very conscious effort to be cognizant of their heartbeat, their facial flush, and so on when they find themselves in these kinds of situations. Wise teachers ensure they are both emotionally and physiologically calm before reacting to a student's challenge.

There were several occasions in my career when students challenged me. Typically, this would happen when I was new to a school, and it was early in the year, and thus I was at the beginning stages of establishing effective working relationships and trust with my students. As well, this happened more often in secondary school settings than in elementary schools. Knowing that my body would automatically kick in with the physiological responses described in this section, when I was confronted by a student, I developed certain strategies that helped me to stay calm and not respond aggressively to the student challenging me. I always tried to remain mindful of the axiom, *You can't unring a bell*, and I didn't want to say something in anger that would severely damage my relationship with the student who was attacking me. After all, we had the bulk of the school year still ahead of us.

I will give you a couple of strategies that worked for me. If a student challenged me or my teaching in front of the class ("This class sucks, and so do you!"), I would—depending on my read of the student and the circumstances—have a reply ready that I had mentally prepared for such situations. I would say to the class as a whole something like: "Leo has just made what he seems to believe is a statement of fact. That this class sucks, and so do I." You can easily imagine how closely the class is now paying attention to Leo and me—thinking "This could be good." I would then look at Leo, and calmly say, "OK, Leo, prove your case. I am going to stop teaching for the next five minutes, and you have that time to convince the class and me that either I suck, or this class does, or perhaps you want to tackle both. It's all yours." And then I would walk to the side of the room, lean against the wall, and just wait.

Most students like the spotlight, but only for a few seconds. The smart remark that flies out of their mouth for their classmates to hear and laugh about before the class moves on is very comfortable for many students. However, having to come up with arguments to prove your point while the whole class looks at you and waits is an entirely different matter. The spotlight lingers too long, and it gets very hot. The social pressure can be enormous.

I would never let the student remain in that position for too long. That would take us into Mr. Hundert's danger zone. So, after a few moments, if I see that Leo is really uncomfortable, I simply interject to say, "Leo might need some time to gather his thoughts. Let's move on, and he can let me know when he's ready, maybe tomorrow."

This kind of event rarely happened more than once. In rare cases, where a student decides to try and make his or her argument and chooses to speak, I listen respectfully and then try and lighten the mood with a few self-deprecating comments about how I may not agree with Leo completely, but yes, I do suck in my teaching on some days. For example, I might say, "Leo, please keep a log and let me know how I am doing at the end of the month. Create a 'Ripley's class sucks' scale and rate each class." The rest of the class would laugh, and I would continue with the lesson.

There were other times when a student might confront me after class when we were alone in the classroom. Mostly, this would occur when the student was attempting to convince me to give them a higher mark on an assignment, and they were challenging my grading system or my interpretation of the rubric. If confronted aggressively in this kind of situation, I would do what I called a body scan. Could I feel my heartbeat getting faster? Was I flushed in the face? Was I about to say something in a loud and aggressive tone? If I answered

yes to any of these, I would tell the student I badly needed to go to the washroom, and I would return in a few minutes, and I would simply get up and leave the room. This little two-minute break was enough for me to gain control of my physiological responses and return and continue the conversation in a calm manner.

The Pack in Your Classroom

At the beginning of chapter 1 (page 9), I asked you to imagine that you are in a fairly large room. There is one door by which you can exit this room. Between you and the door, there are approximately thirty predators, and they are all staring at you. How do you feel?

By now, you understand that your student predators are also a kind of *pack animal*. Like all pack animals, they want to be in groups of their own kind, their in-groups. Within their packs, they understand the hierarchy and their place in that hierarchy. They have been taught through countless interactions with others in the pack where they fit. They know who is physically powerful, they know who is intellectually powerful, and they know who is popular. In short, they know where they fit in the multiple hierarchies that make up any classroom.

Some teachers may take exception to viewing students as pack animals and predators. It can seem a disconcerting, perhaps even shocking assertion. Students are, after all, *human*. Nonetheless, this view is one of several valid ways to look at students. Indeed, were a student to find themselves presenting to a classroom with a ravenous pack of *adult teachers*, they would feel much the same and rightly so. From this particular vantage point, you can begin to more completely understand why your students behave the way they do in certain situations. If you truly want to be more effective at influencing, motivating, encouraging, and inspiring your students, it is essential that you understand them more deeply so you know better how to accomplish these goals.

Natural selection argues (quite successfully in my view) that while we—teachers and students—*are* human, we are at the same time a product of natural selection, a product of our evolutionary history. We *are* a kind of animal, and we still retain our animal traits and our animal instincts. Instincts to survive—both physically and socially—lead us to want to be with others of our own kind and find ways to get along and increase our status within our groups.

Harari (2018) tells us:

> [Humans] have inherited our anger, our fear, and our lust from millions of ancestors, all of whom passed the most rigorous quality control tests of natural selection . . . . Unfortunately, what was good for survival and reproduction in the African savanna a million years ago does not necessarily make for responsible behavior on twenty-first century motorways. (p. 58)

I would add this is equally true regarding responsible behavior in 21st century classrooms.

HUMAN NATURE'S INFLUENCE ON CHOICE

The lens of natural selection provides some very worthwhile insights into student behaviors, and it should be one among many of the lenses you utilize in order to first understand and then influence the students in your classroom. But the term *natural selection* itself prompts the question: What exactly is the nature of your students? What exactly is your nature as a person who teaches? As educators, we must be very careful of the plethora of assumptions we make in our attempts to answer each of these questions. Why? Because the decisions we make based on these assumptions may be illusions. And the actions we take based on those decisions may turn out to be very inappropriate, even destructive, to ourselves and our students.

Harari (2018) reminds us that "the voice we hear inside our heads is never (completely) trustworthy because it always reflects state propaganda, ideological brainwashing, and commercial advertisements, not to mention biochemical bugs" (p. 271). Think about this the next time you make a judgment about a student or plan a course of action in an attempt to change a student's behaviors in your classroom.

There is a famous (and seemingly unattributable) quote that educators would do well to remember: "It ain't what you don't know that gets you into trouble. It's what you know that just ain't so." Remember this before you jump to unfounded conclusions about students based on bias and faulty reasoning.

In 2018, author Malcolm Gladwell gave a presentation to the World Government Summit in which he talked about "new" observations on what constitutes good teaching. Gladwell (2018) tells the audience:

> Good teaching, we now understand, is about an interaction between a teacher and a student. You can't take the student out of the equation. Students are responding to a certain kind of teacher, teaching a certain kind of subject, in a certain kind of situation. . . . Now the task of managing and creating an effective school . . . requires that we shift from thinking about students as groups to thinking about students as individuals.

I—probably like you—found myself chuckling when I heard Gladwell speak about this finding. Every good teacher I have ever met came to this realization very early in their teaching careers. Every student is different. Every class is different. Because of this indisputable reality of teaching, if a teacher wants to be effective and have a positive impact on students, then doing the hard work of getting to know them as individuals *and* as a group is absolutely essential.

Students are like Russian nesting dolls. If you simply look at the outer layer, you will have some sense of who and what they are, but you will miss much and misunderstand even more. You need to look past your assumptions and your preconceptions. You need to look deeper. You need to listen better. You need to understand more clearly. All of this is essential if you are truly going to have the capacity to influence, motivate, persuade, and inspire your students. Without these insights, you are at risk of being like the teacher in the Peanuts (Shatner Method, 2016) cartoons: nothing much more than a "Wah wa wa wah wa wa" noise in the background, not having much—if any—impact at all.

The remainder of this book explores the question of *how* to go about the task of influencing even your most challenging students. As a teacher, you have the power to play the cards you have been given in your classroom in ways that motivate, inspire, and encourage your students to be their very best. Is this not, after all, why you went into teaching?

SUMMARY

As you reflect on this chapter, make sure to remember the following.

- The human brain often makes decisions in a fraction of a second, based on patterns we have come to recognize over time. Unfortunately, some of these patterns are vestiges from the savanna brains of our ancient ancestors, which can mislead us in the kinds of decisions we make in the modern world—including the ones we make in our classrooms.

- When teachers confront students, some students respond in flight mode, while others respond in fight mode. Often, students have little to no control over these emotionally driven responses to teachers.

- You need to understand the basic drivers of your students' behaviors if you are going to successfully influence those behaviors. One way to understand student behavior is to search for the *payoff*, the reward the student is getting from their behaviors.

- Students are hardwired to need and want to belong to an in-group. All classrooms have in-groups and out-groups, and within every classroom, there is a dominance hierarchy that affects how students interact with one another and with their teacher.

- Challenging or embarrassing students in front of their peers are rarely effective in the long run. They are an attack on them individually as well as an attack on their status in the group. This can do very serious damage to the teacher-student relationship and negatively impact a teacher's ability to influence a student going forward from such an event.

- Teachers rarely have much control over which students are assigned to their classrooms. However, teachers do have a great deal of control over how they relate to the students in their classrooms. Play the cards you have been given, and if you do this effectively, every class can be a great class.

Reflective Practice

Take a look at a class you are now teaching, but this time do so through the lens of natural selection. In completing this reflection, consider the following.

1. Think of a time when you chose to challenge or confront a student in the classroom in front of his or her classmates. Why did you choose to engage the student in front of their peers rather than talking to them privately? How did this work for you? For the student? What were the long-term repercussions of your actions in terms of your working relationship with this student?

2. Name the different student groups that you see in class (think in-groups—student groups that choose to belong together for whatever reasons). Use whatever labels you feel are fitting. Name the leader or leaders of each of these groups and the students who are their followers—the members of each of these groups.

Groups in My Classroom	Group Leaders	Group Members

3. Choose the group that you feel is the most influential in your class. Think about your relationship with this group. Good teachers know that it is extremely useful to have class leaders on their side because these leaders can help them steer the class in a positive direction.

4. If you feel you have a good working relationship with this group and they support your efforts in the classroom, take a look at one of the other groups you have noted. If you find that your relationship with one of these groups is not where you want it to be, think about three ways in which you could attempt to improve that relationship. In doing this, remember the concept of payoff, and try to devise a strategy that has payoffs for the students as well as yourself. List three ways you could attempt to improve your relationship with the target group.

   a. _____
   _____

   b. _____
   _____

   c. _____
   _____

Important note: If you find there is a group or group leader that you want to target, but at this point, you find yourself struggling to come up with effective strategies to utilize with this goal in mind, set this step in the exercise aside for now. The rest of this book is dedicated to showing you effective influence strategies that you can implement in the classroom to improve your relationship with students and increase their levels of cooperation and achievement in your class. If you can immediately name three strategies, revisit your answers after reading this book, and consider if you need to make changes.

Part 2

SOFT AND HARD TACTICS

CHAPTER 3

SOFT TACTICS FOR HELPING YOUR STUDENTS CREATE A POSITIVE SELF-IMAGE

When I think about how students see themselves and how that self-image governs their behavior, I often think of the following story as told by spiritual speaker and psychologist Anthony de Mello (1982):

> A man found an eagle's egg and put it in the nest of a barnyard hen. The eaglet hatched with the brood of chicks and grew up with them. All his life the eagle did what the barnyard chicks did, thinking he was a barnyard chicken. He scratched the earth for worms and insects. He clucked and cackled. And he would thrash his wings and fly a few feet into the air.
>
> Years passed and the eagle grew very old. One day he saw a magnificent bird above him in the cloudless sky. It glided in graceful majesty among the powerful wind currents, with scarcely a beat of its strong golden wings.
>
> The old eagle looked up in awe. "Who's that?" he asked.
>
> "That's the eagle, the king of the birds," said his neighbor. "He belongs to the sky. We belong to the earth—we're chickens."
>
> So the eagle lived and died a chicken, for that's what he thought he was. (pp. 3–4)

Anthony de Mello's (1982) story of the eagle who thought he was a chicken is similar to a phenomenon called *baby elephant syndrome* (Telg, Jones, & Barnes, 2016). When an elephant living in captivity is still young, it is tied to a stake with a rope or chain. When it tries to break free, the baby elephant soon discovers that it is not strong enough to break its tether, and eventually, it simply gives up trying to get free. As time passes, the elephant grows older and stronger. While as an adult elephant, it could now easily break the rope or chain holding it, the elephant doesn't even try. Why? Because its prior experiences have conditioned its mind to believe that it cannot break free; thus, an elephant that could uproot a large tree is held captive by a small rope—and the cage of its own beliefs. Let's consider how this story might apply to student behavior.

There is a scene from a movie called *The Help* (Taylor, 2011) in which an African American maid performs a daily ritual with the young White girl in her care. (Visit https://youtu.be/3H50llsHm3k to see a clip of this scene.) Every day, she lifts the little girl onto her lap and says to the child, "You is smart, you is kind, you is important." She then has the child repeat these words back to her.

What's going on here? Why are rituals like this—the ones where parents, teachers, and caregivers consistently tell children about their worth and potential—so powerful in shaping the qualities and characteristics of that child in the future? These are important questions given that, although this example is life-affirming, there can be a dark side to rituals like these, occasions when the significant adults in a child's life put them down with words and labels that are belittling rather than uplifting.

Several years ago, I was registering new students at a junior high and middle school when a father came up to me and introduced me to his twelve-year-old son with these words: "This is Phil, *my little thief*. He will steal anything he can. Don't take your eyes off this one." As this father chuckled at his own words, I looked at this boy, his head down, staring at the floor.

In another example, as a principal, I once suspended a fourteen-year-old boy for fighting in school. He had beaten up another boy quite seriously. The suspended boy's father came to see me after school that day and shouted at me, "There are only two kinds of people in the world: hammers and nails, and I'm teaching my son to be a hammer!"

The odds are strong that children in circumstances like these will ultimately live up to the images their caregivers place on them: one growing into an adult who is smart and kind, one becoming an adult who steals, and the other becoming a man who beats up other people in order to get his way or vent his anger. In this chapter, we begin our exploration of soft tactics by examining the following.

- Understand the impact of other people's views on how students see themselves.
- Be aware of confirmation bias.
- Recognize the placebo effect.

TACTIC: UNDERSTAND THE IMPACT OF OTHER PEOPLE'S VIEWS ON HOW STUDENTS SEE THEMSELVES

When John F. Kennedy (yes, *that* John F. Kennedy) was a teenager at the elite Choate School in Connecticut, he belonged to a prank club (Hamblin, 2019). The club was planning to pile manure in the gymnasium, and school officials found out about the plan. The headmaster strongly suggested that the young Kennedy needed to see a specialist to help him overcome his childish behaviors. The doctor that Kennedy ended up seeing was a young psychologist by the name of Prescott Lecky. About this, James Hamblin (2019), a lecturer at Yale writing for *The Atlantic*, states:

> Lecky paid particular attention to Kennedy's talk of sibling rivalry. 'My brother is the efficient one in the family, and I am the boy that doesn't get things done,' Kennedy says in one of Lecky's records. This constituted what Lecky considered a *self-view*—a deeply held belief about oneself. He wrote that Kennedy had a reputation in the family for 'sloppiness and inefficiency, and he feels entirely at home in the role. Any criticism he receives only serves to confirm the feeling that he has defined himself correctly.' Kennedy's case fit into a new idea Lecky was developing, called *self-consistency theory*. It posited that people are always striving to create a world in which their ideas of themselves make sense. (emphasis added)

Lecky was a psychology teacher at Columbia University, where he developed his self-consistency theory. Lecky believed:

> The prime need of an organism is to maintain its mental organization as a unified whole. The object of integrative forces in the organism is to preserve unity, particularly on the highest psychic levels. All other needs may be conceived of as subsidiary to this primary motive. . . . Lecky recognized that the characteristics of a person on the highest levels of integration are determined by his style of life, i.e. the individual organization of ideas and attitudes which are acquired through experience and which control the highest intellectual functions. The essence of this organization of ideas and attitudes is its

self-consistency. (Lecky & Thorne, 1945, pp. 2–3; emphasis added)

Essentially, Lecky and Thorne (1945) argue that each of us develops certain ideas about who we are and what we are like, and then we work hard to maintain the self-image we have created. This self-image, particularly in students, can be greatly influenced by significant adults such as teachers and caregivers. After extensive study with children, Lecky came to believe that a student's poor self-image significantly impacts poor performance in school (Hamachek, 1995).

In the 1990s, William B. Swann Jr., a psychologist at the University of Texas, took up Lecky's ideas and evolved them into what he referred to as *self-verification theory*, which he later called *identity fusion* (Swann, Gomez, Seyle, Morales, & Huici, 2009). Swann later conducted studies with his colleagues that led them to conclude, "When people become fused with a group, their personal and social identities become functionally equivalent" (Swann et al., 2009, p. 995).

In *Atomic Habits*, author and entrepreneur James Clear (2018) similarly describes how self-identity can be a significant impediment to changing bad habits and achieving our goals:

> Many people walk through life in a cognitive slumber, blindly following the norms attached to their identity. . . . "I'm always late." "I'm not good with technology." "I'm horrible at math" . . ., and a thousand other variations. When you have repeated a story to yourself for years, it is easy to slide into these mental grooves and accept them as fact. In time, you begin to resist certain actions because "that's not who I am." There is internal pressure to maintain your self-image and behave in a way that is consistent with your beliefs. (p. 35)

The idea that students most often act in harmony with their self-image is evident to anyone who has spent time in a classroom. Students who think they are "dumb" will generally not do well on academic assessments and will not put much effort into them. From their perspective, why would they? There is little point in trying to do something when they are convinced they will perform poorly. Similarly, students who think they are uncoordinated and unathletic do not typically do well in physical education for the same reasons. And on it goes.

To a great extent, all students are vulnerable to being *barnyard eagles*, that is, a predisposition of living down to the low expectations and labels placed on them—consistently, over long periods of time—by the significant adults in their lives, such as caregivers and teachers. The opposite is also true. Tell a student repeatedly over a long period of time that they are smart, kind, and important, and watch them soar. Cialdini (2007) says that people have an almost obsessive desire to be consistent: "Once we have made a choice or taken a stand, we will encounter personal and interpersonal pressures to behave consistently with that commitment. Those pressures will cause us to respond in ways that justify our earlier decision" (p. 57).

While acting in a manner consistent with our self-image is something people usually see as desirable in themselves and socially acceptable to others (because we like the stability and predictability of knowing how others will act so we can prepare ourselves for our interactions with them), the flip side of this—inconsistency in behavior—is something people see as undesirable. Cialdini (2007) further notes: "The person whose beliefs, words, and deeds don't match may be seen as indecisive, confused, two-faced, or even mentally ill. On the other side, a high degree of consistency is normally associated with personal and intellectual strength" (p. 60).

In general, you want your teaching colleagues to act in a consistent manner. You want the same from your students, and they, too, want the same from you and their classmates. Why? Because we like the stability and predictability that this brings to our relationships. Randy Burkett (2013), a staff historian for the U.S. Central Intelligence Agency, writes that a desire for consistency is a key motivator of human behavior, stating, "Portraying ourselves as consistent speaks to who we humans are at our essence. Society generally seems to spurn members who are inconsistent" (p. 15).

Cialdini (2007) makes the argument that automatic consistency is also a shield against having to think too much. We simply go on autopilot with our behaviors based on our previous behaviors and our current self-image. Why? Because it's easy.

All of this gives rise to an extremely important question for teachers who are attempting to help students succeed in schools: *If a student's self-image is a significant barrier to their success in school, then what can you do to change this self-image to one that enhances that student's success?* The next two tactics I present in this chapter—(1) awareness of confirmation bias and (2) making use of the placebo effect—will help you answer this question.

TACTIC: BE AWARE OF CONFIRMATION BIAS

One specific aspect of self-consistency we need to explore if you are to help your students create a positive self-image is the idea of confirmation bias. Simply put, *confirmation bias* is our tendency to pay close attention to information that supports the beliefs we already hold and to minimize or ignore information that challenges our beliefs (Kolbert, 2017). Once people form an opinion about some person (including themselves), it is extremely difficult to get them to alter their beliefs. In "Why Facts Don't Change Our Minds," journalist and Pulitzer Prize–winning author Elizabeth Kolbert (2017) argues we evolved this mindset to prevent us from being taken advantage of by other members of our group:

> Living in small bands of hunter-gatherers, our ancestors were primarily concerned with their social standing, and with making sure that they weren't the ones risking their lives on the hunt while others loafed around in the cave. There was little advantage in reasoning clearly, while much was to be gained from winning arguments . . . sociability is the key to how the human mind functions, or perhaps more pertinently, malfunctions.

Confirmation bias is one such malfunction.

There are good reasons why all of us fall victim to confirmation bias. First, it feels good to have our opinions and beliefs validated. This is because our bodies deliver a hit of dopamine when we process information that supports our existing beliefs, creating an instant rush of pleasure (Kolbert, 2017). Who among us doesn't like it when people agree with us and support us?

When people disagree with our beliefs and challenge them—especially when they have solid data to support their contrary views—that doesn't feel good at all. In a study examining why liberals and conservatives tend to avoid being exposed to the opinions of the opposing side, researchers Jeremy A. Frimer, Linda Skitka, and Matt Motyl (2017) find that "people on both sides indicated that they anticipated that hearing from the other side would induce cognitive dissonance (e.g., require effort, cause frustration) and undermine a sense of shared reality with the person expressing disparate views" (p. 1).

Further, researchers Jonas T. Kaplan, Sarah I. Gimbel, and Sam Harris (2016) conducted a study in which participants entered an fMRI scanner, which measures brain activity by detecting changes in blood flow to different parts of the brain. They state:

> [The participants] read 8 political statements and 8 non-political statements with which they had previously indicated strong agreement. Each statement was followed by 5 challenges. Each challenge was a sentence or two that provided a counterargument or evidence against the original statement. (Kaplan et al., 2016, p. 2)

The results show that when people are confronted with challenges to deeply held core beliefs, blood flow to those parts of the brain associated with personal identity and basic beliefs *increases*. In other words, our brains are wired to hold on to the core beliefs we've developed about ourselves and the world, and there is a natural, biological resistance to ideas that challenge these core views. This reaction changes when we learn new information about a topic. For example, when presented with fresh discoveries about quantum computing, not many people would see this information as a challenge to their self-identity. But if someone threatens your core beliefs with new information, accepting that information, in a certain sense, requires you to let go of parts of your former self, creating a somewhat new self. This sort of metamorphosis can result in growth, but the process is often painful.

For this reason, there are a number of issues that confirmation bias raises for you as a teacher. In terms of self-consistency theory and the labeling of students, do you find yourself spending time with colleagues who share the same views as you hold in regard to the students you teach? Do you find yourself saying (or agreeing with others saying) things like the following? "Jackie is really smart and hardworking and will certainly go places" or "Taylor is lazy and disinterested and doesn't have much of a future." If you buy into these kinds of views about your students, they will manifest themselves in your interactions, expectations, and your relationships with them.

It is easy and natural to fall into agreement with those around us. Why? Because as social psychologist and author Jonathan Haidt (2001) tells us in "The Emotional Dog and Its Rational Tail":

> People are highly attuned to the emergence of group norms. . . . The mere fact that friends, allies, and acquaintances have made a moral judgment exerts a direct influence on others, even if no reasoned persuasion is used. . . . In many cases, people's privately held judgments are directly shaped by the judgment of others. (p. 819)

Your colleagues are influencing the views you have about particular students, even if you are unaware of it.

Additionally, confirmation bias can inhibit your professional growth if you find yourself associating *only* with those colleagues who hold the same beliefs that you hold in regard to what constitutes good pedagogical practices. There are many ways to teach effectively, there are many ways to assess effectively, and there are

many ways to relate to students effectively. Perhaps some of those colleagues who do things differently than you may have something to offer that may help you become an even better teacher.

The lessons here are simple. First, if you find that you have labeled a student in any way that would negatively impact his or her chances of success at school, under no circumstances should you ever verbalize or demonstrate these views to that student. No matter how convinced you are that your beliefs about Carson being "a loser" are correct, if Carson senses this, he will more than likely act in ways to confirm your view of him. Instead, work hard at finding something that Carson is good at in your classes, and use that as the seed to let him know that he can be successful when he wants to be. A little water and sunshine help seeds grow. Carson, too, needs a little nurturing and some light. Give it to him consistently over several weeks, and see what happens. And if you find you've already engaged in this sort of labeling with a student, I encourage you to review the positive-word tactic in chapter 5 (page 49), in which you create a series of positive descriptors about a student or students and give this list to them on certain occasions.

A second lesson is that you need to be very careful with regard to how your colleagues may influence your beliefs about the students you teach. Just because Ms. Johnson is having huge difficulties with Tyler's behaviors in her class doesn't mean that Tyler is a poor student. It could be the subject Johnson teaches, or it could be the way she teaches. You simply don't know and shouldn't even try to guess. Take Tyler at face value, the way he is with you in your classroom, and find something positive to focus on and encourage, and go from there.

TACTIC: RECOGNIZE THE PLACEBO EFFECT

The word *placebo* has its origin in Latin and means "I shall please" (Merriam-Webster, n.d.)—and please it does. Often used in medical trials, a placebo is used as a comparative base against the actual medicine that is being tested. However, while the placebo has no active medical components whatsoever, it can nonetheless have a positive effect on the patient's health and feelings of well-being. But what about the application of the placebo effect on cognitive performance? Are there ways that you can use the placebo effect to increase academic achievement in the students in your classrooms? It appears that the answer to that question is *yes*.

Ariely (2008b) describes an experiment he conducted where students received a series of word puzzles to solve. The letters of a series of words were mixed up, and the students had to try and figure out how to rearrange them into actual words. For example, KINRDS would be DRINKS if solved correctly. However, Ariely gave some of the participants a drink he called SoBe, which was a placebo. He then placed the following message on the cover of some of the test booklets:

> Drinks such as SoBe have been shown to improve mental functioning . . . resulting in improved performance on tasks such as solving puzzles. We also added some fictional information, stating that SoBe's Web site referred to more than 50 scientific studies supporting its claims. (Ariely, 2008b, p. 238)

The results? The group that took the drink and read the message on the cover of the test booklet performed better.

These results were in harmony with a subsequent study by researchers Ulrich W. Weger and Stephen Loughnan (2013) titled "Mobilizing Unused Resources." In the study, researchers told forty undergraduate volunteers they were going to be tested in regard to the role of attention in a twenty-question general knowledge test. The test was in a multiple-choice format and had questions such as: "What is the value of pi?" "Who painted *Guernica*?" and so on. However, half of the students (the placebo group) were told that the correct answer to each question would flash across the computer screen just prior to their answering the question. They were told that while they would not be able to read the answer as it would be on the screen for only a fraction of a second, it would register with them at a subconscious level.

Placebo participants were instructed to "just allow their intuition to speak because 'on some level you already know the answer'" (Weger & Loughnan, 2013, p. 25).

In reality, all that was flashing across the screens of the placebo group were nonsense words with random letters. Yet, "participants in the placebo condition who believed that they had been exposed to the correct answers subliminally scored higher . . . than participants in the control condition" (Weger & Loughnan, 2013, p. 25).

Why did that happen? Weger and Loughnan (2013) believe:

> [What probably occurred] is a weakening of inhibitory mechanisms that normally impair performance on a task—for example, self-incapacitating anxieties that have previously taxed cognitive resources that now become available for other tasks and processes. Likewise, our intervention may have primed a success-orientation that activated corresponding behavioral responses. (p. 26)

In other words, the placebo minimized test anxiety.

In the previous section, we explored the idea of confirmation bias, which Weger and Loughnan (2013) contend has strongly connected psychological variables to the placebo effect, particularly our human predisposition to find information that aligns with what we already think. If students *believe* they are going to perform better, whether because they studied more diligently than usual or because they have been primed with a placebo, they will likely perform better in actuality.

Given this information, what kind of placebos might you use in your classroom? For example, you might say any of the following.

- "Deep breathing, through the nose and out of the mouth for thirty seconds, has been proven to increase students' mathematics scores."

- "Sitting quietly and thinking about a time when you were really happy have been shown to improve students' writing abilities by up to 20 percent."

- "Remembering a time when you achieved the highest mark you ever got in this subject has been shown to increase your scores by a minimum of 10 percent."

None of these strategies have been tested, but they do serve as examples of noninvasive placebos you might use in a classroom setting. However, the use of such placebos poses some ethical questions.

By definition, utilizing a placebo is typically grounded in some degree of deception. If you choose to use a placebo in an attempt to enhance cognitive performance or academic achievement, you would normally have to tell your students that the placebo is going to make them better at the designated task, when in reality, you have no proof of this. But is that really true? Is your use of placebos really a deception since the placebo effect is real, and, in fact, your placebo is likely to actually improve student performance to some degree? Chapter 16 (page 193) examines the ethics of influence, and we will explore questions such as this more deeply there. There is, however, another option. You could actually tell your students they were receiving a placebo—that the deep breathing exercise and the exercise in which they think about a happy time are, in fact, placebos.

The obvious question that arises from this strategy is, "Won't this stop the placebo effect from working?" One would think so, but that appears to not be the case in some instances. World-renowned expert on placebos, Ted Kaptchuk of Harvard, conducted a study in which participants were told in advance they were receiving a placebo. The results of the study were astonishing. Patients who knew they received placebo pills (called *open-label* medication) reported twice as much relief from their symptoms as did the patients in the nontreatment group (Kaptchuk et al., 2010). Clearly, there is evidence to suggest teachers can make ethical use of the placebo effect in the classroom.

SUMMARY

There are many factors to consider with regard to set viewpoints, confirmation bias, and whether to use placebos with your students in order to help them improve their achievement. Some of these considerations are practical, while others are ethical. It's another item in the long list of decisions and dilemmas that we face as teachers as we go about our work of trying to have a positive influence on the students we teach. As you reflect on this chapter, make sure to remember the following.

- Significant adults in a child's life have a great deal of influence on the development of the child's self-image. Teachers can be among the most significant adults in a student's life and thus have the potential to have a positive impact on how a student views themself.

- Like the eagle who thought he was a chicken, students will often conform to the image that significant adults in their lives have placed on them, whether these images are valid or not. Most teachers and students act in ways that are congruent with their self-image. This is called *self-consistency theory*.

- Teachers and students can both fall victim to confirmation bias, which is the tendency to seek information and other people who agree with us. This is one of the strategies all people use to fulfill their need to belong.

- It can also be a struggle for teachers to be open to the opinions and pedagogical practices of colleagues when these opinions and practices are different from their own.

- Teachers can purposefully use the placebo effect to enhance students' cognitive performance, although there are practical and ethical issues they need to consider.

Reflective Practice

As you put this chapter's tactics into practice, and if your subject area and student grade level make this feasible, create and distribute a chart like the one included on page 2 of this reproducible, and try the following exercise with your students. Say:

1. "Write down the names of the three most significant adults in your life so far."

2. "Why did you choose these three people? In other words, what makes them so important to you?"

3. "Think about one negative aspect of your character, something that you don't like about yourself—something that you would change if you could. Describe that quality where indicated on the chart."

4. "You weren't born with this quality, so it must have developed or arisen at a certain time in your life. Where did it come from? When and why do you think it developed?"

5. "Discuss this negative quality that you see in yourself with one of the three significant adults that you listed on the T-chart. Ask them if they agree with your self-assessment or if they see something different. If they agree with you, ask them to help you develop a plan to change this aspect of who you are."

You can also apply this approach to your own professional growth. If you find yourself spending most of your time at school with colleagues who share the same views as you, who teach the same subjects or students as you do, choose a colleague you believe to be a good educator who is not in your regular social circle at work. Commit to spending some time with this colleague, and discuss the following topics in your conversations.

- In your colleague's view, what are that colleague's most effective teaching practices?

- How does this colleague establish effective working relationships with students?

- How does this colleague assess students so as to ascertain whether or not students are learning the curriculum content?

- If you teach some of the same students, focus on a student you may be having challenges with. Find out about that student's behaviors and level of achievement in the other teacher's class. Determine if there are any strategies that teacher utilizes that are working effectively and that you might be able to emulate.

Reflection on Life Influences

Follow your teacher's direction to choose the names of three significant adults in your life and how they've impacted you.

Three people you have chosen	Three things that each of these people have told me about myself that I believe to be true
Name of first person:	1. 2. 3.
Name of second person:	1. 2. 3.
Name of third person:	1. 2. 3.

Describe a quality you would change about yourself if you could.

Where do you think this quality came from? When? Why?

The Tactical Teacher © 2022 Solution Tree Press • SolutionTree.com
Visit **go.SolutionTree.com/behavior** to download this free reproducible.

CHAPTER 4

SOFT TACTICS FOR RECIPROCATION

I have a close friend (Barry) whose daughter (Monica) was having some challenges with high school mathematics during her final year of high school. She had become so discouraged that she started talking about not going to university to study nursing, which had been her plan. Mathematics was a required course for admission into the nursing program. Barry was very concerned.

After giving this some thought, Barry went to the University of Alberta campus and obtained the names of several university students who were interested in earning money by tutoring high school mathematics students. Barry interviewed a few students and chose a tutor for his daughter based on three criteria: (1) the tutor had to be an attractive male in his early twenties, (2) the tutor would not go to students' homes (he would only tutor on the university campus), and (3) the tutor had to be very personable.

After choosing a young man who met these criteria, Barry drove his daughter to the university campus once a week for mathematics tutoring. Several things happened over the ensuing months.

- Monica became quite familiar with the university campus. Sometimes Monica and Barry would go to her tutoring sessions a bit early, walk around the campus, then have a coffee or a bite to eat.

- Monica really liked her tutor. She was a seventeen-year-old heterosexual high school student—her tutor was a smart, handsome, pleasant guy who was a few years older than her. What's not to like?

- Because Monica didn't want to look dumb in front of her tutor, she worked harder at mathematics, and her marks improved dramatically. That shouldn't come as a surprise. We all have people in our lives we want to impress.

Monica ended up doing very well in her high school mathematics courses and is now a practicing nurse.

This is the quintessential example of using a reciprocation-focused soft tactic as a form of motivation. This chapter explores the following tactics for using reciprocation to motivate your students.

- Understand how reciprocation motivates your students.

- Give a small gift directly to each student.

- Be involved with student activities.

- Motivate for money.

- Be available and empathetic.

TACTIC: UNDERSTAND HOW RECIPROCATION MOTIVATES YOUR STUDENTS

In June of 1978, *The Washington Post* ran an article with the headline "Ring of Clumsy Forgers Finally Ends Two-Year Run" (Nossiter, 1978). The criminal group in the report was led by a man named Henry Oberlander, who ran a ring of forgers who specialized in fake bank drafts. Although the actual fake drafts his gang produced were of poor quality, Oberlander was able to convince multiple banks to accept the forgeries, as the banks could make a lot of money through the sale and purchase of these bank drafts. Oberlander is famous for a quote known as Henry's Rule: "Everyone is willing to give you something for whatever it is they desire most" (Imiminvestorsworld, 2015).

The quote reveals a great truth that you can utilize with your students. Every one of them wants something—actually, every student you teach wants *many* things. And when you figure out what they want—what they *really* want at a very fundamental level—and you can find ways to give them some of those things or an achievable pathway to those things, you will engender within them a feeling of indebtedness, a sense that they owe you. Once that happens, you can use this to steer them in the positive directions you want them to go.

Cialdini (2007), one of the world's leading experts in the psychology of influence, tells us:

> One of the reasons reciprocation can be used so effectively as a device for gaining another's compliance is its power. The rule possesses awesome strength, often producing a "yes" response to a request that, except for an existing feeling of indebtedness, would have surely been refused. (p. 21)

This is why you should consider ways you can create a feeling of indebtedness toward you from students.

Consider the story of Barry and his daughter, Monica. What did Monica want that Barry's strategy gave her? Barry was very aware that Monica liked guys who were smart and a little older than her. In choosing a mathematics tutor who was a bit older than his daughter and someone he imagined she would find attractive, Barry anticipated that she would want to impress this young man. He was right. She showed up every week with her assignments completed, and she worked hard to be prepared for these sessions in order to impress her tutor. For Barry, the learning of the mathematics material was the primary goal. For Monica, impressing her handsome tutor was her primary goal—but she believed she had to master the mathematics in order to do this.

Student or adult, all of us are tuned into our favorite FM radio station: WIIFM—What's in it for me? That includes your students. Your students don't automatically care about the curriculum and what you are trying to teach. They care about themselves, their dreams, their needs, and their wants. This makes them no different from anyone else, including you. To be influential and inspirational as a teacher, you must show them that what you are selling them will help them obtain the things they want.

Like Oberlander said, everyone will give you something *if* you can give them the things they fundamentally desire. Barry gave his daughter what she wanted—and he did so in such a way as to virtually ensure that he got what he wanted as well.

Before we turn to the other tactics in this chapter, let's take a closer look at two aspects of *reciprocation* that reflect both subtle and direct uses in the classroom: (1) trading and the importance of establishing legitimacy and (2) the rule of reciprocity in our genes.

Trading and the Importance of Establishing Legitimacy

In "The Hidden Curriculum Revisited" (Feinberg & Soltis, 1992), sociologist Paul Willis talks about how important it is for teachers to establish legitimacy very early in the school year. He describes this in terms of an exchange made between the teacher and their students. Willis puts it this way:

> The teacher's authority must be won and maintained on moral, not on coercive grounds.

There must be consent from the taught. This moral authority is cemented for most students when they accept the basic exchange that the teachers offer them in various ways. The bargain is struck along the following lines. If the students give the teachers respect, then the teachers will give meaningful knowledge in return, which will lead to a marketable credential, which will then provide access to a rewarding job. (as cited in Feinberg & Soltis, 1992, p. 66)

Establishing legitimacy—the basic bargain that you will give students worthwhile knowledge in return for cooperation—is fairly simple to generate with academically oriented students. You demonstrate in various ways that you have something they want—that being the knowledge and skills necessary to pass your course, move on to the next level, and ultimately be more likely to become economically successful. In exchange for obtaining their cooperation in terms of both classroom behaviors and the successful completion of the necessary schoolwork, you will give them this knowledge. While teachers and students rarely speak overtly of this agreed-on exchange, it underpins much of the dynamic that happens in most classrooms with students who want to be successful in school. This is because such students see the exchange as necessary to attain future academic and economic success.

However, there are some students who do not buy into this exchange. Willis talks about a group of boys he calls "the lads" (as cited in Feinberg & Soltis, 1992). The lads envision their futures as being much like their fathers' and grandfathers' lives working as laborers in the local factory. Since they cannot see any economic future for themselves but these factory jobs, the academic knowledge their teachers offer them seems of little use. Thus, they spend their time in school joking around, avoiding work as much as possible, and trying to entertain themselves and one another.

Another way to look at the notion of legitimacy is that to be successful in the classroom, you need to establish credibility with your students. Credibility in this sense means that your students know that you mean what you say, you always follow through with your commitments, you show up every day unless something catastrophic prevents this, and you constantly show them how the knowledge you are teaching them will benefit them and is relevant to them.

For students like the lads, the exchange of academic knowledge for future economic payoff simply doesn't work. For such students, you need to use other strategies, such as the forthcoming reciprocation strategies in this chapter and the likability strategies in the next chapter. Reciprocity, by definition, involves an exchange. You have something the student wants, and you give it to them *if* they give you what you want. However, if you fail to show your students that what you are teaching is important *to them*, then you have failed to establish legitimacy. In circumstances such as this, you will have to utilize other ways to engender a feeling of reciprocity.

The Rule of Reciprocity Is in Our Genes

Chapter 1 (page 9) established that many of the behavioral tendencies we find in our students are hardwired in them based on evolution and natural selection. Cialdini (2007) quotes famed anthropologist Richard Leakey, who makes the argument that this evolutionary hardwiring applies to reciprocity as well:

We are human because our ancestors learned to share their food and their skills in an honored network of obligation. . . . A widely shared and strongly held feeling of future obligation made an enormous difference in human social evolution, because it meant that one person could give something (for example, food, energy, care) to another with confidence that it was not being lost. For the first time in evolutionary history, one individual could give away any of a variety of resources without actually giving them away. (p. 18)

Chris Voss (2016), a former FBI hostage negotiator, calls this instinct the *reciprocity reflex* and says that across all cultures, when somebody gives you something, they usually expect something in return. Burkett (2013) warns us, however, that the perceived value of a favor decreases in the eyes of the recipient over time.

Therefore, if you are looking for reciprocation, you need to make your request relatively quickly after doing the favor or giving the gift. Further, a person who does not abide by the rule of reciprocation and gives nothing in return is usually disliked and often excluded from further favors or from the group itself (Goldstein, Martin, & Cialdini, 2008). We use terms like *moocher*, *freeloader*, *sponge*, or *leech* to describe people like this.

I once heard a story about a very successful car salesman. While he used a number of strategies described in this book that helped increase his sales, his most successful tactic was the test drive. He would get in the car, invite the prospective customer to sit in the passenger seat, and without asking, he drove away. He would drive for about twenty minutes, all the while talking and building rapport with the customer. Depending on his read of the customer, sometimes this conversation would be about the car and sometimes it would be about whatever the customer wanted to chat about. Even when customers said they were busy and had to get back, this salesman kept driving and chatting. After about twenty minutes, he would pull over and let the customer drive the vehicle back to the lot.

When I first heard about this, I couldn't figure it out. I thought that if I were in this situation, I would most likely feel that I was being held hostage in the car, and I would probably feel annoyed. However, it turns out that the rule of reciprocation seemed to override most prospective customers' feelings of annoyance. Most customers felt obligated to this salesman after such a test drive. After all, he had spent so much time with them, and he was so nice, there was a feeling that they owed him something.

How can you use this example in adapting the rule of reciprocity to your teaching? Clearly, you have to give an individual student or the class something *they* want. This has to be something above and beyond what teachers normally provide. The tactics that follow in this chapter offer several classroom examples that have worked well in my teaching practice.

TACTIC: GIVE A SMALL GIFT DIRECTLY TO EACH STUDENT

Across all grades—primary through to high school—on occasions such as Halloween, Christmas, Valentine's Day, and Easter, I *give* each student a small gift. On Halloween, I distribute mini-chocolate bars; at Christmas, it's candy canes; on Valentine's Day, it's chocolate hearts; and at Easter, it's chocolate eggs. I do not pour these out on my desk and tell the students to come up and *take* one. I walk around the classroom as they work, and I *give* the treat to each student directly. Why? Because I want the gift to be personal—*directly from me to them*. This may seem like an insignificant difference in distribution methodology, but I assure you it is not. When you walk around and hand these kinds of small treats directly to students, smile at them and say something like "Happy Halloween" or "I hope you have a wonderful Christmas," they naturally respond with something like, "Same to you" or "Thanks so much." The contact is brief and positive. You are sending a small but significant message: "I went out of my way to get this small gift for you, and I am giving it to you because you matter to me, and I like you."

These small gestures will pay huge dividends for you. It is difficult not to like a teacher who gives you something extra, and it is equally difficult not to want to give a little extra in return. While these kinds of things may happen more naturally in elementary schools than in secondary schools, it's my experience that these strategies work equally well in all secondary grades. It appears that students of all ages appreciate receiving candy from their teacher. In fact, I still do these kinds of things in my university preservice teacher-education classes, and they work just as well as they did in elementary school.

TACTIC: BE INVOLVED WITH STUDENT ACTIVITIES

While giving away candy on holidays is certainly a small way to engender some feeling of reciprocation in your students, there are opportunities that will present themselves to teachers to do fairly significant things for students, and thus, the payoff and payback can be more substantial. For example, one of the ways that you can stimulate a feeling of indebtedness in some of your students is through being involved with school teams or clubs. I always made it a point to coach senior teams in any school I taught. If that job was already taken, I volunteered to be an assistant coach. Why senior teams? Because typically, the players on these teams were the older students in the school, and thus, they generally had more influence on the younger students. It is difficult, if not impossible, for a student to be rude to you or disrupt your class on a Monday if you have just spent Friday evening and all day Saturday coaching them at a tournament—irrespective of how well the team performed.

The same applies to working with students via school clubs. It doesn't matter whether it's the student council, the yearbook or debate club, or future entrepreneurs. What matters is that you are providing a significant and extra service to this group of students (particularly student leaders), and they know it. They will reciprocate—many times and in myriad ways.

TACTIC: MOTIVATE FOR MONEY

When I was the principal of a junior high school, our school experienced a problem with *tagging*, which is a kind of personalized signature or symbol a graffiti artist spray paints somewhere to leave their mark. One Monday morning, the school custodian asked me to come outside with him, where he then showed me that two of our school doors had been tagged. I asked him to either remove the graffiti or paint over it right away. I long ago learned that if that kind of vandalism is not cleaned up quickly, it simply promotes further vandalism. He did as I asked, and all was well until the following Monday morning. Once again, two exterior doors had been tagged with the same symbol. Again I asked the custodian to remove the tags as quickly as possible, but I knew that I had to do something before the following weekend, or we would likely be dealing with the same problem again.

I called an assembly of all of the students just prior to lunch break. Once they were seated in the gym, I held up a crisp, new $100 dollar bill. I held the bill in front of me as I explained the following to the students:

For the last two weekends, someone has tagged your school. This is your school, and someone thinks they can vandalize it because they simply have no respect for your school. I know that most of you know nothing about who has done this, and I know that most of you do not approve of vandalism. But I also believe that some of you do know who has done this. I am talking to those students who do know something about this vandalism. After school today, when you go home, phone me. Do not come to my office during the day, but call me after school. The first person to call who has information that leads me to whoever has done this, that student will get this $100 bill—no questions asked. Now, go enjoy your lunch.

You might wonder if it was fair for me to assert my confidence that some students knew who the perpetrator was, but let's face it: no teenager vandalizes something in private and then keeps his or her mouth shut about committing this kind of act. They don't get any social recognition unless they either vandalize in the presence of their friends or do it alone and then brag about it later. So it was no surprise that I received five tipster phone calls that day after school. I learned that the boy who had been spray painting our doors didn't go to our school or even live in the neighborhood, but that he came to visit friends most weekends and tagged our doors at night as they watched. I got the offender's phone number and called his home. His father answered, and I told his dad who I was and why I was calling. I told the boy's father the story of the tagging and how I had received information from several sources that it was his son who was the offender.

"Look," I told him. "I have no interest in involving the police. I simply want the tagging to stop. If it does, you will never hear from me again. If it happens again, I will turn all of the information I have over to the police."

All he said was, "It won't happen again," and he hung up. It never did.

The next day, I gave the first informer $100, with a warning not to show off and be a big spender in front of his friends, who might put two and two together and figure out how he suddenly came into some extra money. I made sure to let all of the students in the school know that the problem had been solved. I wanted it to be well-known that the $100 reward incentive had worked. It was extremely important that all the students knew that I was serious about finding out which students were involved in any serious breaches of our behavioral expectations and that I was willing to pay big money for information that would help put a stop to such behaviors.

In a lot of ways, you could name this tactic, "I ain't no rat—at least, not for free." Most students behave appropriately most of the time. This reward system was aimed at those few students who choose to behave badly and to do so in significant ways. Many of the students at this school did not have a lot of money, so $100 was a huge incentive. I wanted those students who were inclined toward extremely poor behaviors to give some thought to the greatly increased probability that, if they chose to do things like vandalize the school, the likelihood of them being informed on was extremely high. They were well aware of the fact that *they* would turn in their friends for $100, so they rightly figured their friends would do the same to them.

There are, however, some potential problems that can arise from this kind of strategy. If the cash reward is too large, some students may actually be incentivized to commit acts of vandalism, agreeing ahead of time that one culprit will turn in the other, and they will then split the reward. It is, therefore, important that the reward not be so large as to become a motivator for the very kinds of behaviors you are attempting to curtail. We will discuss the idea of using rewards in detail in chapter 12 (page 151). For now, simply consider the possibility that if a reward is too significant, it may backfire and actually become an incentive.

Other educators may argue that schools shouldn't have to pay students for behaviors they ought to be doing on their own. This is a valid argument that applies to those students whose moral compass is well developed. However, that is not the case for all students who walk the hallways of our schools.

This is among the most basic kinds of reciprocation strategies, one that students are very familiar with—one person gives another person money in exchange for goods or services. And while there may be some things money can't buy, as a motivator for information from secondary-level students, money can work very well in select circumstances. Having said that, however, this is a strategy that I used very infrequently and only in situations where I could not obtain the information I urgently needed by more conventional means. I recommend the same for you.

TACTIC: BE AVAILABLE AND EMPATHETIC

Some students may struggle with issues outside of the classroom. Family stresses and personal issues make it difficult, if not impossible, for a student to be successful in school. You want to be the teacher that students can go to with their problems and be confident they will find an understanding ear and a compassionate heart. Youth trauma experts Larry K. Brendtro, Martin Brokenleg, and Steve Van Bockern (2019) classify students' need for trusting relationships as an essential component of survival, rivaling thirst and hunger. But students, particularly those who have experienced trauma, don't give trust freely. Brendtro and colleagues (2019) suggest mistrustful youth need adult figures, including educators, who will turn *toward* them despite unproductive "bids for attention," offering messages to students such as:

- "I am interested in you."
- "I want to understand you."
- "I'd like to help you."
- "I accept you—even if not all of your behavior." (p. 58)

Remember, many students are blind to their own potential. They need an advocate, a champion who will always be there for them because they cannot see the possibilities for their futures in the ways that you can.

Beyond listening, show them the greatness you see in them—over and over and over again, until they start believing in themselves. If you are the teacher that has their backs, they will have yours.

Beyond being an available and empathetic listener who sees the best in students, there are a number of ways you can show your students that you care about them and their success in school. In doing so, you strengthen your effectiveness as their teacher. The following sections offer additional variations on and examples of this tactic.

Visit Students Who Are Hospitalized

If you teach long enough, you will likely experience a situation where one of your students is hospitalized for an extended period, and they may even have to stay at home for a period of time once they are discharged. This presents you with a unique opportunity to strengthen your relationship with this student and to set the stage for even more positive influence opportunities when the student eventually returns to school.

No matter the reason for it, students are generally taken aback when they are in the hospital or homebound, and you take time from your personal life to visit them. It shows your students that they matter, both in and out of school. It shows you care, which is often the motivator a student most needs not just for academics but to feel valued in life. I once received a card in the mail from a student whom I had taught some twenty years earlier. In the card, she reminded me of how depressed she had been during those years and how she had attempted suicide. She then told me that my visit to the hospital, along with some of her friends that I brought with me, had convinced her that she was cared for and that people would miss her if she was gone. For her, that brief visit to the hospital was life changing.

Help Your Students Be Successful Readers

Stay in at recess over and over again to help a student who is struggling to learn to read; give these students books at the appropriate reading level to take home.

Sometimes, you may want to give books to these students as gifts from you to them to help celebrate their successes.

Help Your Students' Caregivers

Sometimes, you can be more effective as a teacher by strengthening your relationship with their caregivers. Having the significant adults in a student's life support your efforts as a teacher can sometimes be the difference between success or failure in your work with a student. I have provided food, furniture, and finances to some of the families of my students. This is always done discreetly and never made public so as not to embarrass the students. I received nothing but cooperation and gratitude from these students and their families in return.

While beyond the scope of this book, in schools where need is rampant, consider how you might spearhead an effort to establish dedicated wraparound services (services ranging from counseling and substance abuse support to tutoring and clothes closets) for your school or district. In *The Wraparound Guide*, experts Leigh Colburn and Linda Beggs (2021) offer essential knowledge for gathering student input to determine essential services, building community partnerships, and finding a variety of funding sources for this purpose.

Make Sure Students Feel Safe at School

Students simply cannot do well in your classroom if they don't feel safe there (Jensen, 2019). When a student comes to you with concerns about bullying behaviors—be it physical, verbal, or digital—take their concerns seriously. Bullying is a complex issue. Peterson (2018) explores the issue of bullying in a chapter titled "Stand Up Straight With Your Shoulders Back." In the chapter, Peterson (2018) looks at bullying from the perspective of why bullies choose particular victims, and he then offers strategies that people can use to avoid being victimized by others. If you teach students strategies from a resource such as this that prevent them from being bullied, they will not only feel indebted to you, but they will also be better students and better persons overall.

SUMMARY

None of this chapter's strategies are easy. None of this will happen quickly. Relationships are built over time and with experiences. However, know that whenever you do something extraordinary for your students, whenever you go the extra mile, whenever you are compassionate and supportive beyond what they would normally get from a teacher, whenever you spend your personal time helping them or their families—they will be grateful, and the rule of reciprocation will kick in. Then, you will be able to accomplish some really astonishing things with these students.

As you reflect on this chapter, make sure to remember the following.

- Reciprocation is a soft tactic in which a teacher gives students something that they want in return for something the teacher wants. (See Henry's Rule, page 40.) Reciprocity is hardwired into our genes because giving back to the group helped our ancestors survive and reproduce.

- It is important that students accept the legitimacy that what you have to give them in terms of knowledge in the classroom is of value to them. What you are teaching or asking of them needs to be presented in ways that your students see as being important to them.

- Giving your students small gifts—like chocolates on Valentine's Day or candy canes at Christmas—can help engender a feeling of reciprocation in your students. Under certain circumstances, money can be used as a reward for specific kinds of behaviors.

- The larger the favor you have done for your students, the larger the perceived debt of reciprocity they will feel. Such favors might include: giving extra academic or emotional support, helping out a caregiver, or making students feel welcome and safe at school.

- See beyond students' presenting behaviors, especially when students act in a negative or self-destructive fashion. Show them the potential you see in them that they may not see in themselves.

- If possible, visit hospitalized or homebound students when they are ill. If you can't visit, send cards or other written messages expressing your concern for the student.

Reflective Practice

Commit to doing at least two of the following three reciprocation strategies in the next few weeks in your classroom. These will, of course, vary depending on the context in which you teach and the time of year.

1. Give each student a seasonally appropriate treat or gift, such as mini-chocolate bars at Halloween, candy canes at Christmas, chocolate hearts or bunnies at Easter, or age-appropriate small toys or puzzles at any time. (Remember, not all students can partake of sweets, nor do they necessarily celebrate the same holidays.)

2. Get involved with a student group in an outside-the-classroom school activity. Whether this is a team or a club already in existence or a new group that you want to establish with your class is up to you. The important thing here is for your students to see that you like to spend time with them and that you are willing to give up some of your personal time to help them and be with them. Additionally, being with students outside of a teaching context gives you and your students an opportunity to build a different kind of relationship, because now the focus of why you are together has shifted.

3. Select one student who you feel needs to change. This could be a student who is underperforming academically in a significant way, a student whose classroom behaviors are inappropriate, or a student who is not engaged in any meaningful way in your classroom. From all of the strategies regarding how to engender a sense of reciprocation in another person, select two that you feel would likely succeed with this student. Put them into practice and monitor the results.

Please remember, none of the strategies discussed in *The Tactical Teacher* will work all of the time with every student. You may have to try several times, or you might find that some of the other strategies that we will explore in subsequent chapters may prove to be more effective.

For now, attempt a reciprocation strategy and see how it works with the student you selected. You can monitor the results of your attempts using the following chart.

Student's name:	
Reciprocation strategy 1:	Observed effects of this strategy on the student:
Reciprocation strategy 2:	Observed effects of this strategy on the student:

CHAPTER 5

SOFT TACTICS FOR LIKABILITY

Many teachers discount the importance of having their teachers like them. In her TED Talk, Rita Pierson (2013), a veteran teacher who began her career in the 1970s, nicely sums up her thoughts about such thinking as she relates a conversation she had with a teacher colleague:

> A colleague said to me one time, "They don't pay me to like the kids. They pay me to teach a lesson. The kids should learn it. I should teach it—they should learn it. Case closed!"
>
> Well, I said to her, "You know, kids don't learn from people they don't like."
>
> She said to me, "That's just a bunch of hooey."
>
> I said to her, "Well, your year is going to be long and arduous, dear."
>
> Needless to say, it was.

The bedrock of teaching is the relationship between you and the students you are attempting to teach. The more challenging or at risk the students, the more critical it is to have an effective teacher-student relationship if you are to have any hope of being successful teaching them.

While the teacher-student relationship can have elements that are also found in a parent-child relationship, or even in some small ways elements of a relationship that a student may have with their friends, the teacher-student relationship is unique. First, it typically has a start and end date. It usually begins at the start of the school year or semester, and it normally ends to a large degree when that term is over (unless a student takes multiple secondary-level classes in a teacher's subject area). Thus, you have a relatively short window of opportunity in which to build an effective working relationship with your students.

Teachers who work hard at having an effective working relationship with their students will naturally find that these relationships have far more depth in June than they did during the first week of September. Thus, the degree of your influence on your students can be directly impacted by how much time you have spent with them. You can have a far greater degree of influence at the end of the term than you can at the beginning— *if* you have laid the necessary groundwork—and being likable is one aspect of this work.

I want to illustrate this point with a story about some high school students I taught. Many in the school community considered these students, for the most part, to be extremely challenging. At the time this event occurred, we had been together for ten months, and I was preparing them for high school completion exams—exams they would have to pass to get their high school diplomas.

We had some out-of-town educators who were observing the class, and after observing us in action for some time, one of them asked me—in front of the entire class—why the students were so cooperative with me. Given the nature of the students, he found this quite surprising. I replied, "Once they *like me* and *respect me* and know how *committed I am to them*, they generally want to have a good relationship with me. They don't want to disappoint me with bad behavior or really poor schoolwork. That's when I can *make them feel guilty* if they do." At that point, a student I had taught for two years immediately interrupted and yelled out to the entire group, "Oh my god, he's soooo good at it too—making me feel guilty if I disappoint him!"

If this student didn't *like* me, if this student didn't *respect* me, then she would have cared little to nothing about disappointing me, and I would not have been able to use this to motivate her to be successful at school. This only makes sense. As researchers Noah J. Goldstein, Steve J. Martin, and Robert B. Cialdini (2008) remind us, "The more we like people, the more we want to say yes to them" (p. 6). This goes for us as teachers, and it also applies to our students. Ultimately, this student, whom many would consider as at risk, went on to university and obtained a degree in social work.

As you put this chapter's tactics to work, and as I have noted in previous chapters, it is important for you to reflect on the ethics of influence, which we will explore in detail in chapter 16 (page 193). As teachers, it is clear that the more our students like us, the more influence we have over them. But influence is like any tool—we can use it for good or for evil. We need to be very vigilant about *why* we want our students to like us and for *whose benefit* we will use this influence. Ultimately, the influence we have on our students must be directed toward *what they need* and *what is good for them*.

This gives rise to the question: If a great relationship (one where our students like us and care what we think about them) is foundational to good teaching—how do teachers establish this kind of relationship? What things can you do to create and sustain this kind of effective teacher-student relationship with your students? To answer these questions, this chapter explores the following tactics.

- Use the power of perceived similarity.
- Create similarities between you and alpha students.
- Use mirroring to establish similarities.
- Speak to the elephant, not the rider.
- Sell yourself first, then the curriculum.
- Use the positive-word strategy with students you dislike.

TACTIC: USE THE POWER OF PERCEIVED SIMILARITY

In chapter 2 (page 17), we looked at the power of in-groups and how human beings generally prefer members of their own group (whomever and however they perceive that to be) to people who are not members of their group (McIntyre & Blanchard, 2012). This is hardwired into our genetic code; it operates within us at the subconscious level. We tend to like people who we believe are like us in some ways, and the more ways they are similar to us, the more we tend to like them. John Ortberg (2017) sums this up nicely in the title of his book, *I'd Like You More If You Were More Like Me.* Who among us hasn't had that thought on more than one occasion? Brown (2013) puts it this way, "One important pathway to liking is perceived similarity. When people see you as similar to them in some fashion, they immediately—and almost automatically—like you more" (p. 6).

It would be unwise to underestimate the power that perceived similarity has to get people to agree to our requests. In a series of experiments designed to test the power of similarity to obtain cooperation, researchers Jerry M. Burger, Nicole Messian, Shebani Patel, Alicia del Prado, and Carmen Anderson (2004) test the impact that having the *same birthday* or having the *same name* has on people's willingness to cooperate. In the study, participants were asked to read an eight-page essay and provide the requester with feedback on the content of the essay. When participants were led to believe that they shared the same birthday as the requester, they agreed to the request 62.2 percent of the time, while those who believed they did not have anything in common with the requester only agreed to the request 34.2 percent of the time (Burger et al., 2004). Almost *twice as many* people agreed to a request simply because they thought they shared the same birthday as the person asking the favor.

In a follow-up study, participants were asked to donate money to a well-known charity (Burger et al., 2004). People who were led to believe they had the *same first name* of the requester donated an average of $2.07. For those who shared no similarity with the requester, their average donation was $1.00. Donations *more than doubled* based simply on the fact that the person asking for a donation had the same first name. Such is the power of perceived similarity to enhance the likelihood of obtaining cooperation from others.

Cialdini (2007) puts it this way:

> We like people who are similar to us. This fact seems to hold true whether the similarity is in the area of opinions, personality traits, background, or lifestyle. Consequently, those who wish to be liked in order to increase our compliance can accomplish that purpose by appearing similar to us in a wide variety of ways. (p. 173)

There are myriad ways you can use similarity to establish a connection with your students and thus enhance the likelihood of obtaining their cooperation. Burger and colleagues (2004) look at the power of having the same first name or sharing the same birthday, and these are strategies you can use as a teacher *if*, in fact, you actually share these similarities with some of the students in your classes. Obviously, you will not share the same name and birthday as most of your students. However, the power of similarity works in many other areas as well. For example, you might share any of the following with your students.

- Play or like the same sports
- Come from the same hometown or country
- Play the same musical instrument
- Live in the same neighborhood
- Have gone to the same school when you were a child
- Like a particular movie or the same TV shows
- Have the same hobbies or share similar interests (coins, cars, cooking, music)
- Share similar opinions about certain things
- Admire the same people

For your target students to know the ways in which they are similar to you, you will have to find out about the likes and interests of these students. As a classroom teacher, one way I accomplished this was to start the year with an assignment that I called the *Newspaper of the Self*. I would have students write a newspaper in which they were the only topic. In the sports section, they would tell about the sports they played or liked to watch. If they hated sports, they would tell me why. The TV section was about their favorite TV shows, and the same with music and movies. The travel section talked about the best holiday they ever had or the fantasy holiday they would take if they could go anywhere they wanted. You get the idea. This assignment was a gold mine of information that I could then use to establish similarities with each of the students I taught. In my experience, if you maximize what you know about your students, you will almost always find something you share in common.

Note: You will find a complete description of the Newspaper of the Self assignment in the appendix (page 217).

TACTIC: CREATE SIMILARITIES BETWEEN YOU AND ALPHA STUDENTS

There will be times when you have a student or group of students who are natural leaders. They have established themselves as the alpha students among their peers (students whose peers like and respect them; the leaders and influencers in your classroom), and perhaps they have held this position for several years before they arrived in your classroom. It is highly unlikely that you will be able to change this kind of well-established social hierarchy. Instead, you need to figure out ways to have it work for you. You need to get these alpha students on your side in order to vicariously influence the students who follow them.

This is of particular importance when these alpha students impact your classes in a negative way. You need these student leaders to be supportive of your classroom goals. This is simply a reality of teaching that effective teachers are well aware of. However, this prompts the question: How can you win these kinds of students over? What can you do to get them to like you a little bit so that you have a starting point from which to work on building an effective student-teacher relationship?

Your first step is to use the guidance in the previous section to look for similarities. If you have had conversations with these kinds of students, and you discover there is nothing that you have in common with them at that point, then you need to *create similarity*. As in the previous section, find out what the target student is interested in outside of school. How do they spend their free time? What movies, TV shows, or Netflix series do they follow? Are they into any kinds of sports—and if so, what kind of sports? What is their favorite team? Who are their favorite athletes?

Once you have this information, begin to familiarize yourself to some degree with a few of the things your target student is interested in. This may involve you watching a movie or an episode or two of a TV series you are unfamiliar with. It may involve you listening to some hitherto unknown music or looking up *zorbing* online. Once you have some familiarity with something this student is interested in, initiate a conversation on that topic. The fact that you know about this particular sport or music or TV show tells the student you have similarities, and that can be the way in as you seek to build an effective working relationship.

When I taught eighth grade, I was trying to win over a particularly challenging student who was quite influential in my class in a very negative way. Let's call her Nicole. When I went on my exploration mission to see if we had anything in common, I discovered that Nicole liked a show I had never heard of called *Jersey Shore*. So, I watched a few episodes. To say this was a painful undertaking would be an understatement. To this day, I can remember a character on the show named Snooki relieving herself in a plant pot on an outdoor deck. However, when the opportunity presented itself, I mentioned something to Nicole about Snooki. It was amazing to see this student instantly open up and start babbling on and on about Snooki and the show. I was careful not to say anything negative about the show. I was in, and things just got better and better after that.

TACTIC: USE MIRRORING TO ESTABLISH SIMILARITIES

Another simple but powerful way to establish similarity and enhance likability is through *mirroring*. Voss (2016) tells us:

> [Mirroring] follows a very basic but profound biological principle: We fear what's different and are drawn to what's similar. . . . Mirroring, then, when practiced consciously, is the art of insinuating similarity. "Trust me," a mirror signals to the unconscious, "You and I—we're alike." (p. 36)

How can you mirror students you are trying to connect with? One simple verbal mirroring technique is by repeating the last one to three words of what the student has just said. If you use the student's exact words, they will feel that you are really listening, that they have been heard. It's a subconscious feeling of, "My teacher gets me—we're alike."

In other circumstances, you may want to repeat whole sentences or phrases—again, using *the exact same words in the exact same order*—that the student has used. In a study done with restaurant servers (Lynn, 2003), one group of waiters was trained to mirror the customers' orders by repeating the order back *using the exact words* of the customers. The other group of servers responded to the customers' orders using phrases like "OK" or "Coming right up" to indicate they had heard the order. Mirroring increased the number of customers who chose to leave a tip by 26 percent compared to the non-mirroring servers, and the amount of the tips *doubled*. Mirroring speaks to the subconscious, an area that we have little awareness of and even less control over—but an aspect of our personalities that silently and most assuredly drives many of our feelings and behaviors.

TACTIC: SPEAK TO THE ELEPHANT, NOT THE RIDER

In *The Happiness Hypothesis*, social psychologist and professor of ethics Jonathan Haidt (2006) uses the image of a rider on an elephant to describe how little awareness and control we have over our subconscious:

> The image that I came up with for myself, as I marveled at my weakness, was that I was a rider on the back of an elephant. I'm holding the reins in my hands, and by pulling one way or the other I can tell the elephant to turn, to stop, or to go. I can direct things, but only when the elephant doesn't have desires of his own. When the elephant really wants to do something, I'm no match for him. (p. 4)

In Haidt's (2006) analogy, the rider represents conscious reasoning, the things we are aware of as we analyze and size up the various options and the potential consequences of our choices. Everything else going on is the elephant—the automatic, unconscious processes, the things going on in your subconscious mind that you are totally unaware of. Haidt (2006) argues that most people spend their time and energy trying to persuade other people's riders by using arguments based on logic, facts, and reasoning. Teachers do this often. It is an arena in which most teachers are quite comfortable.

The notion of appealing to reason rather than emotion in order to persuade others has been around for centuries. The 17th century French philosopher René Descartes (1637) is well-known for this famous quote, "I think, therefore I am." Over two centuries later, however, neuroscientist Antonio Damasio (2005) argues in *Descartes' Error*:

> Reason may not be as pure as most of us think it is or wish it were, that emotions and feelings may not be intruders in the bastion of reason at all: they may be enmeshed in its networks, for worse *and* for better. The strategies of human reason probably did not develop, in either evolution or any single individual, without the guiding force of the mechanisms of biological regulation, of which emotion and feeling are notable expressions. Moreover, even after reasoning strategies become established in the formative years, their effective deployment probably depends, to a considerable extent, on a continued ability to experience feelings. (p. xvi)

Damasio worked at the University of Iowa and studied people who had damage to the part of the brain where emotions are formed. He examined the famous case of Phineas Gage, who was a Vermont railway worker (Damasio, 2005). In 1848, Gage, who was twenty-five years old at the time, had a metal tamping rod thrust completely through his skull as the result of an explosion. Gage survived and even went back to work but lost virtually all ability to make judgments relating to socially appropriate behavior.

In examining the medical records of Gage and in working with his own patients, Damasio (2005) finds they all had one thing in common: when the part of the brain that generates emotions was damaged, the patients could no longer make decisions. They could describe in logical terms what they thought they should do, but they couldn't actually do it. They could not make even the simplest choices.

This led Damasio (2005) to hypothesize that contrary to the common belief that people make most of their decisions based on reason and logic, in fact, what really occurs is that most of us may use reason to move us toward various options in our decision-making processes, but *the final decisions we make are governed primarily by emotions*. In *Homo Deus: A Brief History of Tomorrow*, Harari (2017) agrees with this view, arguing, "Sapiens don't behave according to a cold mathematical logic, but rather according to a warm social logic. We are ruled by emotions" (p. 140).

The Undoing Project (Lewis, 2017) explores the work of Nobel Prize–winning psychologists Daniel Kahneman and his colleague Amos Tversky, who came to the same conclusion. In conducting experiments that investigated how doctors arrived at diagnoses, the researchers concluded: "Most physicians try to maintain this facade of being rational and scientific and logical and it's a great lie . . . a partial lie. What leads us is hopes and dreams and emotion" (as cited in Lewis, 2017, p. 229).

In attempting to influence your students to do what is in their best interests for the long term, you can certainly appeal to reason and logic on occasion. However, Haidt (2006) argues that the more effective way to persuade people is to try to persuade their elephants. You will often be more effective if you appeal to your students' emotions in your attempts to have an impact on the decisions they make than if you appeal to reason.

A teacher who attempts to get an underperforming fourteen-year-old to work harder at school through reason alone may say something along the lines of:

> *If you work harder, you can get into high school on the academic track. Then you can work hard in high school for three years and get into university. Then you can work hard at university for four years and get a degree and a good job. Then you can work hard at your job and advance and make more money. See, you need to work hard now, and it will pay off for you in the long run.*

What the teacher is telling this student is rational, logical, truthful—and most likely useless. Why?

Think about what the student hears. The student hears the phrase "work hard" over and over, as well as "in the long run," which is a future years down the road—a future he or she can barely imagine, let alone feel motivated by.

What does the student *feel*? Perhaps exhaustion—something along the lines of, "This is insane. This teacher is talking about years into the future and me working hard for years and years into the future. I'm interested in my life *now* and my friends *now* and what we're doing this Friday night."

If you want to increase your impact on students, you need to appeal to their feeling and emotions much more often than making an appeal based only on reason. Getting your students to like you is a cornerstone of that kind of appeal. In *The Righteous Mind*, Haidt (2012) tells us that "if there is affection, admiration, or a desire to please the other person, then the elephant leans *toward* that person and the rider tries to find the truth in the other person's arguments" (p. 68).

These are powerful strategies that you can use to great effect in your classroom. If your students like you, this increases the probability of the elephant going in the directions you want it to go and taking the rider (your students) along with it. However, if the elephant digs in its heels and doesn't want to go where you want it to go, there isn't much you can do, even if the rider agrees with you at a rational level. Why? Because we are mostly emotional-social creatures. Thus, speaking to the emotional elephant is likely going to be a far more effective persuasive strategy than speaking only to the rational rider.

TACTIC: SELL YOURSELF FIRST, THEN THE CURRICULUM

In the introduction to this book, I intimated that as teachers, we are all salespeople. While we don't sell furniture, fridges, or financial planning, we do sell the idea that knowledge has value, we should treat other people respectfully, students should learn to read and write and speak effectively, and so on.

In *The Tipping Point*, Malcolm Gladwell (2002) takes a close look at a man who excels at sales, Tom Gau. Gau is a financial planner who makes millions of dollars a year through sales. At the time of the writing, he was in his forties and wealthy, with no need to work. Yet, he went to work early each morning and stayed late. Why? In Gau's words:

> I love my clients, OK? I'll bend over backward for them. . . . I call my clients my family. I tell my clients I've got two families. I've got my wife and my kids and I've got you. . . . I love my job. I love my job. . . . I manage a lot of money. I'm one of the top producers in the nation. But I don't tell my clients that. I'm not here because of that. I'm here to help people. I love helping people. I don't have to work anymore. I'm financially independent. So why am I here working these long hours? Because I love helping people. I love people. *It's called a relationship.* (as cited in Gladwell, 2002, p. 71; emphasis added)

Gau once helped Donald Moine, a behavioral psychologist who studies persuasion, put together a kind of script book of the responses he uses when clients ask him questions about financial planning. Gladwell (2002) observes that while anyone could memorize these responses and use them verbatim, this in itself is *not* sufficient in order to be persuasive. There is something else in the mix besides giving great answers to clients' questions.

Gladwell (2002) describes it this way:

> [Gau] seems to have some kind of indefinable trait, something powerful and contagious and irresistible that goes beyond what comes out of his mouth, that makes people who meet him want to agree with him. It's energy. It's enthusiasm. It's charm. It's likability. It's all those things. (p. 73)

Gladwell (2002) then goes on to describe how incredibly happy and positive Gau is in all aspects of his life.

Think about the very best teachers you had as a student, the ones who persuaded you to work hard, to do your best, to reach your potential, the ones you didn't want to disappoint. I suspect they had many of the same qualities as Tom Gau. I would bet that the great teachers you had as a student and the great teachers you work with could be described as being *energetic, enthusiastic, charming, happy, positive,* and *likable*—the qualities that Gladwell (2002) observes in Tom Gau. Most students want to be in *that* teacher's class—the teacher who loves to help them and genuinely cares about them; the teacher who is energetic, enthusiastic, charming, happy, positive, and who is ever so *likable*.

You can be that teacher. What's stopping you?

TACTIC: USE THE POSITIVE-WORD STRATEGY WITH STUDENTS YOU DISLIKE

So far, this chapter has explored the importance of likability from the perspective of how much more effective you can be when your students like you. I now want to look at the flip side of this same coin.

No matter how much we like students in general, no matter how much we want to help our students be successful in school, there will come along—hopefully on rare occasions—a student that you just don't like. For various reasons, no matter how much you try and connect with this student, their attitudes, behaviors, and values just rub you the wrong way. They are disrespectful, disengaged, devious, and no matter how much you try, you really don't like them. In fact, on days when they are absent, you quietly smile to yourself and maybe even utter a quiet prayer of gratitude.

In some sense, this is completely understandable. We all have our preferences in terms of the qualities that we like and can relate to in other people, and we will come across students whom we just cannot seem to connect with and whom we simply do not like. When this happens, it will most certainly have negative consequences on how well this student performs in your classroom. What can you do in circumstances such as this?

One strategy that can work very effectively is the positive-word strategy. On the surface, this strategy is quick and simple. All you do is write *one positive word or short phrase* about that particular student each day. You write this in your plan book or a notebook, somewhere that is private. That's it—one word or short phrase each day. While it may sound simple, be assured that there will be days where you may find it challenging to find even one positive word to write about this particular student—and writing "Stacey was away today" doesn't count.

Then, on an occasion of your choosing, give this student the list of words and phrases you have created. I know one teacher who does this on Valentine's Day. She gives each student a valentine with a list of positive words and phrases that she created for each student in the preceding weeks and months. Each student's list is unique, and the positive descriptors apply only to them.

Two things are likely to happen when you utilize this strategy.

1. It prompts you to find something positive among all the negative aspects of that student. The exercise forces you to shift your focus from the negative to the positive. When you build on this daily, somewhere along the journey, you are likely going to find yourself beginning to view this student in a more positive light. There is a commonly quoted proverb, ostensibly originating from China, that says, *Two-thirds of what we see is behind our eyes.* By placing some positive thoughts behind your eyes, you are going to see them come alive in these kinds of students.

2. When the student (who in many instances will likely feel the same about you as you do about them) receives the list of positive attributes that you see in them, their attitude toward you will likely soften. They now have concrete evidence that you can and do see positive qualities in them. Watch their behavior—and your relationship with them—change, and change for the better.

SUMMARY

As you reflect on this chapter, make sure to remember the following.

*   For many students, the teacher-student relationship is fundamental to whether or not they will be successful in your classroom. Getting your students to like you is one of the most powerful ways you have to influence their behaviors.

*   Perceived similarity is one way to engender likability because we tend to like people who are like us. You can achieve this through simple actions such as liking the same sports teams, sharing the same hobbies, liking the same music or TV shows, and so on.

*   Mirroring is an effective tool to get students to cooperate with you and to make them feel understood. Simply repeating the last few words they say is one way to mirror a student.

*   Teachers who only use logic and reason to motivate students are, in effect, speaking only to the rider and not to the elephant. The elephant represents how students feel, and it is often more effective and more essential to address how a student feels when attempting to change attitudes and behaviors.

*   If you have a student whom you don't like and cannot seem to work with, use the positive-word strategy to change both your attitude and the student's.

Reflective Practice

As a way to form a connection with specific students, complete the the following actions.

Identify Students to Connect With

Fill out the chart in this section while completing the following steps.

1. Select three target students—students whom you have purposely chosen because you want them to change certain aspects of their classroom performance. The changes you desire for them can be in the areas of greater academic performance, more engagement, or more positive classroom behaviors.

2. In the first column, write the names of these three students.

3. In the second column, write at least two things that you have in common with these students. It is important that these similarities be things that involve your students' lives *outside* of school.

    Important: You may find that you cannot complete the list. In other words, you may discover that you do not have at least two similarities for each of your students. If this is the case, then you will have to create similarities. If you have to do this, use the strategies described in this chapter.

Name of student 1:	Similarity 1: Similarity 2:
Name of student 2:	Similarity 1: Similarity 2:
Name of student 3:	Similarity 1: Similarity 2:

Remember, perceived similarity is only effective as an influence strategy if students are aware of the similarity they have with you. Therefore, it is essential that you spend some time discussing your areas of commonality. Do this in casual conversation where it arises naturally. Think hallways and the lunchroom or cafeteria. A casual inquiry such as, "Hey John, did you see that amazing three-pointer that clinched the game for the Lakers last night?" is far more effective than, "Hey John, do you know that I like basketball too?"

Engage in Mirroring With a Student

Select one of the three students you targeted in the chart. For one week, practice mirroring with this student. That is, deliberately repeat the last three words they say to you in the exact order they say them in several of your interactions with them throughout the week. This should appear natural, not automatic. You do not need to do this all of the time. Do this when you believe it will help the student to feel that you understand what they are saying and where they are coming from.

Use the following questions to record your observations.

- How did the student respond when you used mirroring in the conversation?

- In what ways, if any, do you feel your relationship with this student has been impacted by your use of mirroring?

The Tactical Teacher © 2022 Solution Tree Press • SolutionTree.com
Visit **go.SolutionTree.com/behavior** to download this free reproducible.

Create Positive-Word Associations With a Student

Select a student in your class that you either don't like very much or the one student you like the least. For the next week, each day, think of one positive thing you have seen that student do or one positive thing you can say about that student. Complete the following chart with your thoughts and observations.

Student's name:	
Day of the week:	**Positive comments or observations:**
Monday	1. 2.
Tuesday	1. 2.
Wednesday	1. 2.
Thursday	1. 2.
Friday	1. 2.

After you complete this chart, ask yourself whether your feelings toward this student have changed. If so, in what ways? Think about sharing your chart with this particular student in some fashion if this feels comfortable to you. Doing so will likely have a positive impact on your relationship.

The Tactical Teacher © 2022 Solution Tree Press • SolutionTree.com
Visit **go.SolutionTree.com/behavior** to download this free reproducible.

SOFT TACTICS FOR THE POWER OF COMMITMENT

A school director and old friend once asked me to establish an accredited high school program on a First Nations Reserve. She had been there one year, and the high school program that was in place was not working well. She thought I might be able to help, so we talked, and I went to "the Rez" to take a look.

What I observed were a few students dropping by the high school when they got bored. These students were working on self-paced modules, so if they missed one day or several days of school, they weren't really missing any work because when they decided to show up at school, they simply picked up wherever they had left off. In reality, the school work didn't much matter to them anyway. I agreed to see if we could build something more akin to a conventional high school, so I started to teach these students.

They *hated* me! Really, there is no other way to put it—they hated me. In their eyes, I was this White guy from the city coming out to the Rez who had no business being there and nothing to offer them. They swore at me—sometimes in English, other times in Cree—sometimes in a whisper, other times loudly enough to ensure I had heard them. That was the start of the school year in the fall.

Fast forward to spring of the same year. It was a beautiful evening in May. The school had put on a spring concert that evening, and I was walking around the building after the concert making sure that all the doors and windows were properly shut. One of my students, Annie, was walking with me—chatting about the concert, her friends, school, and so on. It was about 9:00 in the evening. I couldn't help but wonder, what was this sixteen-year-old Indigenous girl doing walking the school hallways, helping me on a beautiful warm spring evening? She was popular and had a lot of friends. Surely she had better things to do.

So, as I wrote in *The Successful Teacher's Survival Kit* (Ripley, 2019), I asked:

> Annie, why are you here? Your mom and sister have already left. I'm sure you have lots of other things you could be doing, yet here you are, chatting with me and helping me lock up. And, as I recall, when I first started teaching here last fall, you hated me! You refused to do any work. When I gave the first assignment in our English class last fall, you yelled at me, 'I don't read, and I don't write!' What's changed? You and the other kids are nice to me now. Seriously, I want to know. What happened? Why the change? (pp. 12–13)

This young lady then proceeded to teach me a lesson that I have never forgotten, one that I believe is essential to what it means to be a good teacher. "Well, Ripley," she replied, smiling:

> You're right. We did hate you back then. You wanted us to come to school every day, and you made us work when we did. You were pushy and demanding and always wanted more from us. So we made a bet as to how long it would take us to get you to quit. We were mean to you and swore at you and refused to do any work because we figured you would quit—just like so many of the other white guys who come to the Rez to teach.
>
> But you didn't. You kept coming back. You came every day. *You never even took a sick day.* Finally, after several months, you wore us out. We just gave up. We knew that no matter how badly we treated you, you would show up the next day anyway and try to teach us. (Ripley, 2019, pp. 12–13)

At the end of the school year, Annie wrote me a beautiful letter about all she had learned that year and what a great experience the year had been for her. I still have that letter. There it was: the incredible power of commitment for both teachers (to their students) and students (to their learning). This chapter details the following commitment-themed tactics you can use to motivate and influence students.

- Understand the importance of teacher commitment.
- Implement an Adopt-a-Kid program.
- Understand habits and the power of consistency.
- Start with small commitments focused on self-identity.
- Use four steps to achieve student commitment.

TACTIC: UNDERSTAND THE IMPORTANCE OF TEACHER COMMITMENT

The lesson that Annie taught me applies to all teachers. You cannot be effective unless you are *there*—there at school with your students, working hard every day to teach them. If you want to have an effect on your students, if you want to be influential and persuasive and inspire them, well, you can't do that from home. Nor can you hope to achieve those things if your students don't believe that you are going to be there *for* them and *with* them the entire year, at a very minimum.

Why is this? Because effective teacher-student relationships take time to develop. Trust and respect do not come automatically in the first week of school, particularly as students age into adolescence. If your students have experiences with high rates of teacher turnover, they may even ask you about your commitment to them in the form of questions such as "How long are you planning to stay and teach us?" Researchers Melinda Adnot, Thomas Dee, Veronica Katz, and James Wyckoff (2017) find that "higher rates of teacher turnover are legitimately thought to negatively influence student outcomes" (p. 72). In an eight-year study of over 850,000 upper-elementary students, researchers Matthew Ronfeldt, Susanna Loeb, and James Wyckoff (2013) further find that "students in grade levels with higher (teacher) turnover score lower in both English language arts (ELA) and math" (p. 4).

As teachers, it's clear we all need to be there for our students, making a genuine commitment to them. *Be there* when they don't deserve it. *Be there* when they behave badly. *Be there* when they fight with you because you are trying to get them to do their best and learn something. Make a commitment to your students to be there for them. Let them see and feel and know for certain that you will be there for them—today, tomorrow, and the day after that—because you believe they are worth it, even if they don't think they are.

Consider the following example. In the July 2018 issue of *Wired*, Daniel Duane describes his experiences enrolling his daughter at Willie Brown Middle School in San Francisco. This school was state of the art—opening in August of 2015 at the cost of $54 million. The curriculum focused on science, technology, engineering, and mathematics (STEM) and supported this focus with robotics laboratories, Apple TVs in each classroom, and Chromebooks for every student.

Yet, after only one month, the principal had resigned, and there were extensive reports of violence at the school in the local media. By October of the first year, the school was on to its third principal, and stories circulated in the community that six teachers had resigned.

What happened? Why had this school, with its beautiful architecture and all of the support it had in terms of modern technology, suffered such an abysmal start? Economist and policy expert on education Eric Hanushek (2018) says that of all of the reforms that have been attempted to improve schools over decades—reforms such as smaller class sizes, more technological support, new buildings, and the like—all miss something very fundamental to school success. If schools are not staffed with good teachers who clearly demonstrate they are effective in the classroom in helping students learn—educators who have made a *long-term commitment* to the school and the students who go there—most of these other reforms are merely window dressing. They look good, but they don't matter much.

A significant part of a teacher's commitment to their students is to be there and to *be there for the long haul.* It is virtually impossible for a teacher to develop an effective working relationship with students if the students think you are likely to leave them sometime in the near future. This makes sense. Why would they invest in *you* if they believe you have failed to invest in *them*?

Just as Annie's words taught me, if your students (especially those who are the most challenging) do not get a sense from you that you are there for them and there for a significant length of time, they will not invest in you. They will not give you the chance to build an effective student-teacher relationship with them, they will not trust you, and they will not respect you. Because of this, it is highly unlikely that they will learn from you. However, if you make that kind of commitment, and your students know that you believe in them and are going to be there *for them* and *with them* day after day, then even the most challenging students may give you a chance to truly teach them.

Fancy furniture and the latest technology are no substitute for competent and committed teachers. That is why schools like Willie Brown Middle School failed to live up to expectations—they focused on those things that can be seen and look good—the veneer of education—but not nearly enough attention was given to the hearts of the teachers and their willingness to commit and connect with their students.

TACTIC: IMPLEMENT AN ADOPT-A-KID PROGRAM

One strategy that I used very effectively in a number of junior high and middle schools with a high percentage of students at risk was an Adopt-a-Kid program. In October of each year, after teachers had an opportunity to get to know students fairly well, staff would identify students who they felt were at risk in some capacity—poor grades, social issues, dropping out, and so on. Then, every staff member who was interested in participating in the program (this included non-teaching staff) would meet, and each volunteer would choose one or two students to "adopt" for the year, typically a student they knew and cared about. They would then work diligently to develop a special relationship with that student to let them know someone at the school really cared about them and their success and assist them when appropriate.

The results were truly remarkable. Not every Adopt-a-Kid story was a success, as no attempt at intervention is successful 100 percent of the time. But I witnessed firsthand many students stay in school and change their behaviors because they didn't want to disappoint a mentor who really cared about them. Knowing that someone went out of their way to connect with them on a personal level, to ask how things were going—at home and with friends and at school—meant a great deal to most of these students. You'll find a complete description of the Adopt-a-Kid program in the appendix (page 217).

TACTIC: UNDERSTAND HABITS AND THE POWER OF CONSISTENCY

You know from our discussions in chapter 3 (page 29) that your students have, for the most part, an innate drive to act in ways that are consistent with their self-image and their previous behaviors. If you look closely at these behaviors, you will likely see certain patterns that fall under the category of habits. For your students, habits are those patterns of behavior that are routine for them, the typical ways in which they think and act in your classroom.

Author of multiple books on the power of habits, Charles Duhigg (2016), describes a *habit* as "a decision that you made at one point, but then stopped making but continued acting on." It is vital that you understand that your students once made very conscious decisions about how to behave in school, perhaps many years before. Yet, after a short time, these behaviors became habits. They often behave the way they do (be those behaviors productive or disruptive) at a very unconscious level, much like the way many teachers drive to school not really thinking about it, just doing it out of habit. Duhigg (2016) puts it this way: "Habits feel so automatic because once something becomes a habit, your brain has kind of gone to sleep. You are no longer participating in decision making around that activity."

You will be aware of the fact that some students have developed poor habits in your classroom, behaviors that occur on a consistent basis that hold them back from achieving their potential. Examples of poor classroom habits can include the following (when such behaviors occur on a regular basis and with key exceptions).

- Drawing during presentations
- Spending time on their phones
- Being disorganized
- Paying more attention to their friends than to you
- Consistently coming late or without the necessary supplies
- Not participating in class activities

If you are attempting to change a student's bad habit, you may have to look both outside and inside the classroom to understand more fully what is going on and why. For example, you may have a student who comes to school habitually late, and you want to change this habit. You can't be effective in your influence attempts here without understanding *why* this behavior is happening. A student who fidgets or doodles may have so much excess energy their behavior signals a coping mechanism rather than inattention. If the student is consistently late because he or she gets a ride to school from a parent who is late, or maybe he or she is responsible for ensuring a younger sibling gets to school on time, that would lead you to address the problem one way. However, if the student is constantly late because he or she is playing video games until 2:30 in the morning, that would lead you to address the problem in a completely different way.

Comedian Jerry Seinfeld (2017) does a routine about *night guy* and *morning guy*. He explains that night guy stays up late drinking, having fun, and doing whatever he wants because waking up late and hungover the next morning are the morning guy's problems. Night guy is living in the moment and doesn't really think too much about morning guy. Psychologists call this *future-self continuity* (Kluger, 2018), which is a term that describes the degree of connectedness between our present self and our future self. For many students' night guy, there is little connectedness between him and morning guy. There are countless students who live in the moment as a matter of habit and do not factor in future consequences while making decisions about what they want to do at any particular time. This is particularly true of students on the attention deficit hyperactivity disorder spectrum (Barkley, 2021), including students who have no idea they are on that spectrum or why they make the choices they do.

So how do you go about helping your students break bad habits that may be holding them back in the classroom, such as continually being disengaged? Markham Heid (2018) states: "by definition, habits are repeated, nearly automatic actions that are triggered by contextual cues" (p. 68). Take note of the fact that habits are *contextual*; they happen at a certain place and time—in this case, *your* classroom. You cannot assume that the habitual behaviors you are seeing in a student—the ones you want to change—are going on in other classrooms as well (assuming that the student has more than one teacher) unless you investigate the accuracy of your assumption.

In *Talking to Strangers*, Malcolm Gladwell (2019) calls this *coupling*: "Coupling is the idea that behaviors are linked to very specific circumstances and conditions" (p. 273). The idea that a student's behaviors are closely tied to place and context is very difficult for many teachers to accept. In most instances, teachers simply assume that a student's behaviors—be they deemed appropriate or inappropriate—are the same or very similar in the other teachers' classrooms as they are in their own. This assumption may or may not be correct and bears looking into.

If, for example, you find that a student is consistently disengaged in your class, check with that student's other teachers to determine whether or not this behavior manifests itself in their classrooms as well. If you discover that the student's behavior patterns are relatively consistent across a number of classes, you can assume with some confidence that the root of the problem lies with the student. If, however, you find in talking to your colleagues that the student in question behaves quite differently in your class than in other teachers' classes, you can assume that the problem is either the student's relationship with you, the subject you teach, or perhaps the classroom peers around him or her.

If you want a student to change a particular habit in your classroom, there are a number of things you need to keep in mind. First, you need to recognize that changing a habit is *not* simply a matter of willpower. You may ask the student to change his or her bad habit and be more active and engaged in your class, and the student may genuinely want to do this. Simply resolving to change a behavior that has become a bad habit is very unlikely to work. (How consistently do your New Year's resolutions work out for you?) About this, medicine and biology writer Jerome Groopman (2019) writes for the *New Yorker*:

> The path to breaking bad habits lies not in resolve but in restructuring our environment in ways that sustain good behaviors. . . . Psychologist Kurt Lewin argued that behavior was influenced by "a constellation of forces" analogous to gravity or to the fluid dynamics that make a river run faster or slower. Those forces work depending on where you are, who's around you, the time of day, and your recent actions. We achieve situational control, paradoxically, not through will power but by finding ways to take will power out of the equation.

Take special note of that. If you want to change a student's bad habit (or even one of your own), such as being disengaged, you need to *change the context*—which involves changing things like *where* the student is and *who* is around him or her.

Heid (2018)—whose work derives from Benjamin Gardner (Gardner, Lally, & Wardle, 2012; Gardner & Rebar, 2019), an expert on habit formation and senior lecturer in psychology at King's College London—supports this approach. He argues there are three facets that are necessary in changing habits. The first aspect is the *initiation phase*, which involves choosing the new behavior and the context in which it will occur. For a disengaged student, once you get agreement that becoming more engaged in class is something the student wants, you *must* move him or her to a new place in the classroom. *You must change the context*. Determine in consultation with the student where the best place would be to increase their level of engagement, then move the student there.

A second aspect to this change process is to *keep the changes small at first*. Clear (2018) tells us:

> It is so easy to overestimate the importance of one defining moment and underestimate the

value of making small improvements on a daily basis. Too often, we convince ourselves that massive success requires massive action. . . . improving by 1 percent isn't particularly notable—sometimes it isn't even *noticeable*— but it can be far more meaningful, especially in the long run. The difference a tiny improvement can make over time is astounding. (p. 15)

The message here is clear. Don't try to alter the target student's behaviors in significant ways. If you do, you will likely fail. Rather, try for a very small change—a *1 percent change*—and do this consistently and over an extended period of time. It will be easier on the student, and you are more likely to see some early wins that will encourage you to keep going.

For example, you and the student may agree that you are going to put a checkmark on a chart or click a clicker in your pocket every time you glance at the student during class, and the student makes eye contact with you. Set a goal for a minimum number of times you both agree this should occur for each class for a week, then you can increase the number. After a few weeks, you will no longer have to do this because a new habit has been formed that replaces the old one.

The third aspect to the process of changing a habit is that the change should be enjoyable in some way. Heid (2018) reminds us: "The trick to habit formation is repetition, repetition, repetition, and we are most likely to repeat actions that we enjoy" (p. 68). Find ways to make the change enjoyable for the student, perhaps in the form of a small reward if the student achieves ten clicks or checkmarks per class for paying attention.

In *The Power of Habit: Why We Do What We Do In Life and Business*, Duhigg (2012) uses a similar construct that he calls the *habit loop*:

This process within our brains is a three-step loop. First, there is a *cue*, a trigger that tells your brain to go into automatic mode and which habit to use. Then there is the *routine*, which can be physical or mental or emotional. Finally, there

is a *reward*, which helps your brain figure out if this particular loop is worth remembering for the future. Over time, this loop—cue, routine, reward; cue, routine, reward—becomes more and more automatic. (p. 19)

For example, think of our aforementioned disengaged student as Bob. A cue can be anything in the student's classroom surroundings—where the student sits (or with whom), the teacher (or substitute), the topic, the time of day, even the weather outside the window. Bob's cue might simply be whom he sits beside in your classroom. The routine is the behavior—the way a student acts after having been stimulated by the cue. Bob's routine might be to play it cool in front of his friends by not engaging in class activities or making smart comments to the teacher. So, if Bob sits with his friends, he is cued to this routine; Bob's reward is having his friends laugh approvingly at his behaviors.

Duhigg (2012) argues that if you want to change a student's habit, you need to focus on the routine, not the cue or the reward. Many teachers in this example situation would simply move the student to a different part of the classroom, attempting to address the cue. The problem with this approach is that the routine has not changed, nor has the reward: Bob can still make smart remarks in order to get a laugh from his friends, only now he simply turns up the volume so his friends can hear from across the room.

How, then, do we address the routine in this example? It's actually quite simple. Bob likes getting a laugh. This is not a bad thing. Most people want to have good relationships with their friends, and most of us don't mind being entertaining in a social setting and making our friends laugh. The approval of his friends is the reward that lies beneath Bob's behaviors. While his goal is understandable, his methods are disruptive to your classroom.

When I have students who take on the role of the class clown (and other attempts to change their behavior have failed to work), I do what I call "giving them the spotlight." I tell them that I recognize they like to get a laugh, and yes, some of their comments in class are really quite funny. I then invite them to prepare and deliver a stand-up comedy routine to the class. If I am teaching English, I tell them I will give them bonus marks for their presentation based on its quality.

Most students turn down this opportunity. Having to get a laugh through deliberate planning is difficult. Just ask any stand-up comic. I tell those students who decline my offer that their refusal is OK, no worries at all. However, the next time they make a smart remark in class in an attempt to get a laugh, I will invite them up to the front of the room to deliver a five-minute comedy routine. I make sure to note that I will set a timer, and I will not teach for those entire five minutes. The addition of using a timer is even more frightening for most students. I then tell them that if they think they have something really funny to say, they can either give me a signal that we arrange (hand up with the peace sign), and I will call on them to deliver their quip, or they can write it down and pass it to their friend.

Having permission from the teacher to say funny things in class changes the routine. Having permission to pass notes to your friend changes the routine. Most students do not take advantage of these options. If they do, they tire of them quickly and develop other classroom habits instead.

The habits that your students manifest in your classroom are often one aspect of the role that they see themselves playing in school. Your students will tend to act in a somewhat consistent manner in order to fill the various roles that they have chosen for themselves—roles such as the jock, the geek, the Goth, the kid who doesn't care about school, the popular kid, the reject, the skater, the cool kid, the rebel, the bully, and so on. While these kinds of roles have been common among students for decades, the digital world presents students with several additional roles they can try on for size: the online social justice warrior, the student with their own YouTube channel, the online entrepreneur who sets up their own business, and so on. Sometimes students choose these roles for themselves. At other times, the

significant adults in their lives are the ones who label them as *kind*, or *a thief*, or *a bully*. How can teachers use this desire for consistency in their students to obtain positive commitments from them—commitments that will help students be successful in school?

Cialdini (2007) advises getting the student to make a commitment, stand, or otherwise go on record: "Once a stand is taken, there is a natural tendency to behave in ways that are stubbornly consistent with the stand" (p. 67). Even better, if you can get the student to make a *public* commitment, such as a verbal statement to commit to a course of action, then you have increased the likelihood that the student is even more committed to this new behavior. As Burkett (2013) says, "Public commitments create more lasting change" (p. 15). At times, all this takes is for the student to make a promise to you and shake on it.

TACTIC: START WITH SMALL COMMITMENTS FOCUSED ON SELF-IDENTITY

A particularly challenging aspect of choosing what tactics to include in this book has to do with the origins of the strategy. I write this to note that this section discusses some strategies related to changing behavior that derived from what Chinese military members did to American captives during the Korean War. I thought for a long time about whether or not to include this section. On one hand, the strategies described here are extremely effective. On the other hand, you may rightly find these tactics' origins deeply troubling. However, by being aware of the ethical guidance in chapter 16 (page 193) and knowing that you should apply these kinds of strategies *only* if they benefit your students, but *never* if you are using them entirely for your own gains, I have chosen to include this information in this chapter.

During the Korean War, North Korean soldiers and their Communist Chinese allies captured several thousand American soldiers. However, the strategies these two countries used to obtain compliance from their prisoners were quite different. While the North Koreans employed tactics of fear and harsh punishment, the Chinese employed what they called their *lenient policy* or *policy of tolerance* (Keckeisen, 2002). They opted to see their prisoners as victims of their imperialist leaders and of Wall Street capitalists. Thus, they saw American prisoners as needing re-education so that they would be able to see the truths within the communist view of the world.

Cialdini (2007) writes of these practices:

> An examination of the Chinese prison-camp program shows that its personnel relied heavily on commitment and consistency pressures to gain the desired compliance from prisoners. Of course, the first problem facing the Chinese was how to get any collaboration at all from the Americans. These were men who were trained to provide nothing but name, rank and serial number. Short of physical brutalization, how could the captors hope to get such men to give military information, turn in fellow prisoners, or publicly denounce their country? The Chinese answer was elementary: *Start small and build.* (p. 70; emphasis added)

Captors started by asking prisoners to make statements that seemed so trivial and so obviously true that it was hard not to agree with them, statements such as "America is not perfect" or "Full employment is good, correct? In communist countries, we have full employment."

Once prisoners agreed with these seemingly small statements, captors then asked prisoners for a little bit more (Cialdini, 2007). If a prisoner agreed that the United States wasn't perfect, they might ask him to describe the ways in which he saw the United States as flawed. Once answered, they might ask him to make a list of the failings of his country, perhaps even write a short essay describing these faults or make a recorded statement describing them.

Once a prisoner committed this criticism of his country to paper or to a recording, he was lost. The Chinese would then broadcast the prisoner's criticisms to his camp, to the other POW camps in North Korea, and across South Korea as well. His captive countrymen would brand him as a *collaborator*, which, for the soldier, was a new adjective. It was a descriptor no one had applied to him before because it neither fit with how others saw him or how he saw himself. But now, there was a piece of paper or a recording that provided proof that, yes—in fact—he was a collaborator. Cialdini (2007) writes:

> Aware that he had written the essay without any strong threats or coercion, many times a man would change his image of himself to be consistent with the deed and with the new 'collaborator' label, often resulting in even more extensive acts of collaboration. Thus, while 'only a few men were able to avoid collaboration altogether' . . . the majority collaborated at one time or another by doing things which seemed to them trivial but which the Chinese were able to turn to their own advantage. (p. 71)

There are numerous studies that demonstrate the power of persuasion by starting small and building. For example, in a study by Goldstein and colleagues (2008), two groups of people in the same neighborhood were asked if they would be willing to put a large, unsightly sign on their front lawns that said, "DRIVE CAREFULLY." Only 17 percent of one group agreed to do this, but an incredible 76 percent of the other group agreed to post the sign on their lawn. (Remember, this was the same neighborhood.) What was the difference? Two weeks earlier, the second group of people had been asked if they would be willing to place a small sticker in their window that read, "BE A SAFE DRIVER." Because this seemed like such a small request, most of them agreed (Goldstein et al., 2008).

Why would such a small act result in so many people in this group agreeing to post the lawn sign when asked two weeks after posting the window sticker?

> The evidence suggests that after agreeing to the request, the residents came to see themselves as committed to worthy causes, such as

safe driving. When these homeowners were approached a couple of weeks later, they were motivated to act consistently with this perception of themselves as concerned citizens. (Goldstein et al., 2008, pp. 64–65)

Remember our chapter 3 (page 29) discussion about Prescott Lecky's self-consistency theory (Lecky & Thorne, 1945), which basically said that people develop certain ideas about themselves and then work hard to maintain this self-image? We see the results of that in the homeowners who agreed to post the large *drive carefully* signs on their lawns after posting a small sticker in their windows, and we see it as well in the American POWs who—once they had collaborated on little things—were much more likely to collaborate on larger issues.

How can you *ethically* utilize the foot-in-the-door strategy in your classroom? If you start with large requests for changes in behaviors or academic performance of a student, you will very likely fail to attain a change in behavior with that student. What we have learned here is to *start small*. If a student talks too much, set aside five minutes each hour during which he or she commits to being quiet. If a student rarely does homework, get a commitment that homework will always be done on Mondays—just on Mondays. If a student has disorganized notebooks, choose one subject only for them to organize their materials.

The point is, start small, get a commitment, and grow from there. It is critical that you have a focus, that you start by focusing on a small change in behaviors. When you are dealing with challenging students, it is easy to see the countless changes that you want these students to make in their behaviors in your class. This is a trap, and it is virtually guaranteed to result in failure and frustration. You need to begin with a very small focus on one thing. Start small, achieve success, then take the next step. As a teacher looking to persuade your students to adopt behaviors that will help them grow and be more successful in school and in life, I advise you to remember the words of Taoist philosopher Lao

Tzu from the *Tao Te Ching*, "A journey of a thousand miles begins with a single step" (as cited in Mitchell, 1988, p. 64). In *The Soul of America: The Battle for Our Better Angels*, Jon Meacham (2018) quotes Theodore Roosevelt, who similarly advised that we "Begin with the little thing, and do not expect to accomplish anything without an effort" (p. 255).

Lao-tzu and Theodore Roosevelt both knew a thing or two about influence.

TACTIC: USE FOUR STEPS TO ACHIEVE STUDENT COMMITMENT

What does transforming student behavior look like in a classroom with your students? What is the process that you as a teacher can implement that may bring about a significant change in some hardcore negative student behaviors?

Know that this will not be easy, and know that this will not happen quickly (remember, your students can't take a thousand steps at once, only one at a time). You need to get *partway there* before you can get *all the way there*. However, if you use the four steps described in the following sections, there is a very good chance that even the students with the most negative habits will begin to change their ways.

Step 1: Focus on One Student at a Time

Achieving the kind of commitment we are referring to here is not something you can typically do with a group of students; you need to choose one. How you choose this student is up to you. You may want to focus on a student who is fairly negative but who has some followers, believing that if you can turn this student around, others will follow.

Step 2: Start Small and Build From There

Think of this step as your foot-in-the-door approach. You simply cannot ask a student whose image is the class clown, the renegade, or the chronic procrastinator to suddenly become a serious student focused on academic success. This is not going to happen because of a single conversation you have with this student.

You can, however, do this by asking the student you have chosen to work with to agree to specific actions, like the following.

- "You haven't done homework for two weeks. How about you do it *just once* next week?"

- "You haven't achieved a mark over 30 percent so far this year. How about you shoot for a *35 percent minimum* on the next assignment?"

- "You have come late for class every day this week. How about you come on time, *just for tomorrow*?"

- "You haven't handed in a writing assignment so far in this course. How about you hand in *three sentences* by the end of this class?"

The idea is that you start by obtaining a small, one-on-one commitment to some course of action that is the first step down the path you want the student to take. A student's self-image is based on how they act. Therefore, to get them to change, you need to change their actions—first in very small ways, then you can build from there.

While the kinds of requests given in these examples are best discussed with the student quietly and privately, take note of the fact that many of the student's actions will have some degree of public display. Classmates see if the student comes on time, turns in an assignment that was done in class, or hands in their homework.

As well, think back to the ideas we explored earlier around the power of self-image and students acting in harmony with their self-image. What you are doing here is making subtle changes to the student's self-image. The student whose self-image was "I don't do written assignments!" is now the student whose self-image is "I do three-sentence written assignments." Or the student whose self-image was "I don't do homework!" is now the student whose self-image is "I do homework once a week."

How these students view themselves is likely how they will behave on a consistent basis. Therefore, you need to change the way they view themselves by changing the way they act in small but meaningful ways. Cialdini (2007) writes:

> Once an active commitment is made, then self-image is squeezed from both sides by consistency pressures. From the inside, there is a pressure to bring self-image into line with action. From the outside, there is a sneakier pressure—a tendency to adjust this image according to the way others perceive us. (p. 77)

Step 3: Label the New Behavior in a Discreet and Positive Way

We discussed in chapter 3 (page 29) how students often feel influenced by how they are labeled ("You is kind . . . " and "My little thief"). Labeling "involves assigning a trait, attitude, belief, or other label to a person, and them making a request of that person consistent with that label" (Goldstein et al., 2008, p. 69).

When a student has begun to change behavior you've targeted, you need to reinforce these changes in their self-image. Comments such as "You are a good writer" and "These three sentences are really well done" can impact the non-writing student's self-image in the direction you want them to go. While labeling can be a very effective strategy in getting students to comply with what you want from them, you do have an ethical responsibility to your students to only apply labels that are honest and accurate—labels that authentically reflect the student's behavioral changes and accomplishments.

Step 4: Obtain Agreement and Gradual Commitment to More Substantive Requests

As you use steps 1–3 with students, you may notice a change in their attitude as they comply with a small request and begin to see themselves as the kinds of students who, for example, do homework once a week or come to class on time occasionally. Once you feel a student has internalized these steps, you can move further down the road you want the student to travel.

For example, with the student who comes to class on time once a week, it is a small step to say to this student,

"It's pretty clear that you can make it to class on time if you choose. How about you shoot for coming to class on time three days next week?" Or for the student who hands in three sentences on written assignments, you can say something to the effect that, "Clearly you can write, and your three sentences are pretty good. I wonder what you could do with six sentences."

Once you have changed the student's self-image to where you would like it to be to maximize their chance of success in school, the student will be more likely to comply with a range of requests that you make if these requests are congruent with their new self-image.

SUMMARY

Do you remember Annie from earlier in this chapter? The "I don't read, and I don't write" Annie? By using likability, commitment, and the four steps outlined in this chapter, I was able to help Annie change her self-image. She changed from a student who didn't read and who didn't write at all to a student who could both read and write *well*.

There is no magic in what I was able to accomplish with Annie. I made a long-term commitment to her. I never gave up. I always showed up. And I utilized the four-step process to earn her buy-in. You can do the same thing with your most challenging students. It is not easy, and it does not happen quickly, but it is achievable. And the rewards—for both you and your students—are priceless.

As you reflect on this chapter, make sure to remember the following.

- Students need to know very early on in your relationship with them that you have made a commitment to be their teacher for a significant period of time. They also need to know from your actions that you will show up every day unless there is something substantial keeping you away, they cannot scare you away, and when they show up at school, you will be prepared to teach.

- Students all enter your classrooms with a sense of self-identity. Sometimes this self-identity is negative and destructive and works counter to what you are attempting to achieve. You will need to understand a student's self-identity and, if that identity is a barrier to their success in school, guide him or her to make positive changes to it.

- Students come to the classroom with ingrained habits, some of which may be detrimental to their success in school. You need to be able to recognize these negative habits and take students through a process that has proven effective in changing people's habits.

- Asking for small changes in behavior or small commitments is far more effective than asking for big changes when beginning the process of working with a student to help them change. Remember, you must first get partway there before you can get all the way there.

- There are four steps a teacher can take in helping a student to make positive changes.

  a. Work with one student at a time. You cannot implement this process with an entire class.

  b. Start small and build from there. Utilize the foot-in-the-door strategy.

  c. Label the new behavior in a discreet and positive way.

  d. Obtain agreement and gradual commitment for more substantive changes.

Reflective Practice

This chapter stresses the power of long-term commitment to the students you are teaching. Use the following three actions to consider your approach to getting a commitment from your students.

1. Answer the following questions to get a sense of your long-term commitment to your students.

   ♦ If all things go according to your plans, how long do you see yourself remaining in your current teaching position?

   ♦ If you believe that your answer to the first part of this question is significant enough to have your students invest in a relationship with you, are your students aware of how long you plan to stay in your current teaching position? If not, devise some ways to communicate this to them.

2. Choose one student whom you see as manifesting some habits in your classes that are inhibiting his or her progress. Utilize the steps outlined in the chapter by completing the following chart to see if you can help the student to change these negative habits.

Student's name:	
Four Steps to Change Behavior	**Observed Results**
1. Choose the target student. Give some thought to this. Make your choice based on the likelihood of success and the potential impact of the behavioral change for this student.	
2. Start small and build from there. Think of and describe your foot-in-the-door strategy, and make sure it is time-specific ("For one week I am asking you to . . . .").	
3. Label the change and positively reinforce it when and where appropriate.	
4. Obtain agreement and gradual commitment to more substantive changes from the student.	

The Tactical Teacher © 2022 Solution Tree Press • SolutionTree.com
Visit **go.SolutionTree.com/behavior** to download this free reproducible.

3. This chapter looked at several strategies you can use to change some of your students' poor habits in the area of their classroom performance. However, you can also use these same strategies to improve your teaching practices. Think about what Duhigg (2012) said about the habit loop and how, if you want to change a habit, you should focus on the routine. Think about what Clear (2018) said about how you should focus on changing very small things rather than attempting to make significant changes that may, in the end, prove to be too challenging. Now, think about one aspect of your teaching practice that has become habitual for you but might hinder your teaching practice. For example, it might be in the area of assessment, where you are slow to get marked assessments back to students. Or, it might be in the area of the emotional energy you project in the classroom, where you find yourself getting a bit sluggish near the end of the day. Now, think about how you can change that one habit (and I stress, please focus on only *one* aspect of your practice for this exercise) using some of the strategies we explored in this chapter.

Your habit: _____

Sources: Clear, J. (2018). Atomic habits: An easy and proven way to build good habits and break bad ones. *New York: Avery; Duhigg, C. (2012).* The power of habit: Why we do what we do in life and business. *New York: Random House.*

The Tactical Teacher © 2022 Solution Tree Press • SolutionTree.com
Visit **go.SolutionTree.com/behavior** to download this free reproducible.

CHAPTER 7

SOFT TACTICS FOR MAKING THE INVISIBLE VISIBLE

It was early November in my first year of teaching. At the end of the last class on a Friday afternoon, my eighth-grade students had come back to homeroom to receive their first report card of the year. After I had finished distributing the report cards, one young man came up to me and said, "Mr. Ripley, I think you made a mistake on my social studies mark. It says here that I got 55 percent. That can't be right. I did really well on the final unit exam and the major assignment. I got over 80 percent on both of those."

"Well," I replied, "Stay after the other students have left, and we will check. I have been known to make a mathematical mistake or two in my life."

A few minutes later, he and I sat down at my desk. I opened my mark book, and we had a look at what was there. "You are correct," I said. "You did get over 80 percent on the final unit exam and on the major assignment."

He looked relieved, even a bit smug. I continued. "However, you also got a 35 percent on a smaller test and a 42 percent on another test. As well, you didn't hand in one of the homework assignments—which was worth 10 percent—even though I asked you for it directly and phoned home to let your parents know you had not handed it in."

He looked stunned. Up until that point, he had completely forgotten about the poor marks he had achieved as well as the homework assignment he had failed to complete. He only remembered the good marks, the tests and assignments that he had done well on. The poor marks and the missing assignments didn't exist for him; they were gone—completely invisible.

Many aspects of school are virtually invisible to both students and teachers. If you want to test this out, ask some of your lower or mid-range students to take a guess at what their current average is in your courses or how many days of school they have missed in the year thus far. I find that while high-achieving students often have a fairly good handle on their marks and attendance, students who struggle tend to overestimate their marks and underestimate their absences. Much like the eighth-grade student who thought his social studies mark was in the '80s, to students who are struggling or less engaged, actual achievement and actual attendance patterns are often invisible.

Therefore, you need to find ways to *make the invisible visible*. Why? Because the things students don't see or know about can't motivate or impact them. Why would students try to improve their attendance or achievement if, in their mind, both aspects of their school performance were just fine as is? Finding ways to make students cognizant of what is real is a critical first step in getting students to improve.

I developed the following strategies to increase students' awareness of what was actually happening at school in regard to their behaviors and achievements. Once students become aware of these things, you can work with them to develop strategies to address areas for improvement. The following tactics have had a profound impact on student performance and achievement throughout my teaching career by making the invisible visible.

- Use mark charts for achievement.
- Display posters to motivate attendance.
- Get a public commitment for grade goals.
- Consider physical and emotional contagion.
- Understand how mood affects fast and slow thinking.

TACTIC: USE MARK CHARTS FOR ACHIEVEMENT

Most teachers have experienced situations where students have no real sense of their current level of achievement for a course. You can attempt to overcome this problem using several different approaches. A fairly common one many schools utilize is to have *students* list their marks in their school agendas, planners, or homework books. I find this strategy can be somewhat effective if utilized on a consistent basis; however, this strategy has a number of problematic factors.

First, students have to open their agendas or planners to specific pages to see their marks. The students who most need a sense of their learning progress rarely review their previous scores. Usually, the only time many students look at their marks is when they are entering their most current one. Second, this approach is not visually impactful to students as it is often simply a list of percentages. And third, this strategy does nothing to categorize a student's assessments into meaningful information. It is simply a list of numbers—the raw data—and it does not sort their assessments into

different categories such as exams, assignments, class presentations, and so on.

Many schools have teachers post their marks on web-based platforms such as School Zone (www.schoolzone.com) and PowerSchool (www.powerschool.com). Thus, a student's marks are available online at any time to both students and caregivers. The problems with using only this strategy to keep students informed of their actual progress are similar to having the students list their marks in a school agenda or notebook. First, students have to log in to the database to see their marks. Second, they simply see a listing of marks and assignment names and dates without context. They do not get a *visual display* that shows them not only their marks but their marks in different aspects of assessment. In other words, they see what they are good at and where they may need to improve.

Another strategy that some teachers use is to give students their current average in their course each time the students receive an assessment. For example, if a student achieved a mark of 74 percent on an assessment, the student's assessment would say: 74 percent / 82 percent. The first mark is their percentage on that particular assessment, and the second mark is their current average in the course. This is an effective way to keep students informed of their current overall progress in a course. However, providing a student with their current weighted average means that a teacher needs to know all of the assignments for an entire term and their relative weightings in advance. This can be challenging, and it still doesn't provide students with insights into where they need to focus.

I decided I needed an approach that would keep assessments *visible* to my students in a way that was meaningful and ever-present. Eventually, I settled on the mark chart pictured in figure 7.1.

For each course or subject I taught, whenever I would pass back the first marked assessment, I would give each student a blank copy of the mark chart, placed inside a nonglare page protector. I then instructed all students that they were required to put this in the front of their

Course: _____

	1	2	3	4	5	6	7	8	9	10	11	12	13	14	15
100%															
90%															
80%															
70%															
60%															
50%															
40%															
30%															
20%															
10%															
0%															

*(Left axis label: **Weight of Marks in Percentage**)*

Write the *date* and *name* of each assignment or exam in the lower boxes—then color-code your mark using the following codes: *red* for exams; *blue* for assignments; *green* for class presentations.

Figure 7.1: Mark-chart template.

*Visit **go.SolutionTree.com/behavior** for a free reproducible version of this figure.*

binder for that subject, modeling how to fill in the chart. I directed them to complete their mark chart by entering the mark they just achieved, and I would walk around the room to ensure that each student was doing this correctly, providing additional guidance as needed. I then told students they would do this each time they received an assessment and that I would check to ensure they were completing their mark charts properly.

Given the prevalence of technology in many schools and classrooms, you may have students who prefer to track their grades using their laptop, tablet, or phone. For example, students could track their marks on an Excel spreadsheet that they then convert to a graph that is similar to the mark-chart examples pictured in this section. That approach can work, but it doesn't ensure students see the data frequently. If students want to keep an electronic record, encourage them to do so, but I suggest that you still make it a requirement that they have a notebook of some sort in which they keep all handouts and all returned assessments and a completed

mark graph. By keeping this physical record as a focal point of your classroom, you ensure students see their marks every time they open their notebooks.

In addition, keep your own copies of students' marks, so that when a student inevitably loses their binder, you can give him or her both a blank mark chart and a fresh printout of their current marks to re-enter on the replacement mark chart.

This system has several advantages over simply listing marks in a student agenda or notebook or a digital file. For one, the mark chart was always the first thing that a student would see whenever they opened their binder. No longer did I have a student come up to me at report card time in shock because their report card mark was a huge surprise. They had recorded and observed each of their achievements throughout the entire term. While the chart did not show the relative weightings of the marks, it did show achievement over time in the various areas of assessment. The other advantage was the color-coding. This enabled students and me to see where there might be strengths and weaknesses in the three areas of assessment: (1) assignments, (2) tests, and (3) presentations.

While I never taught a student who was severely color blind, if you have such a student in your classroom, allow them to adapt your color-coding system to shades or patterns that work best for them. For example, you could have them do vertical lines to fill in the bar graph for assignments, horizontal lines to fill in the bars for exams, and crisscrossed lines for class presentations.

Let's look at some anonymized samples of my students' mark charts from the first few weeks of school at levels ranging from elementary to high school. Note that *E* indicates *exams*, *A* indicates *assignments*, and *P* indicates *presentations*.

If you look at figure 7.2, you see a student who has missed no assessments and who does quite well on assignments and exams. However, this student did not do nearly as well on the presentation assessment. If the student did the class presentation independently (not as part of a group), this indicates to a teacher a need to more deeply explore this aspect of the student's performance. Why was this student's performance so much lower on this type of assessment than on the other types? What additional guidance or supports might this student need in the area of public speaking and presentations?

Now consider the student whose work is represented in figure 7.3 and is clearly struggling with taking exams. It's impossible from these data alone to determine whether the cause is a lack of study time, poor study skills when preparing for exams, exam anxiety, or a need for special accommodations (extended time, large print, and so on) while writing exams. But from this information, teachers have a clear area of focus to investigate and help this student develop strategies to successfully deal with whatever is causing weak performance on exams.

Figure 7.4 shows the profile of a student with one obvious performance outlier. This is a student who typically excels with assignments, so what happened on the third assignment? There is a story here that this student's teacher needs to explore. As well, this student—who is clearly quite capable of achieving high

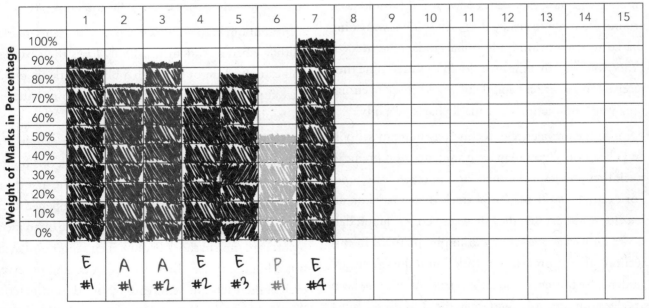

Write the *date* and *name* of each assignment or exam in the lower boxes—then color-code your mark using the following codes: *red* for exams; *blue* for assignments; *green* for class presentations.

Figure 7.2: Example student mark chart showing a struggle with presentations.

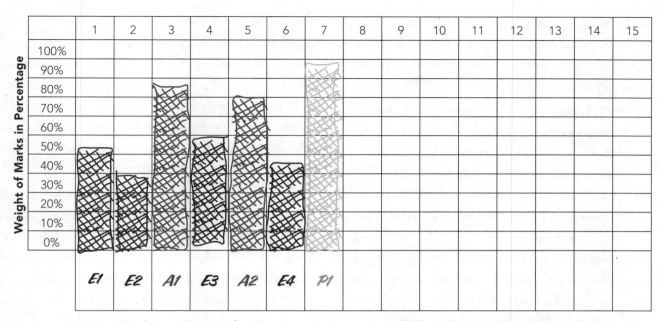

Write the *date* and *name* of each assignment or exam in the lower boxes—then color-code your mark using the following codes: *red* for exams; *blue* for assignments; *green* for class presentations.

Figure 7.3: Example student mark chart showing a struggle with exams.

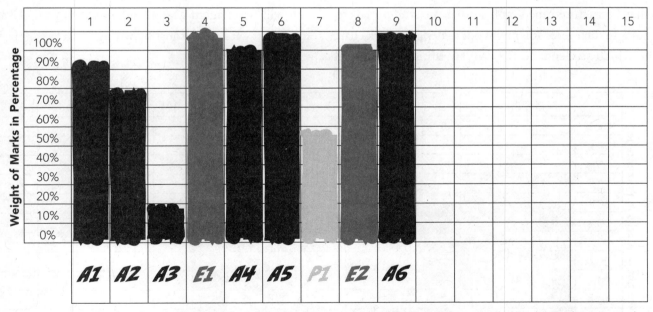

Write the *date* and *name* of each assignment or exam in the lower boxes—then color-code your mark using the following codes: *red* for exams; *blue* for assignments; *green* for class presentations.

Figure 7.4: Example student mark chart showing on outlier assignment result.

marks on assignments and exams—did not do so well on the one class presentation shown here. Was this an anomaly, or does this student need some help in this particular area?

Figure 7.5 shows an intriguing profile. If you look only at the clusters of assessments (that is, all the assignments together, the exams together, and the presentations together), you see a student who shows very inconsistent performance. For example, this student's assignments range from a low of 30 percent to a high of 90 percent, with a lot of marks in between on the other assignments. We see this pattern again on presentations, though not as dramatically on exams. Why is this student's performance so erratic? A teacher won't know from these data alone, but again, an avenue for deeper inquiry exists.

Last, take a close look at the achievement profile figure 7.6 depicts. This student is fairly consistent across all of the eleven assessments shown on the mark chart, with the exception of assessment 7. The student did not do that assessment and achieved a mark of 0. Notice that I structured the graph so that the student has to color in their zero. You might opt to design a mark chart in which students don't fill in anything for a missed

assignment. I find that by making students color in any zeros, it reinforces the choice they made not to do an assessment and accept the consequences of that choice, but either approach works. In a situation such as this, with the anomaly of the missed assessment, you will want to have a conversation with the student to find out what happened and determine an appropriate course of action based on what you discover.

Using mark charts with your students works incredibly well in helping them stay consistently aware of their level of achievement. As well, the color-coding helps both you and students see areas of strength and areas that may need some additional support or changes in regard to how the student approaches a particular type of assessment. In any case, achievement that was invisible is now visible—it is the first thing students see when they open their notebooks.

Whatever way you choose to utilize this mark-chart strategy, not only will you help your students improve their performance in a much more targeted fashion, but you will never again hear a student say to you, "Hey, my report card mark must be wrong!"

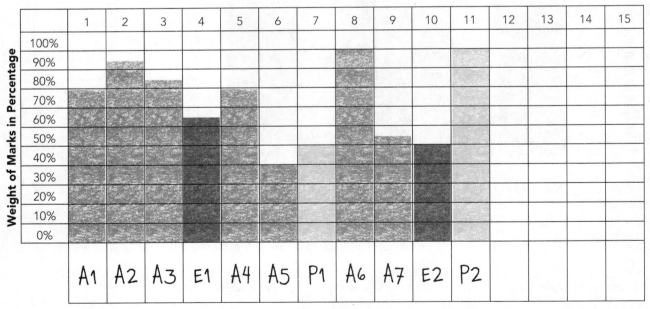

Write the *date* and *name* of each assignment or exam in the lower boxes—then color-code your mark using the following codes: *red* for exams; *blue* for assignments; *green* for class presentations.

Figure 7.5: Example student mark chart showing inconsistent results.

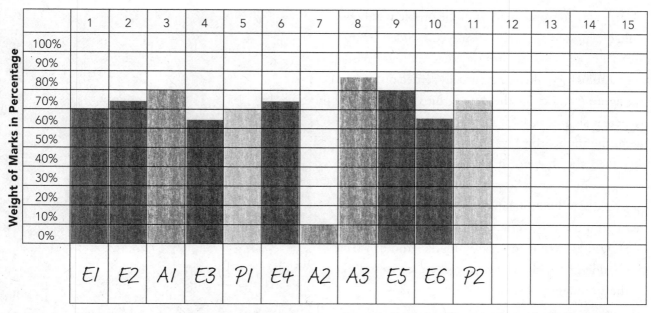

Write the *date* and *name* of each assignment or exam in the lower boxes—then color-code your mark using the following codes: *red* for exams; *blue* for assignments; *green* for class presentations.

Figure 7.6: Example student mark chart showing a missed assignment.

TACTIC: DISPLAY POSTERS TO MOTIVATE ATTENDANCE

It is common knowledge among educators that good attendance is a critical factor for success at school. Students cannot learn what you are teaching if they are not in class. In an interview with the Canadian Broadcasting Corporation, award-winning pediatrics educator Mandy Allison states:

> As early as kindergarten, missing more school affects things like third-grade reading scores, third-grade math scores. What we also know is that missing school in younger grades leads to missing school in older grades, and missing school in older grades is linked to school dropout. (as cited in Birak & Cuttler, 2019)

Allison further notes the degree to which school dropout and poor attendance in adolescents is linked to drug and alcohol use, as well as a greater likelihood of unemployment or work in lower-paying jobs: "It's this chain of events that starts at a very young age" (as cited in Birak & Cuttler, 2019).

Exacerbating this problem even further is the downward spiral that happens once a student begins to experience chronic absenteeism. They are absent and fall behind. Upon returning, these students can feel left out because they don't know the new material. At times this translates into feelings of "I'm dumb" or "I'll never catch up." From that mindset, it doesn't feel good to be at school, and this can lead to even further absenteeism.

Most North American organizations and educators with expertise in this area define *chronic absenteeism* as missing 10 percent or more of the school year (Alberta Government, 2015; Balfanz & Byrnes, 2012; U.S. Departments of Education, Health and Human Services, Housing and Urban Development, and Justice, 2015). In most jurisdictions, this equates to two days per month. Missing only one day every couple of weeks may not seem like much, but the consequences can be dire and long-lasting. Yet, many students—in particular lower-achieving students—are often unaware of how much school they are actually missing. They can grossly overestimate how often they attend.

I struggled for some years with the problem of how I could design something that displayed a student's actual attendance and absences in a way that was highly visual and meaningful to them. I eventually settled on a poster (see figure 7.7). I chose the thunderbird because it had particular significance for my students. Culturally, for them, the thunderbird was a symbol of strength, and we talked about the obstacles many of them had to overcome in order to be successful in school and how they needed to be strong in order to be successful. Note that if you use this tactic, the specific image is not as important as how it impacts students. You can have your students decide whatever image they would like on the attendance posters.

In my use, each poster had one hundred peel-off stickers. Students would write their names on the bottom of the poster, leaving ninety stickers intact—the exact number of days in the semester at our high school. The row of ten stickers at the bottom was simply so the students had a place to print their names. After the students had printed their names along the bottom row, they were told that these attendance posters would be placed along the top of the wall at the front of the classroom. Each time they missed an entire morning, I removed the top half of a sticker. Each time they missed an afternoon, I removed the bottom half of a sticker. If they missed an entire day, I removed an entire sticker.

On occasion, a student might complain that their attendance was a private matter and that I shouldn't be displaying it. I would reply, "You do realize that both I and your classmates can see your empty desk, don't you? There is nothing at all secret about you being away. We noticed."

Figure 7.8 shows examples of five attendance posters. (Visit **go.SolutionTree.com/behavior** to access color versions of these images.) While I have changed the names, these are the thunderbird attendance posters of actual students.

As you look at each one, see what you can discover about each student's attendance. Do you see any patterns? How do you think each of these students did

Figure 7.7: Attendance poster template.

in terms of achievement for the term illustrated? Let's take a look at each of these in turn.

- You can readily see that Alex J. has missed six full days and eight half days of school. This is reasonably good attendance, assuming this is the total attendance at the *end* of the semester. It would not be good if this is his attendance at the end of the first month. Now, take a good look at the half days. Alex *only misses in the mornings*, never in the afternoons. This should prompt you to wonder what is going on with this kind of attendance pattern. Does he stay up too late and, therefore, have a hard time getting to school some mornings? Does he have unreliable or inconsistent transportation to school? You cannot know the answers to these questions without investigating further,

Figure 7.8: Examples of student attendance posters.

but if this is Alex's attendance after only twenty school days, you know you need to have a conversation with Alex to determine what is happening and how to address it.

- What do you notice from Casey B.'s poster? Would you discuss attendance with this student, and if so, what might you explore during this conversation?

- Riley S. has missed thirteen full days; there are no half-day absences whatsoever. This student is either always at school all day or absent completely. Given that there were thirty days of school up to this point, Riley has missed 43 percent of classes to date. This is both clear to Riley and obvious to her teacher. It's time for a chat.

- Let's consider Sandy S. and Taylor M. together, both of whom missed substantial classroom time. I took these images at the end of a semester, before final exams. I conducted several conversations with these two students throughout the semester in an attempt to address attendance issues. While those conversations resulted in some slight progress for both students, the visual data here suggest they will both have difficulty being successful in their courses. Nonetheless, the attendance issues are *visible*.

There are several ways to use a visual image such as my use of the thunderbird to make attendance patterns move from the invisible to the visible and to initiate discussions with students in regard to their attendance. Sometimes I would quietly and privately ask, "How's your thunderbird doing?" At other times, when a student's attendance was good, I would say to them with a big smile, "Please keep up your attendance. It would break my heart—I might even cry—if I had to peel the head off your thunderbird!"

You don't have to use posters like this that have peel-off stickers, which can get expensive. A more cost-effective alternative is to simply draw the appropriate number of squares (which would represent the number of days of attendance you are tracking) on an 8 1/2 × 14-inch sheet of paper, then draw the graphic that you and your students have chosen. Copy and laminate this, one for each student. You or your students can then simply color these squares over with a permanent felt marker to accomplish the same visual display of attendance patterns as I accomplished with the attendance posters.

In any case, this is a powerful visual. I have seen students whose attendance was mediocre at best change their ways and work diligently to keep their thunderbird intact or plead with me to only peel away the blue background, not their thunderbird itself. Other students set a goal at the outset of a term to not have *any* stickers removed at all—perfect attendance.

I want to emphasize that this strategy to improve attendance is generally unnecessary in most classes and for most students. It can, however, be utilized to great effect where attendance issues are serious and need to be addressed. For example, you may not need to do this kind of visual tracking for an entire class, but you may want to use this strategy *privately* with specific students instead of the whole class. Whichever way you choose to implement this strategy—to improve the attendance of a class as a whole or that of individual students—one thing *is* guaranteed: no student will ever again be able to say to you, "Oh, I didn't know I had missed so much school."

TACTIC: GET A PUBLIC COMMITMENT FOR GRADE GOALS

I was once assigned to a school as the new principal, and when I walked the halls for the first time, I was struck by the dreadful shape of the bulletin boards in the hallways. There was writing on the corkboard, faded and torn construction paper, and posters that had seen better days. At my first staff meeting, I got the staff to agree that each of them would take responsibility for maintaining one of these hallway bulletin boards.

Nothing changed. The boards were left in their state of disrepair . . . until the next Monday morning. The staff walked in, and above each of the bulletin boards was an engraved plaque that read: "This bulletin board is proudly maintained by _____" with the appropriate teacher's name in the blank. Within a week, every bulletin board in the school looked fantastic. Such is the power of public commitment.

Some students enter our classrooms like twigs floating on a stream. They simply drift from one day to the next with no discernible direction or intent. Other students begin the term filled with wishes and hopes: they wish to be successful in the course, and they hope to get a great final mark. Neither of these attitudes is conducive to success.

As educators, we know the potential power that lies in having students set clear goals. SMART goals—goals that are strategic and specific, measurable, attainable, results oriented, and time bound (Conzemius & O'Neill, 2014)—have been around for a long time, and they work. However, they are challenging to

articulate and can be somewhat complex for students to work through.

Some teachers ask their students to set achievement targets at the beginning of the term. They will ask the students to write the grade or mark they want to achieve in the course. While this strategy is somewhat useful, it has two limitations that need to be addressed.

1. If the student writes the grade they *want* to achieve, this is akin to a wish. Any student who thinks clearly about the question would write down 100 percent. Asking a student *what* mark they want to achieve is not a good question. Again, most students reply to this question with an answer that is more along the lines of what they *hope* to get. A better question is, "What mark *are you prepared to work to achieve* in this course?" If you ask this question, followed by a clear description of what it takes to achieve an 85 percent or an A+, for example, students can write a grade goal that is much more realistic.

    An important part of this process is to let your students know there is nothing wrong with them aiming for a 65 percent or a C+ if that is what is realistic for them. Some students have a great deal going on in their lives, and they must balance their out-of-school demands or interests with in-school achievement. For students in these kinds of circumstances, a C or a C+ may be a perfectly legitimate and realistic goal.

2. The second problem with this strategy is *where* the student writes the grade they want. Often buried in a notebook, this achievement goal is too soon forgotten. In chapter 6 (page 59), we looked at the power of commitment. Cialdini (2007) tells us that public commitments become more hardened than private commitments. Burkett's (2013) research indicates, "Public commitments create more lasting change" (p. 15). Goldstein and colleagues (2008) suggest that if we really

want someone to truly commit to a particular change, then the commitment needs to be ". . . voluntary, active, and *publicly declared to others*" (p. 74; emphasis added).

This makes a great deal of sense, especially if the people we share our goals with are people who are important to us. Public accountability enhances the likelihood that students will perform better than if they keep their academic goals known only to themselves.

In asking students to record the grade they are prepared to work to achieve, this strategy becomes more powerful if the grade goal is *public* in some fashion. Whether you have students record this on the name plates on their desk or on a laminated chart taped to their desk or in some other fashion, the important thing is that they see it every day. (Be mindful of school or regional guidelines or laws related to parental consent and protecting the privacy of students' marks.)

Of course, we know that objects such as posters and words that are in our environment on a day-to-day basis can become somewhat invisible over time. We simply fail to notice them after a while. That is why it is important to regularly ask your students if they are on track to achieve their goal mark. A great time to do this is when they receive an assessment back.

This strategy does not work for all students—no strategy does. But I consistently used the strategy of choosing a grade goal and making it public, and I have found that it has had a definite impact on many students. I find that students who come to class highly motivated and with a track record of academic success in school don't seem to be impacted very much by this strategy. However, students who are not as highly motivated and who may not have achieved the level of academic success they wanted in the past seem to be the ones this strategy most impacts. These students benefit the most when teachers implement this approach.

Table 7.1 (page 84) lists some verbatim responses I have received in answer to the question: "Did seeing your grade goal every class have any effect on your achievement in this course?" The top section lists some of the positive responses with negative responses in the bottom section.

While this strategy does not impact all students (as you can see from table 7.1, it does have a significant influence on the majority of students. I kept track of the impact of this strategy on student success for two years and found that the number of students who indicate that seeing their grade goal had a positive daily impact on their achievement consistently hovered at around 80 percent.

TACTIC: CONSIDER PHYSICAL AND EMOTIONAL CONTAGION

How many times have you smiled at a student, and he or she immediately responded by smiling back, even if just for a fraction of a second? This happens often in classrooms. Why is this? Why do students so often respond to teachers with in-kind expressions and emotions? Why do teachers respond to students in much the same way? Pink (2018) says it's because "Moods are an internal state, but they have an external impact. Try as we might to conceal our emotions, they inevitably leak—and that shapes how others respond to our words and actions" (p. 17).

In chapter 5 (page 49), I noted that this type of behavior is called *mirroring* or *mimicry*, an approach I noted that Voss (2016) used as a professional negotiator for the FBI. It is a form of copying or imitating the behavior of those around us that acts as a contagion of positivity. In *Yes! 50 Scientifically Proven Ways to Be Persuasive*, Goldstein and colleagues (2008) describe the power of mirroring *words* to increase influence if we repeat the students' words back to them *exactly*, because mirroring words and body language increases the students' feelings of being understood. Voss (2016) describes mirroring as:

> Another neurobehavior humans (and other animals) display in which we copy each other to comfort each other. It can be done with speech patterns, body language, vocabulary, tempo,

Table 7.1: Positive and Negative Student Responses to Public Grade Commitments

Positive Responses	
"Yes, because it was staring at me *every single day*! If I didn't put enough effort into my work, it would stare at me, and I'd feel guilty."	"It was a clear reminder of my goal and helped me to be accountable to myself. It pushed me to do better because it reminded me of my own potential."
"Yes! Not only did I see it every day, but the students around my table saw it. I believe it held me to a state of accountability. It was bold, it was out there, and *I wanted it*!"	"Yes! I wanted to prove to myself that I was capable of receiving that grade. It motivated me to work extra hard."
"The grade in front of me every day was like a goal that I could see, and I knew that everything I did that specific day was toward that goal."	"When I got my first mark back and it wasn't near to my grade goal, I knew I had to step up my game if I was going to get the mark I wanted."
"Yes, it encouraged me to work hard and push myself to achieve the letter grade I set for myself."	"Yes, because mentally it helped me to keep my goal in sight."
"Yes, because I didn't want to disappoint myself."	"It kept me accountable to myself."
"Yes. It encouraged me to work hard so I didn't let myself down."	"It was a visual reminder of the work I needed to put in to get the mark I wanted."
"Yes, it was always a reminder of what I wanted to achieve, and it kept my mind more focused on getting it."	"Yes! It inspired me and pushed me to try harder."
Negative Responses	
"After I got the first assignment back, I felt bad because it was below the grade I had assigned myself. I wanted to work harder to get to the grade, but I also felt a bit discouraged because I figured I wouldn't be able to reach it anyway."	"No, because I intended to give this course my best effort regardless of seeing my goal mark or not."
"No, because I already had that mark in my mind before ever walking into the course."	"Not really because I'm always motivated to do well."
"No, because I feel like I came into this course aiming for that grade or higher anyway."	"No, I wanted to do really well in this course from the beginning already."

and tone of voice. It's generally an unconscious behavior—we are rarely aware of it when it's happening—but it's a sign that people are bonding, in sync, and establishing the kind of rapport that leads to trust. (p. 35)

Students trusting teachers is critical if we are to have any kind of positive effect on their behaviors in our classrooms. But how effective is mirroring or strategic mimicry in helping us gain trust with our students, especially with those students who are the most challenging?

Any teacher who has ever attempted to negotiate behavioral changes with a difficult student will see the truth in the following statement (Maddux, Mullen, & Galinsky, 2008):

A negotiation is an inherently interpersonal interaction . . . final outcomes are largely dependent upon one's ability to influence, persuade, and interact effectively. . . . Thus, it is not surprising that interpersonal variables, such as liking, trust, familiarity, and rapport are associated with more favorable negotiation outcomes. (p. 461)

Clearly, the more a student likes and trusts us, the greater our chances of being able to influence them. Can mirroring and mimicry help us earn this trust? Can mirroring and mimicry help us to establish an emotional connection with our students?

Maddux and colleagues (2008) tested the power of mimicry to influence others in two studies, the first involving negotiations between a job candidate and a recruiter, and the second involving the sale of a gas station. In "Chameleons Bake Bigger Pies and Take Bigger Pieces," they describe two experiments they conducted to test the power of mimicry and the concern that subjects would negatively view *obvious* mirroring and mimicry. So, those doing the mimicking received the following instructions five minutes prior to the experiment:

> Successful negotiators recommend that you should mimic the mannerisms of your negotiation partner to get a better deal. For example, when the other person rubs his/her face, you should too. If he/she leans back or leans forward in the chair, you should too. However, they say it is very important that you mimic subtly enough that the other person does not notice what you are doing, otherwise this technique completely backfires. Also, do not direct too much of your attention to the mimicking so you don't lose focus on the outcome of the negotiation. Thus, you should find a happy medium of consistent but subtle mimicking that does not disrupt your focus. (Maddux et al., 2008, p. 463)

As a teacher, pay particular attention to the phrase, *your negotiation partner*. If you are at a stage where you find yourself attempting to persuade a particularly difficult student to change his or her behaviors, then clearly this student has already demonstrated that he or she is strong-willed and self-motivated, albeit in a negative way from your perspective. If your plan is to attempt to simply use your power and authority as a teacher to change student behaviors, then you are utilizing *hard tactics*, strategies which we will explore in chapter 14 (page 171). Here, we are looking at *soft tactics*, and in using soft tactics, we want students to come *willingly* to our way of thinking. So, in a very real sense, we *are* negotiating with them, and they do have a voice in the negotiations.

Back to the question of how effective mirroring or strategic mimicry is in helping us achieve our goals in a negotiation. In the first experiment involving negotiations between a job candidate and a recruiter, the candidate scored *significantly more points* when he or she followed the mimicking instructions (Maddux et al., 2008).

In the second experiment involving the sale of a gas station, 67 percent of those who followed the mimicking instructions achieved a deal, while only 12.5 percent of those who did not mimic were able to achieve a deal (Maddux et al., 2008). In other words, by following the simple instructions, participants were over *five times more successful* in achieving their goals. Why? Maddux and colleagues (2008) conclude: "The current research not only demonstrates the robustness of mimicry's ability to facilitate even complex types of interpersonal interactions, but also offers some insight into the underlying processes responsible for these benefits, namely *instilling perceived trust of the mimicker*" (p. 467; emphasis added).

Why does mirroring or strategic mimicry work so effectively to gain trust and win people over to our ways of thinking? Pink (2012) cites social psychologist Adam Galinsky who says this is something that goes back to early humans:

> Our brains evolved at a time when most of the people around us were those we were related to and therefore could trust. But "as the size of groups increased, it required more sophisticated understandings and interactions with people." . . . People therefore looked to cues in the environment to determine whom they could trust.

"One of those cues is the unconscious awareness of whether we are in synch with other people, and a way to do that is to match their behavioral patterns with our own." (p. 77)

Your students will, albeit at a subconscious level, be looking for clues as to whether or not they can trust you, open up to you, and be honest with you. In other words, they will look for clues as to whether or not there is any kind of emotional connection. One clue will be your body language. How you sit when talking to a student with whom you are trying to connect is important. Arms crossed can be interpreted as being closed or guarded, while an open body posture can be seen as welcoming and signaling, "Come on in!"

Eye contact is one of the most powerful subconscious signals we can send. When your eyes are focused on the student with whom you are working to connect, and your facial expressions mimic his or hers, the student will often feel more important in your eyes, that you "get it," and that you are a safe person to form some degree of emotional connection with.

Additionally, when you want to connect at a deeper level, you must pay close attention to setting the stage of the context in which the conversation will take place. Just as your arms folded across your chest may signal a barrier to the student, so too might objects that separate you from the student do the same. If you sit behind your desk and talk to a student who is seated on the other side of your desk, you have set limits to the level of connection that is possible. Instead, think about setting the stage so that there is nothing physical separating the two of you. You can easily accomplish this by moving the student's chair in front of you or sitting at a table where you sit side-by-side, not across from one another. This can enhance a feeling of connectedness.

In *Emotional Contagion*, Hatfield and colleagues (1994) argue that in addition to the physical mimicry that affects us, we are often impacted emotionally—often unconsciously—by what we see and hear. "Emotional information processing is not always accessible to conversant awareness. . . . People often have

powerful emotional reactions to others, yet are at a loss to explain just *why* they responded as they did" (p. 11).

The phenomenon of emotional contagion can have a significant effect on how well groups function, be they adults in a work environment or students in a classroom. Researcher and teacher Sigal G. Barsade (2000) conducted a study of emotional contagion, which she describes as "a process in which a person or group influences the emotions or behavior of another person or group through the *conscious or unconscious* induction of emotion states and behavioral attitudes" (p. 6).

At the conclusion of her study, Barsade (2000) describes people as *walking mood indicators* who continuously influence others' judgments and behaviors:

> The process is a subtle one, however, in terms of people's awareness of both its occurrence and its effects, which makes it both a powerful and possibly problematic process in organizational life. Thus, there is a combinatory effect of organization members not realizing that their seemingly cognitive and rational consideration of the facts is actually a product of other people influencing their mood and that this mood, in turn, is influencing their cognitive processes. (p. 38)

Perhaps the most significant finding in Barsade's (2000) research is that the people who are in positions of power (like teachers in a classroom) are the most emotionally influential members of the group. We mirror their emotions more than those of the other members of the group. Why? Because we pay a great deal of attention to the powerful people around us. We need to be tuned in to them because of their power over us. *The Science of Emotions* (Lombardi & Joshua, 2020) discusses Barsade's thinking about the impact of the leader's emotion on a group: "The primary mechanism for creating a healthy emotional culture is through leaders. . . . How did the leader walk in this morning? Are they upbeat, or is the weight of the world on their shoulders?" (p. 43).

Substitute *leader* with *teacher*, and you see the point. You are the leader; you are the most influential person in the classroom; you are the alpha mood inductor. Your mood will have a considerable impact on the emotional climate in your classroom. In turn, this has a significant influence on the cognitive processes in your students' minds.

How do we determine how someone else is feeling, like our students? We scan the faces of those we are conversing with for signs of emotion and mood change. We listen to the volume, cadence, pace, and pitch of their voices for cues to the emotions behind the words. This outside-in perspective assumes that whatever emotions a person is showing on the outside are what they are feeling on the inside. We have done this kind of scrutiny instinctually since infancy. It helps us successfully navigate the complex world of other human beings. However, there is a way to look at emotions as an inside-out exercise:

> Emotion is contagious. In a way, this is perfectly intuitive. All of us have had our spirits picked up by being around somebody in a good mood. If you think about this closely, though, it's quite a radical notion. We normally think of the expressions on our face as the reflection of an inner state. I feel happy, so I smile. I feel sad, so I frown. Emotions go inside-out. Emotional contagion, though, suggests that the opposite is also true. If I can make you smile, I can make you happy. If I can make you frown, I can make you sad. Emotion, in this sense, goes outside-in. If we think about emotion this way—as outside-in, not inside-out—it is possible to understand how some people can have an enormous amount of influence over others. (Gladwell, 2002, pp. 85–86)

What Gladwell (2002) is saying is both insightful and obvious to any teacher who has taught longer than a month. Our moods, our emotions, our tone, and our feelings impact the students in our classrooms in significant ways. Because of this, we must be constantly tuned in to our feelings and in control of them.

This can be difficult in a classroom setting. There will be times when things don't go well, when some students are disruptive or defiant. At times like these, it is particularly important to be in touch with your feelings and to be initially *non-reactive* if expressing your feelings will interfere with what you are teaching, or more importantly, damage the relationship you have with these students. In circumstances like this, expressing your anger immediately with words you can't take back can do a great deal of damage—think back to *The Emperor's Club* (Hoffman, 2002) and the flippant comment, "Stupid lasts forever." When this happens, you will need to pause, slow down, and check your heart rate and breathing. Pause some more. Then respond when you are calmer and you have chosen your words carefully. (We discussed specific strategies you can use in this regard in chapter 2, page 17.)

It takes a great deal of self-awareness and maturity to hold our negative emotions in check when the students we are working with are doing quite the opposite. This is, however, one of the things that differentiates poor teachers from good ones—good teachers are aware of their emotions, and they have the maturity to protect their students from expressions of negative emotions that can damage their relationships with them.

Think about it. Have you ever seen a teacher arguing with an eleven-year-old? Yelling at the student to "Smarten up, and act your age!" That's like trying to put out a fire with gasoline. From the outside, it looks ridiculous, and it is difficult to see the point. I have always believed that if a student and a teacher are having a disagreement, one of the people in the conversation ought to take on the role of an adult and work to de-escalate the tension and find a resolution to the conflict that leaves the student feeling he or she was heard.

In a quote often attributed to Maya Angelou, but originally spoken by Carl Buehner, Buehner (1971) reminds us of a lesson that is of preeminent importance to teachers in regard to students: "They may forget what you said, but they will never forget how you made them feel."

TACTIC: UNDERSTAND HOW MOOD AFFECTS FAST AND SLOW THINKING

In the seminal work *The 48 Laws of Power*, author Robert Greene (1998), who specializes in influence tactics, describes how a heckler interrupted Nikita Khrushchev, the first chair of the Soviet Union Communist Party, in the middle of a speech in which he was denouncing the crimes of Stalin:

> "You were a colleague of Stalin's," the heckler yelled, "why didn't you stop him then?" Khrushchev apparently could not see the heckler and barked out, "Who said that?" No hand went up. No one moved a muscle. After a few seconds of tense silence, Khrushchev finally said in a quiet voice, "Now you know why I didn't stop him." Instead of just arguing that anyone facing Stalin was afraid, knowing that the slightest sign of rebellion would mean certain death, he had made them feel what it was like to face Stalin—had made them feel the paranoia, the fear of speaking up, the terror of confronting the leader, in this case Khrushchev. The demonstration was visceral and no more argument was necessary. (p. 73)

As you consider the impact of this exchange, let's return to Kahneman (2011b), whom you read about in chapter 1 (page 9), and how he describes every person using *two systems* for thinking: (1) fast and (2) slow. As a reminder, Kahneman (2011b) describes System 1 as operating "automatically and quickly, with little or no effort and no sense of voluntary control" while System 2 "allocates attention to the effortful mental activities that demand it, including complex computations" (pp. 21–22). This is the thinking most often aligned with agency, choice, and concentration (Kahneman, 2011b).

In *The Art of Choosing*, author and professor of business and management Sheena Iyengar (2010) describes System 1 behaviors as "a continuously running 'stealth' program that analyses sensory data and triggers feeling and behavior in rapid response" (p. 114). Like the heckler who yelled at Khrushchev, the response Khrushchev gave made the heckler immediately *feel* what Khrushchev had felt in front of Stalin. When System 1 kicks in, human instinct overrides human intellect, which makes triggering a System 1 response an extremely powerful persuasive strategy.

Kahneman (2011b) further describes System 1 thinking as including less-intense but equally automatic behaviors, such as determining that one object is closer than another, turning toward a sudden noise, completing phrases like "bread and . . .," and answering simple questions like, "What is 2 + 2?" We go on autopilot in experiences like these and expend little to no effort in the doing.

System 2 tasks, however, require that we pay attention to them, and we don't perform System 2 tasks very well if our focus is distracted. Kahneman's (2011b) examples of System 2 tasks include things like bracing for the starter's pistol to go off in a race, attempting to focus on only one voice in a noisy room, searching our memory for a sound we recognize but can't name, performing complex calculations, and checking the validity of an argument.

For this strategy, what is most essential for teachers to understand is how mindset influences performance with System 1 tasks. Kahneman (2011b) reports:

> Putting the participants in a good mood before the test by having them think happy thoughts *more than doubled accuracy*. An even more striking result is that unhappy subjects were completely incapable of performing the intuitive task accurately; their guesses were no better than random. Mood evidently affects the operation of System 1: when we are uncomfortable and unhappy, we lose touch with our intuition. . . . When in a good mood, people become more intuitive and more creative but also less vigilant and more prone to logical errors. (pp. 68–69; emphasis added)

The implications for classroom teaching here are *significant*. Simply put, if you are having your students perform a System 1 task, a task that requires things like intuition and creativity, then establishing conditions that put your students in a good mood will likely significantly enhance their performance. You can do this with upbeat music or spending a brief period of time having your students think of something they do that makes them happy. Another strategy is to have your students put a pencil between their teeth. This puts their facial muscles into a similar position as a smile, and there are studies that suggest smiling, whether sincere or simulated, has beneficial effects during stress (Kraft & Pressman, 2012).

However, if you are asking your students to perform System 2 tasks—tasks that require logic, critical analysis, complex problem-solving abilities, and the like—then you are likely to improve performance by ensuring that the mood in the room is serious, focused, and perhaps even a bit somber. Knowing that the mood of your classroom can affect your students' performance on certain kinds of tasks, and knowing that you want your students to feel relaxed and happy while performing System 1 tasks and more serious and focused while performing System 2 tasks, shows how important it is for you to be able to project the appropriate emotions in your classroom. Researchers Howard S. Friedman, Louise M. Prince, Ronald E. Riggio, and M. Robin DiMatteo (1980) developed a test to measure our ability to project emotions, called the Affective Communication Test. There are thirteen statements on this test, such as, "When I hear good dance music, I can hardly keep still," and "I like to remain unnoticed in a crowd" (Friedman et al., 1980, p. 335).

In scoring people who took this test, Friedman finds, "People who scored high on this test were able to 'move, inspire, and captivate others.' . . . They were charismatic, colorful, and entertaining" (as cited in Hatfield et al., 1994, p. 138).

Do you find yourself wondering how you would score on a test such as this? That is certainly a good question, for we know that in a classroom setting that emotions are contagious, and your students are catching your emotions on a daily basis. This will be one of the key reasons why your classroom feels the way it does. It will also be one of the fundamental reasons as to why your students are behaving the way they are and why they are attaining the levels of academic achievement that are evident in your classroom.

So I leave you with this question: Since your students are catching your emotions, what emotions are you throwing their way?

SUMMARY

There are many things that happen in a classroom that are invisible unless you purposefully bring them to an awareness level. Student attendance, student achievement over time, and the effect of your emotions on your students are just some of the examples we have explored in this chapter. Since your emotions are contagious and have a powerful impact on both how your students behave in your classroom as well as on their level of academic achievement, it is critical that your classroom has the right feel to support student success.

As you reflect on this chapter, make sure to remember the following.

- There are many things that happen in classrooms that are virtually invisible to both students and teachers, but teachers can use specific soft tactics to make the invisible visible.

- Often, having a person actually experience what you are going through is far more effective at gaining understanding than simply explaining something to them.

- Requiring students to make a public commitment in regard to achieving a goal, such as a grade goal, can be an effective motivational strategy.

- Students feel better when they feel understood. Mirroring and mimicry are two effective strategies that help students feel they are being understood.

- Emotions are contagious. How you feel has a powerful impact on your classroom's emotional state, and how your students feel can be a significant factor in determining their success in your classroom, especially prior to assessments.

- Putting students in a happy emotional state prior to assessments can have a dramatic increase on student performance, especially on tasks that require System 1 thinking. For tasks that require logical thinking, critical analysis, or complex problem solving (System 2 thinking), student results often improve if the teacher sets a mood that is serious and focused.

Reflective Practice

Use the following steps to help make the invisible visible in your classroom.

1. Think about the class or classes you teach. Do your students generally have a good sense of their overall academic progress in a consistent fashion? If you are unsure, ask a few of your students, especially those students who are not doing as well as you expect them to.

   If you answered *no* to this question, think about how you could incorporate the mark-chart strategy with your class. You can access the template shown in figure 7.1 (page 75) at **go.SolutionTree.com/behavior**, or you may wish to modify this strategy to make it more contextually specific for the students you are teaching. Whatever strategy you finally choose to enact, the key element to having this impact your students is that you have incorporated structures in your classroom whereby students see their progress at least twice a week.

2. Think about the attendance patterns of your class or classes. If you find that there are students whose attendance is causing them to underperform, think about implementing something akin to the thunderbird attendance poster strategy.

   Please remember what you learned in chapter 6 (page 59) about changing habits—small steps, then bigger steps. You may want to create an attendance image for a student that only tracks attendance for one month or, if the problem is significant, even one week. The intention behind the image is to provide a visual prompt on a continual basis so the student can set an attendance goal and see the degree to which he or she has succeeded in meeting it.

3. Think about having your students write down a grade goal they are willing to work to achieve in your class. Be sure to phrase the question along these lines: "What grade are you prepared to work to achieve in this course?" Follow this question with a clear description of what it takes to achieve an 85 percent or an *A+*, for example. Thus, students can select a grade goal that is realistic.

   Next, have students post their grade goal in a public place. This can be on their nameplates if you use these, on a corner of their desks—whatever works given your classroom context.

4. The next time you find yourself negotiating with a student to agree to change their behaviors (be this about attendance, academic performance, or classroom disruption), try using the mimicking strategy. However, remember the instructions given to the Maddux and colleagues (2008) participants who were able to gain a lot of cooperation from their counterparts. In the following, I modified their instructions for teacher use (Maddux et al., 2008):

   Successful negotiators recommend that you should mimic the mannerisms of the student you are trying to persuade in order to increase your chances of getting them to cooperate with you. For example, when the student rubs his or her face, you should too. If he or she leans back or leans forward in the chair, you should too. However, it is very important that you mimic subtly enough that the student does not notice what you are doing; otherwise, this technique backfires. Also, do not direct too much of your attention to the mimicking so you don't lose focus on the outcome you are attempting to achieve with this student. Thus, you should find a happy medium of consistent but subtle mimicking that does not disrupt your focus.

5. Think about Kahneman's (2011b) findings in regard to how much better students perform on intuitive tasks when they are in a good mood before the test by having them think happy thoughts. Remember, *student accuracy more than doubled*. The next time you are having your students perform a System 1 task, try establishing conditions that put your students in a good mood, and you will likely see a significant improvement in their performance. This can be as simple as having them remember the last time they laughed really hard or the most recent time they felt really happy. This is a relatively quick and easy way to improve student performance and make everyone feel better at the same time.

Sources: Kahneman, D. (2011b). Thinking, fast and slow (7th ed.). Canada: Doubleday Canada; Maddux, W. W., Mullen, E., & Galinsky, A. D. (2008). Chameleons bake bigger pies and take bigger pieces: Strategic behavioral mimicry facilitates negotiation outcomes. Journal of Experimental Social Psychology, 44(2), 461–468.

CHAPTER 8

SOFT TACTICS FOR EMPATHETIC PERSUASION OF STUDENTS' THINKING

In *Never Split the Difference*, professional negotiator Christopher Voss (2016) shares the following compelling insight about human behavior:

> It all starts with the universally applicable premise that people want to be understood and accepted. Listening is the cheapest, yet most effective concession we can make to get there. By listening intensely, a negotiator demonstrates empathy and shows a sincere desire to better understand what the other side is experiencing. Psychotherapy research shows that when individuals feel listened to, they tend to listen to themselves more carefully and to openly evaluate and clarify their own thoughts and feelings. In addition, they tend to become less defensive and oppositional and more willing to listen to other points of view, which gets them to the calm and logical place where they can be good Getting to Yes problem solvers. The whole concept . . . is called tactical empathy. (p. 16)

I had been teaching for over thirty years before I came across this book and quote. Voss spent twenty-four years working for the FBI in the Crisis Negotiation Unit. He was the FBI's primary kidnapping and hostage negotiator for four years, and over his career with the FBI,

Voss worked on over 150 international hostage cases. The title of his book is a reference to a situation where someone has taken four hostages and is threatening to kill all of them. In this circumstance, you cannot make a deal by saying something like, "I want all four hostages released, and you are threatening to kill all of them. Let's split the difference, and you release two and kill the others."

After reading the book as well as researching some other publications by Voss (2018, 2019), it struck me how well Voss's strategies transferred so effectively to the classroom. There were times when I had students who continually wanted to disrupt class. I couldn't cut a deal with a student like that and say, "Well, how about you only disrupt half of my classes?" Disruption of none of my classes was the goal. Nor can a teacher say to a student who likes to hit other students, "Let's make a deal. You only hit kids on Mondays, Wednesdays, and Fridays but not on Tuesdays and Thursdays." As teachers, we simply can't split the difference in situations like these.

Whereas Voss wrote about the successful strategies he utilized with kidnappers and hostage takers, I immediately saw numerous applications to teaching, especially when working with very challenging students. Voss (2016) points out that in a negotiation, you have to fundamentally understand what you are *really* trying to sell. He gives the following examples.

- A babysitter is really selling a relaxing evening out.
- A furnace salesperson is really selling cozy rooms.
- A locksmith is really selling a feeling of safety.

There are numerous other examples, and they all come to a pair of fundamental questions: (1) What are you *really* selling to your students as their teacher? and (2) What is it that you are trying to convince them to do or to believe when you teach them every day? These are questions every good teacher has thought about on some level and answered.

Some educators may take exception to the term *hostages*, arguing that students are not at all like hostages—people who are held against their will by robbers or kidnappers in an attempt to force others to give them large sums of money and a safe escape. In a certain sense, these educators are correct. However, in another sense, teachers who do not see *students as a kind of hostage* on occasion are incorrect. Any teacher who has taught for a while recognizes that many students (like people being held hostage) are in school or in specific classes *against their will*. Simply put, *they don't want to be there*. There are a lot of students who do not want to be in school, but they are forced to attend either by law or by their caregivers.

Additionally, any school that offers option courses (courses where students are supposed to have a choice in regard to which course they take) find that when some options get filled, students have to take option classes other than the ones they want. In other circumstances, schools have invested a great deal of money into certain programs (band and orchestra programs, for example) and, thus, teachers and administrators want these programs filled. I have seen schools name these such options with a very creative oxymoron—*compulsory options*. These kinds of options often have many students in them who do not want to be there,

and many may not want to be at school at all, but they have no choice. For our purposes, this makes them a kind of hostage.

As a teacher, your goal isn't to negotiate a better deal with your school so that they release these student "hostages." Your students *do* need to be there, after all. But you can apply the strategies Voss (2016) used while with the FBI as a means to persuade your students to engage with your instruction. This chapter demonstrates how these same strategies can also work successfully in a teaching context—sometimes in a classroom and sometimes (with exceptionally challenging students) in a one-on-one context. The strategies include the following.

- Determine what isn't negotiable.
- Know when to ask open-ended and irrational questions.
- Practice tactical or empathetic listening.
- Use six key listening skills during conversations.
- Apply FBI negotiation tactics in your classroom.
- Know how to use game theory.
- Give your students the illusion of control.
- Use the F word.
- Find the black swans.
- Persist until you are successful.

TACTIC: DETERMINE WHAT ISN'T NEGOTIABLE

I learned a long time ago that if I wanted to be a great teacher, I had to learn to be a great negotiator. In *The Successful Teacher's Survival Kit* (Ripley, 2019), I told the story of a famous animal trainer that illustrates this point quite effectively:

> Some time ago there was a documentary on TV about a man who trained animals for movies. This individual was quite famous for the effectiveness of his work, and the documentary showed the techniques he used to train birds, dogs, cats, and finally it showed him working with a very large

tiger. This particular tiger still had both its claws and its teeth—very large claws, very large teeth.

The interviewer asked the animal trainer, "What do you do when the tiger doesn't obey you—when the tiger doesn't do what you want her to do?"

The trainer smiled and replied, "Well, sometimes I get what I want, and sometimes the tiger gets what she wants."

Life in a classroom is a bit like that—sometimes the teacher gets what they want; sometimes the students get what they want. This is especially true as students get older, more aware and develop ideas and opinions of their own. Any teacher who thinks students ought to "Do what they're told because I'm the teacher" is in for a very quick wake-up call. While this can be more of an issue in junior high-middle school or high school, students in elementary grades can challenge a teacher's authority as well. (p. 74)

In an online discussion on mastering the art of negotiation, Voss (2018) reminds us that "Just because you're right doesn't mean you're going to get your own way." I would modify this for teachers to say that just because you're the *teacher* doesn't mean you're going to get your own way. Experienced teachers know this.

Ultimately, it's simpler to determine what isn't negotiable in your classroom than to iterate what is. Therefore, it is absolutely essential that you have a clear understanding of what the *nonnegotiables* are in your classroom. For me, they are my classroom procedures, the routines I establish at the beginning of each school year that describe how we will conduct day-to-day operations in my classroom. Every successful teacher establishes classroom procedures very early in the year that explain to students such things as how they are expected to handle the following.

- Enter and exit the classroom.
- Hand in homework assignments or exams and what to do when they come to class with incomplete homework.
- Transition from one subject to another or from one activity to another.
- Have questions they want to ask or comments they want to make.
- Know what to do when they come to class late or need to leave class early.
- Deal with forgetting to bring the necessary classroom supplies

These kinds of activities go on in most classrooms on a daily or sometimes weekly basis. Teachers hone and refine their classroom procedures over many years so that they work, and if a particular student doesn't like them, well, that's OK. They don't have to. They do have to follow them. Why? Because they work for both teachers and a majority of students.

I had two other non-negotiables in my classroom: (1) never lie to me, and (2) treat everyone in this classroom with respect. That's all, just two nonnegotiable rules. At that point, everything else is negotiable at least to some extent.

TACTIC: KNOW WHEN TO ASK OPEN-ENDED QUESTIONS AND IRRATIONAL QUESTIONS

Since intense listening helps us to understand another person's feelings and point of view, and this helps us to determine the best ways to influence them, why doesn't this happen more often in schools? Why is the kind of listening that Voss (2016) recommends so rare in classrooms and in schools?

The answer is simple: schools are filled with noise, and classrooms are filled with constant demands. There are too many students, too many bells, too much work, and too little time. Yet, even with this being the reality in virtually all schools, nonetheless, for some students, it is essential that you find the time to ask the right questions *and* really listen to their answers. If you don't do these things, you will never convince them to start moving in the direction you want.

There are times a student will confront you or make a statement that takes you completely off guard, and your body will want to respond not all that differently from how it might if you received a phone call that someone has kidnapped a loved one and will harm them if you don't pay a huge ransom within twenty-four hours. How can you respond in a situation when your whole system floods? Voss (2016) tells the story of an interview he was subjected to when he was looking to move into hostage negotiation with the FBI. The two interviewers sat down across from him, and one of them started by simply saying, "We've got your son, Voss. Give us one million dollars, or he dies" (p. 2). They followed shortly with graphic descriptions of what they'd do to harm his son. Voss responded, in a soft, calm voice, "How am I supposed to do that?" followed by, "I'm sorry, Robert, how do I know he's even alive?" followed by "I really am sorry, but how can I get you any money right now, much less one million dollars, if I don't even know he's alive?" (p. 3).

This is an extreme context, but pay close attention to what Voss (2016) does here. He speaks using a soft tone of voice, uses one of the kidnappers' first names (the beginning of establishing a relationship), and he has apologized—not once, but twice—giving the kidnapper some sense of control. Voss uses several tactics here, but the predominant one is the *open-ended question*, sometimes called *calibrated questions*. These are questions that the other side can respond to, but they have no predetermined answers. The intent in using these kinds of questions is not to solve the problem but to *keep the conversation going*, give the other side *the illusion of control* (as if they are the ones formulating the answers to solve the problem), and buy time.

In this example, Voss now has the kidnappers (interviewers) attempting to figure out answers to his questions—ways in which they can prove his son is alive and ways in which he can get one million dollars.

And Voss keeps asking the same open-ended questions, over and over and over again, and working very hard at really listening to the answers.

What might this look like in a classroom? Examples abound, but two will make the point. A student (Lee) has failed to hand in an assignment for no valid reason, and after four days of reminders, you tell him that he will receive a zero. Lee replies, "That's not fair. Other kids have handed in assignments after four days and got marks."

How do you respond to Lee using calibrated questions? You might say something like:

> Well, Lee, you're right. There have been times when a student has done exactly that. If a student has a valid medical reason for not being able to hand in their work on time and gives me a doctor's note, I will take in their work after four days. But you were not away ill; you were at school every day this week. How can I treat you differently than I treat the other students? Do you think that would be fair? Are you asking me to give you special treatment?

I have asked the question, "Are you asking me to give you special treatment?" many times in classrooms from elementary to high school. Depending on the student, his or her age, and my relationship with him or her, I may reframe the question into "Are you asking to be a teacher's pet—a special student for whom the rules of the classroom don't apply? Hmmm. How do you think the other students in the class will react to you when they notice that?"

Never once has a student replied "Yes" to that question. The reasons are obvious.

Consider also a common scenario in which a student complains to you about the mark they achieved on an assignment or an exam: "How come I only got 60 percent on this assignment? I worked really hard on this, and I deserve more."

As this student's teacher, you might respond:

It's great to see you working hard on your assignments [empathy; mirroring back some of the student's words to show you are listening]. Did you look at how you scored on each of the sections of the scoring rubric? Did you notice that there is no category for assessing how hard a student worked on the assignment? I have no idea how I could assess how hard each student worked on an assignment. Are you asking me to assess you differently than I assessed the other students? Are you asking for special treatment?

You can see the theme emerging here. Most students want to believe they are special in some ways, and they are. However, *being special* and *being treated differently* are not the same things. Most students are well aware that if their classmates see them as getting special treatment from their teacher, they will be subjected to ridicule and varying degrees of ostracism from their pack—neither of which they typically want.

You can also use what Daniel Pink (2012) calls *irrational questions* to uncover students' inner motivations and to get them to bring to a conscious level what is really going on behind the scenes. A wonderful example of this kind of irrational questioning that you can use with students goes like this:

Teacher: On a scale of one to ten—with one being not at all ready and ten being completely ready—how prepared are you to study really hard for next week's major exam?

Student: [Gives a number]

Teacher: Why didn't you choose a lower number?

Yes, you read that correctly. You are going to ask the student why it was that they didn't choose a *lower* number, a number that would mean they would be doing *less* work. This may take the student completely off guard, as they most likely expect you to ask them why they didn't choose a *higher* number and why they

aren't committed to studying harder. Thus, you may have to repeat your question.

For example, if the student replies, "Five" and you ask, "Why didn't you choose a *lower* number?" the student then must explain his or her reasons for studying at a level five rather than at a level four or lower. This also requires the student to explain to you *why* he or she is prepared to study harder than necessary. In this verbalization, the student clarifies his or her reasons for studying that hard, which can *increase* the chances the student actually studies.

Irrational questions have myriad uses. "Kelsey, what mark are you shooting for on this assignment?" Kelsey replies, and the teacher asks, "Why that mark? Why not a *lower* mark?" And then it happens once again: a student starts explaining to you why they are going to work that hard, not less.

TACTIC: PRACTICE TACTICAL OR EMPATHETIC LISTENING

In *The Seven Habits of Highly Effective People*, Stephen Covey (2005) contends that "Most people do not listen with the intent to understand; they listen with the intent to reply. They're either speaking or preparing to speak" (p. 251). As a result of this, there is little in the way of understanding. Covey (2005) argues a better way to listen is to practice *empathetic listening*:

When I say empathetic listening, I mean listening with the intent to *understand*. I mean *seeking first* to understand, to really understand. . . . Empathetic (from *empathy*) listening gets inside another person's frame of reference. You look out through it, you see the world the way they see the world, you understand their paradigm, you understand how they feel. (p. 252)

In *The Art of Impossible*, author and entrepreneur Steven Kotler (2021) describes it this way: "Active listening is the art of engaged presence. It's listening with genuine curiosity, but without judgment or attachment to outcome. No daydreaming. No thinking about whatever smart thing you're going to say next. Patience is key" (p. 147).

This can be very hard to do in your classroom because there will be times when interactions between you and your students become tense. A student challenges you in front of the class over an alleged violation of classroom rules. The student's tone is loud, aggressive, and belligerent. It is natural for any teacher to kick into autopilot and get defensive. Natural, but it's typically not helpful. Empathetic listening requires that if we want to be successful as teachers, we need to have a highly developed sense of emotional intelligence, and one of the essential skills of emotional intelligence is:

> Learning how to navigate the sometimes choppy waters of human interactions. . . . One of the most powerful tools for effectively managing interpersonal challenges . . . is reappraisal, or putting a more positive spin on someone else's bad behavior. (Lombardi & Joshua, 2020, p. 13)

For example, if an elementary student who is normally outgoing is suddenly acting sullen and snaps at you, instead of seeing this as rude or defiant, you can reframe or reappraise the behavior as a possible sign there has been a very upsetting event in this student's life. If a high school student who is normally quite engaged in class is now acting withdrawn and has his or her head down on the desk, instead of seeing this as boredom, you can reappraise the behavior and imagine that perhaps the student is upset, tired, or stressed for reasons that likely derive from outside the classroom.

I find it helps to remember when you were a student the same age as the students you are teaching. What kinds of behaviors did you and your friends manifest when you were tired, upset, stressed, or feeling down? Doing so can help you cut your students some slack when they may need it the most. Listening to your students is a very difficult thing to do. By this, I mean *really listening* to *what* is said, the *feelings* behind the words, *how* it is said—the *tone* of voice, the *pace* of the words, what is *not* being said—and so on. That is one of the reasons why the FBI uses a *team* to listen in hostage situations (Voss, 2016). It is simply too difficult for one person to catch everything another is communicating during a long conversation with someone else.

If you are in a negotiation with a student where you are trying to get the student to change a particular behavior, you need to be "curious about the other side's needs and priorities" (MacLellan, 2018). Remember, a negotiation is first *a mission of exploration*. To do that well, you need to listen very carefully, paying particular attention to a student's words. If the student says, "I don't want to do that," what you hear is, "OK, you don't want to do *that*, so how about *this* alternative." If a student says, "I can't do that right now," what you hear is, "OK, *when* can you do that?"

As simple as it may sound to listen, let's be honest, listening well is a very challenging thing to do. Voss (2016) writes:

> In one of the most cited research papers in psychology, George A. Miller persuasively put forth the idea that we can process only about seven pieces of information in our conscious mind at any given moment. In other words, *we are easily overwhelmed*. For those people who view negotiation as a battle of arguments, it's the voices in their own head that are overwhelming them. When they're not talking, they're thinking about their arguments, and when they are talking, they're making their arguments. Often those on both sides of the table are doing the same thing, so you have what I call a state of schizophrenia: everyone just listening to the voice in their head. . . . It may look like there are only two people in a conversation, but really it's more like four people all talking at once. (p. 28; emphasis added)

I have had many one-on-one conversations like this with students, when in reality, there were four of us doing the talking—the student and I talking aloud, and the other two participants chatting away inside each of our heads. How about you? Does this sound familiar from conversations you've experienced with your students?

There are ways to avoid these types of conversations—exchanges that are so often unproductive and can easily slip into situations where each side feels the need to win by defeating the other side and showing it is they who are right. As Peterson (2021) reminds us, "Negotiation is exceptionally difficult" (p. 279). When you ask a student to come into the hallway outside of your classroom due to some wrongdoing, and you inquire, "Why did you do that, and what are you going to do to make sure that doesn't happen again?" the reply is often, "I don't know." This "I don't know" really means, "Go away; leave me alone; I don't want to talk about this." It also means, "I don't want to do the hard work of figuring out why I behave the way I do and how I can change my behaviors going forward." You are now in the beginning stages of an important negotiation, and it will likely not be all that easy.

One important thing to keep in mind is that, as tempting as this may be, do not simply tell the student what to do. While the solution to the problem under discussion may be really obvious to you, simply telling students what to do is not likely to work for two reasons: (1) at this point, you really don't understand the reasons behind the behaviors (the student may not understand these as well), and (2) telling students what to do does not involve them in the process of finding solutions and figuring out next steps. Without their involvement in this process, they have no ownership over the outcome. You need to ask them for their ideas and work together with them to find solutions.

However, when attempting to resolve an issue with a student in the hallway, you need to be prepared for the silent treatment. Some students will simply look down at their shoes and not respond to your questions at all. Since you have left the rest of your class, you will feel significant pressure to get back inside the classroom and attend to your other students. You are under time pressure, but the student you are trying to converse with is not. In situations where, for example, a student did not respond after thirty seconds or more (and assuming the student is old enough to have at least basic writing skills), I would typically give the student a piece of paper and a pen, asking him or her to provide me with a written response. Most students didn't like this, as talking is so much easier than writing, and thus they would often open up at this point. With students who cannot yet write (either due to age or language barriers), I would calmly ask them to sit in the doorway, signaling me when they were ready to talk.

Be prepared to be surprised. I have had students come up with some very creative solutions to their classroom behavior issues—solutions that I would never have thought of on my own. If you find success with this strategy difficult, don't worry. The subsequent strategies in this chapter will also help you in these kinds of situations.

TACTIC: USE SIX KEY LISTENING SKILLS DURING CONVERSATIONS

Bruce Lambert (2018) has taken Voss's work and summarized tactical listening into six key listening skills that work well with anyone when you are engaged in conversation. Lambert (2018) advises us to use any of the following six skills; however, he adds that they are more powerful when used all together.

1. **Effective pauses:** Ask the student an open-ended question, then pause. Be silent. Do not be in a rush to fill the silence. For example, if you say, "Janessa, it seems to me that you are really angry today and that you are not your normal self in class. Can you tell me what's going on?" Be prepared to wait. And wait. And then wait some more. You can be assured you will get an answer. If all else fails, and as noted earlier in the chapter, you can ask the student to write an answer.

2. **Minimal encouragers:** *Minimal encouragers* are the small phrases like: *OK, I see, Yup, Uh huh, Yeah,* and so on. They are words and phrases you can say to students to let them know you are really listening while they speak. This is easy to do and comes quite

automatically to people—*when* they are truly listening.

3. **Mirroring:** Chapter 5 (page 49) introduced the concept of mirroring, repeating the last few words a student said, exactly as the student said them. For instance, to continue with my example of Janessa appearing angry in class, if she responds to your query with something along the lines of, "I am mad. My best friend said something really mean about me, and I don't know what to do about it," you might mirror this by asking, "Your best friend said something really mean about you?" and then just wait.

4. **Paraphrasing:** This tactic requires you to repeat the meaning of what you think the student is saying. Unlike mirroring, use your *own* words, not the student's exact words: "Wow, Janessa. It seems to me that it really makes you angry when your friends are mean to you."

5. **Labeling:** Name the student's feelings. Don't hesitate to do this for fear of getting it wrong. Even if you get it wrong, the student will know that you are trying and will correct you if necessary. Right or wrong, you have shown engagement with what the student is trying to tell you and opened the door to a deeper conversation.

6. **Summarizing:** Summarizing is when you feel that the student has said all he or she wants to say, and then you recap what you heard the student say in its entirety. The goal, which is critical, is to get the student to eventually say, "That's right!" When the student says that, you know the student feels you have heard and understood him or her.

TACTIC: APPLY FBI NEGOTIATION TACTICS IN YOUR CLASSROOM

One of the reasons I find FBI hostage-negotiation tactics valuable in the classroom is that it's very common for students to feel in crisis, and when that happens, they can't function normally or as you would want them to (Vecchi, Van Hasselt, & Romano, 2005). About this, negotiation specialists Gregory M. Vecchi and colleagues (2005) state:

> What is normally resolved at a rational or cognitive level is now dealt with at an emotional or affective level. Therefore, restoring the ability of a [student] to cope through the reestablishment of baseline functioning levels is the primary purpose of crisis intervention. (p. 538)

Any teacher who has worked in schools for a number of years has seen this kind of situation. A student has lost all rationality, any semblance of self-control, and is now running full throttle on adrenaline and emotion. In circumstances like this, reason and logic simply cannot work until the student has calmed down. Some teachers call this *resetting* or *starting over*. That leaves us with the question: What is the most effective way to get a student to a calm enough place that you can begin to reason with him or her and begin the process of resetting? What does this process look like?

To address these questions in its work, the FBI's Crisis Negotiation Unit developed and uses the Behavioral Change Stairway Model (BCSM; Voss, 2016). While successful teachers may not use the same terminology, I have seen many effective teachers walk students through a process that is remarkably similar.

The BCSM consists of the following five stages. (For the purposes of explaining the model, where the FBI would use the term *subject*, I use the term *student*.)

1. **Active listening:** This recognizes the student's need to be both heard and understood. At this stage, you utilize the listening strategies we have discussed previously in this chapter, such as mirroring, paraphrasing, summarizing, and

so on. It is critical that you speak in a calm, soft voice, as this will have a calming effect on the student (see Consider Physical and Emotional Contagion, page 83 in chapter 7).

2. **Empathy:** You want the student to feel not only that you hear him or her but also that you truly understand the student's point of view and feelings. This is not the same thing as agreeing with the student, but it is critical for conflict resolution that the student believes you understand how he or she views the situation and the reasons behind his or her feelings.

3. **Rapport:** Up until now, you have been doing most of the listening, letting the student know you understand him or her. Increased levels of trust will help establish rapport. You can then begin to discuss ways for the student to save face, reframe the situation into something that could have a positive outcome, and work together to figure out ways to resolve the situation.

4. **Influence:** As you build initial trust with the student, and he or she begins to listen

to a degree, you are in a position to offer suggestions as to how to move forward and resolve the conflict. You are seeking ways that work for both you and the student.

5. **Behavioral change:** If you have successfully walked the student through the first four stages, you have likely arrived at a place where the student is apt to agree to your suggestions about how to change his or her behavior and resolve the conflict.

Figure 8.1 illustrates the five steps of the BCSM.

At this point, you may be asking yourself if it's truly plausible to apply strategies such as this in your work as a teacher. After all, Chris Voss has much more time to negotiate than you do as a teacher, and he has a team of trained listeners helping him out—all valid points.

First, using the entire process is usually only necessary in the most challenging kinds of situations with your most challenging students, and working your way through it step-by-step is something you would likely need to do only on rare occasions. At the same time, it is important to understand that *parts* of the process work incredibly well on a day-to-day basis in your work with most students. Let's look at one of the more

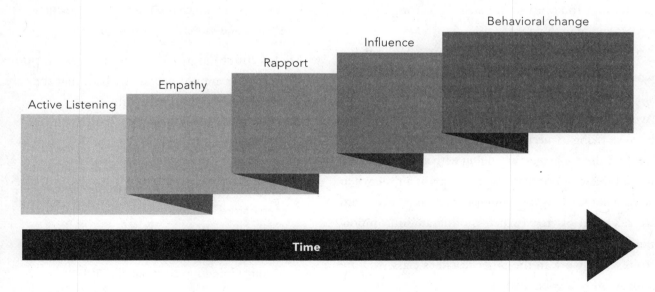

Source: Adapted from Voss, 2016.

Figure 8.1: The BCSM.

extreme situations you might have to deal with in your teaching, if you haven't already.

Imagine you are working with one of the most difficult students you have ever taught. It is early in the school year, you don't really know this student well, but this student continually disrupts your class, rarely does any schoolwork in the classroom, and never does homework. This student has no use for you or what you have to offer. Let's name this student Reese.

When it comes to Reese, you feel like you and the rest of the class are being held hostage—hostage to the outbursts, the verbal abuse, the sullen moods, the foul language, and so on. If you have tried some of the other strategies discussed throughout this book, such as reciprocation and likability—and these have not succeeded—then perhaps it is time to try the FBI's BCSM.

The following sections detail what that might look like.

Step 1: Setting the Stage

Understand that you cannot deploy these kinds of strategies inside a classroom during regular teaching times. There are too many students requiring your attention, there are too many distractions, and the student you are working with is likely to stunt for their peers. These kinds of strategies are best utilized in a one-on-one setting. You must set the stage by getting Reese in a room alone with you.

The choice of room is important. If you feel Reese would be most comfortable in your classroom (after all, it is large and somewhat familiar), then meet there. Avoid having this meeting after school or at lunchtime because asking to meet at those times may cause Reese to feel punished. I suggest arranging with another teacher to pull Reese out of that teacher's class at a time when you are not teaching and your classroom is empty. From Reese's point of view (which is of paramount importance in this entire process), you have just freed him from schoolwork in the other teacher's class. You are already off to a good start.

Step 2: Adopting a Discovery Mindset

Did you ever receive a birthday or holiday gift that was still wrapped, and you had absolutely no idea what it was? As you tore off the paper, you were on a mission—a mission of discovery—to find out what was inside the box. You need to enter the process of working with challenging students with the same kind of mindset: trying to discover what's inside the box.

This is easy to say, but it can be very challenging to do. Why? Because, as teachers, we often think we have students like Reese pegged. We have taught students who display such behaviors before, and we already think we know them.

Where do these assumptions come from? Why do we jump to these kinds of conclusions so quickly? Speaker and physician Hans Rosling (2018) believes this trait is there because it helps us survive:

> The human brain is a product of millions of years of evolution, and we are hardwired with instincts that helped our ancestors to survive in small groups of hunters and gatherers. Our brains often jump to swift conclusions without much thinking which used to help us to avoid immediate dangers. We are interested in gossip and dramatic stories, which used to be the only source of news and useful information. (p. 15)

Ariely (2008b) argues these kinds of assumptions and stereotypes are not necessarily bad, that they are, in fact, necessary and quite useful:

> A stereotype, after all, is a way of categorizing information, in the hope of predicting experiences. The brain cannot start from scratch at every new situation. It must build on what it has seen before. For that reason, stereotypes are not intrinsically malevolent. They provide shortcuts in our never-ending attempt to make sense of complicated surroundings. (p. 212)

Any teacher who has worked with seven-year-old or seventeen-year-old students for a number of years has certain stereotypes and assumptions about these students—*as a group*. These group stereotypes can be both accurate and useful. The problem arises when these stereotypes and assumptions blind you from seeing the *individual* students in front of you, who may or may not have these same characteristics.

If you have any hope whatsoever of working with a challenging student, like Reese, you must put aside your stereotypes as well as all of the stories and gossip you may have heard about this student. You must let go of all of the assumptions you carry about "these kinds of kids." *You must enter the conversation as an explorer, with a mindset of discovery*. You want to get to know Reese at a fundamental level. Voss (2016) describes the mindset of discovery this way:

> Your goal at the outset is to extract and observe as much information as possible. Which, by the way, is one of the reasons that really smart people often have trouble being negotiators—they're so smart they think they don't have anything to discover. Too often people find it easier just to stick with what they believe. Using what they've heard or their own biases, they often make assumptions about others even before meeting them. . . . Great negotiators are able to question the assumptions that the rest of the involved players accept on faith or in arrogance, and thus remain more emotionally open to all possibilities, and more intellectually agile to a fluid situation. (p. 25)

In the YouTube video "Why 'Scout Mindset' Is Crucial to Good Judgment," Julia Galef (2016), cofounder of the Center for Applied Rationality, argues we can have two mindsets, the *mindset of the soldier* or the *mindset of the scout*. The mindset of the soldier is to protect yourself and the other members of your side and ultimately to defeat your enemy. However, the mindset of the scout is entirely different. Galef (2016) says, "The scout's job is not to attack or defend. The scout's job is to understand. . . . Above all, the scout wants to know what's really there, as accurately as possible." According to Galef (2016), a scout's mindset is based on emotions:

For example, scouts are curious. They're more likely to say that they feel pleasure when they learn new information. . . . They're more likely to feel intrigued when they encounter something that contradicts their expectations. Scouts also have different values. They're more likely to say that they think it's virtuous to test your own beliefs, and they're less likely to say that someone who changes his mind seems weak. And above all, scouts are grounded, which means their self-worth as a person isn't tied to how right or wrong they are about any particular topic.

Seeing students like Reese through a *scout mindset* can be difficult, but if you are to have any chance of reaching challenging students and changing their classroom behaviors, you must first find out as much as possible about who they are and what the fundamental causes underlying their behaviors are.

There is a wonderful example of the need for a mindset of discovery in the film *All the Money in the World* (Scott, 2017). The movie tells the true story of the kidnapping of John Paul Getty's grandson in Rome in 1973. The kidnappers demanded $17 million from Getty for the safe return of his grandson. In the film, Mark Wahlberg plays the role of Fletcher Chase, the man responsible for negotiating with the abductors. He tells Gail Getty, the kidnapped boy's mother:

> $17 million does *not* guarantee you get your son back. I've had to bargain with a lot of people . . . and one thing I've learned is that money is never just money. It always stands for the one thing they've never had. Until you know what that one thing is, you're just beating your head against the bricks. (Scott, 2017)

Pause for a moment and think about how "money is never just money" applies to your most challenging students. *Bad behavior is never just bad behavior*. There is always something behind it. Until you discover what that something is, you're just beating your head against the bricks.

Step 3: Negotiating for the Long Haul

Don't think that you are going to spend a magical prep period of fifty minutes or so with Reese where you reach a mutual understanding of why he behaves the way he does, and now you are both going to agree on a successful action plan that will improve the situation immediately. It is highly unlikely that will happen. You may have to spend significant time with Reese to really understand him and the motives behind his behaviors. Voss (2016) tells us:

> Going too fast is one of the mistakes all negotiators are prone to making. If we're too much in a hurry, people can feel as if they're not being heard and we risk undermining the rapport and trust we've built. There's plenty of research that now validates the passage of time as one of the most important tools for a negotiator. (p. 30)

You need to let Reese know that you are in this for the long haul—and that you will be seeking more of these conversations—as many as it takes, for as long as it takes. This is challenging in a school context, where time is one of the most precious and rare commodities. Voss (2016) tells the story of standing outside an apartment door in the hallway of a Harlem high-rise. Reports were that there were three heavily armed fugitives inside, who several days earlier had been involved in a shoot-out with a rival gang. Snipers were on the roof, the SWAT team was poised for action, and there was no phone in the apartment to facilitate communication. All Voss could do was to talk to the fugitives through the locked apartment door. Speaking in a soft, calm voice, Voss (2016) describes the encounter:

> "It looks like you don't want to come out," I said repeatedly. "It seems like you worry that if you open the door, we'll come in with guns blazing. It looks like you don't want to go back to jail." For six hours, we got no response. . . . And then, when we were almost completely convinced that no one was inside, a sniper on an adjacent building radioed that he saw one of the curtains in the apartment move. The front door of the apartment slowly opened. A woman emerged with her hands in front of her. I continued talking. All three fugitives came out. None of them said a word until we had them in handcuffs. Then I asked them the question that was most nagging me: Why did they come out after six hours of radio silence? Why did they finally give in? All three gave me the same answer. "We didn't want to get caught or get shot, but you calmed us down," they said. "We finally believed you wouldn't go away, so we just came out." (p. 51)

You have to convince Reese that you are not going to quit, that you are not going to go away. In a sense, you need to wear him down and outlast him. This is similar to the story we looked at in chapter 6 (page 59), the story that Annie told me about the high school students on "the Rez" trying to drive me out, and how they eventually gave up because they realized that I wasn't going to go away.

You can accomplish a great deal when you convince the Reeses in your classroom that you are not going away.

Step 4: Exploring New Territory

Consider how Voss (2016) spoke to the fugitives in step 3: "It looks like you don't want to come out. It looks like you don't want to go back to jail" (p. 51). While this example was not a two-sided negotiation, nonetheless, the statements Voss began with are good starting points for you as a teacher as well. Too often, conversations with challenging students like Reese begin with something like this, "Why are you behaving that way? You can't act like that in my classroom!"

The mindset of discovery is missing when you speak to a student in this manner. When you ask, "Why are you behaving that way?" the very question assumes that the student knows the cause of their behaviors. That assumption is often a foolish starting point for a conversation with a student like Reese. Think about it this way: many adults have trouble really understanding why they behave the way they do. Why would we possibly expect this kind of insight from a student?

Instead, it is far better to start with open-ended questions or prompts, such as the following.

- "It seems that you don't like school . . ."
- "It looks like you would rather be doing something else . . ."
- "When you say that this school sucks, it sounds like you would rather not be here . . ."
- "It seems that you are angry when you are at school a great deal of the time . . ."

Voss (2016) calls what we are doing here *labeling the emotions* and suggests that labels almost always begin with roughly the same words: "It seems like . . .," "It sounds like . . .," "It looks like . . .," and so on. Voss (2016) says the word *I* raises people's defenses and conveys self-interest instead of interest for the other person—which makes the passive phrasing, "it seems like," important in establishing trust.

The volume, tone, and pace of your voice are also critical, and they will convey as much—if not more—than the words you use. While *what* people say can be persuasive, negotiators Alex B. Van Zant and Jonah Berger (2019) wonder whether or not *how* people speak has an impact on their level of persuasiveness. They conclude from their research that use of paralanguage and controlled pitch and volume of speech:

> Support this possibility, demonstrating that communicators engaging in paralinguistic persuasive attempts (i.e., modulating their voice to persuade) naturally used paralinguistic cues that influence perceivers' attitudes and choice. . . . Even when they are detected, paralinguistic attempts succeed because they make communicators seem more confident without undermining their perceived sincerity. (Van Zant & Berger, 2019, p. 2)

Therefore, when you are attempting to persuade a student like Reese to change his or her behaviors, you need to be attentive not only to *what* you say, but also *how* you say it. Proper presentation is critical. You will want to speak softly, slowly, and calmly. Lowering your pitch to make it sound deeper than usual can be helpful as well. I call this my *DJ voice*—the voice that I use in one-on-one situations where I am trying to calm or persuade a student to give me some information about their behaviors and to then explore how they might change those behaviors.

Your tone will set a mood, and you want that mood to be one in which Reese feels safe and free to speak without fear of judgment or reprisal. The response you get from students like Reese to such prompts will always contain emotions. That is the power of prompts: they invite the student to freely express what he or she is feeling. And so begins the process of the student revealing his or her self to you.

Step 5: Exhibiting Tactical Empathy

Next, comes . . . *silence*! Once you have asked your open-ended prompt, be quiet and listen, even if there are very long periods of silence. This may prove difficult because teachers generally don't like silence. Mary Budd Rowe (1972) published a seminal research paper that discussed her research into wait times in classrooms. She discovered that, on average, elementary teachers allow only *one second* while waiting for a student to respond to a question and that they follow a student's response with a comment within *nine-tenths of a second*. Teachers seem to have a desire to fill the quiet spaces as quickly as possible.

Nevertheless, no matter how challenging this is for you, *be quiet and wait*. Reese will begin talking, because like you, he is uncomfortable with silence and likely lacks the self-discipline to wait you out.

Now that Reese is talking, your most important job has begun, *the job of really listening*. Voss (2016) calls this *tactical empathy*, hearing what is behind the feelings a subject expresses:

> Empathy is not about being nice or agreeing with the other side. It's about understanding them. Empathy helps us learn the position the [student] is in, why their actions make sense to them, and what might move them. As negotiators, we use empathy because it works. (p. 53)

Remember, the goal of these conversations is for you to find out as much as you can about what the student *wants*, what the student *needs*, how the student *feels*, and what the student is *getting out of behaving the way they do*. In situations such as this, you are a scout on a mission of discovery.

TACTIC: KNOW HOW TO USE GAME THEORY

One way to think tactically about the notion of payoffs is to think in terms of *game theory*, which is essentially a way of looking at social situations where the players (usually in a competitive situation) are trying to win by outmaneuvering and ultimately defeating their opponents. In some circumstances, this is how a student will see an interaction with a teacher. Think of game theory as a science of strategy. It explores how the players (students) make decisions based on various kinds of information and their conjecture of possible outcomes. It's also been a serious field of study in mathematics since the 20th century, so we are not working with something new here (von Neumann & Morgenstern, 1944/2004).

There is also *competitive game theory*, which applies to situations where there are winners and losers. Team sports, buying a car from a salesperson, renting an apartment from a landlord, and wars between nations are all applicable examples of competitive game theory. Why? Because each side in these examples wants to win, and *winning comes at the expense of the other side*. Remember, when you are in a conflict situation with a student, if both you and the student are working in a competitive mode, there has to be a winner and a loser, and neither of you wants to be the loser. Remember as well, we still often think and act at an instinctual level. We have the brains of our hunter-gatherer ancestors, and it is through that lens that we often view the world. "In our hunter-gatherer minds, we suspect that life is a zero-sum game—that for someone to have more means that we might end up with less" (Holiday & Hanselman, 2016, p. 299). That is competitive game theory. The student may believe that if they give in to you, they have less, and you have more; they have lost, and you have won. No one wants to feel like a loser.

So, game theory looks very closely at the notion of *payoffs*—the reward that a player obtains if he or she achieves a particular outcome. Slot-machine designers use the notion of payoff in very effective ways to keep people playing. When a player puts in one dollar and pushes the button—lights flash, noises emerge, and then bells ring—announcing that the player has "won" eighty cents—not that the player just *lost* twenty cents.

Think back to the chapter 1 (page 9) exploration of teenage-boy driving habits. You will recall that when placed in the driving simulators *by themselves*, teenage boys took risks at about the same rate as the adults did. However, when the teenagers' friends were brought into the room to watch, these young drivers took *twice as many risks* getting across town as they had when driving unobserved by their friends. Why? Because for them, the payoff had changed. The reward of obtaining their friends' approval for risky behaviors far outweighed the risk of losing time by driving dangerously.

Let's explore the classroom through the lens of game theory. Specifically, let's look at the notion of payoffs and how they work in a classroom. Students are rational beings at some level and in some ways. Thus, if they are behaving in a certain way and continue with that behavior, they are undeniably getting some reward from the behavior (even if they are not consciously aware of it). This reward is their *payoff*. As I've previously written:

> Their payoff might be respect from important peers achieved by defying you; it might be getting a few laughs from the class (and thus being in the spotlight); it might be getting out of doing undesirable schoolwork. Whatever it is, you need to figure out what payoff they are getting from their "poor behaviors," because if you don't, you have little chance of taking the best course of action to change those behaviors. (Ripley, 2019, p. 79)

In other words, if you are going to *change the behavior*, you need to *change the payoff*. And you can't change the payoff unless you first understand what a student's particular payoff is—what, specifically, the student is getting from these behaviors. To do this, you have to ask the right questions, start with the right prompts, and then *really listen* to the student's response with a discovery mindset.

When entering into this process, it is essential that you *leave your assumptions at the classroom door*. Voss (2016) writes, "In basic terms, people's emotions have two levels: the 'presenting' behavior is the part above the surface you can see and hear; beneath, the 'underlying' feeling is what motivates the behavior" (Voss, 2016, p. 57). If you believe that you have already figured out what the payoff is for a particular student's poor behaviors, you have significantly decreased your chances of really finding out what is going on and why. Such thinking makes you blind and deaf—you will fail to *see* the student in front of you, and you will fail to *hear* what is behind the words they are saying. With this attitude, the odds are no longer in your favor.

As a teacher working with a challenging student whose behaviors you are trying to change, you need to guard against simply accepting the presenting behavior as being fundamentally true. Instead, utilize devices such as prompts and mirroring to get to the underlying reasons and feelings that are motivating these behaviors.

Many times in my four decades of teaching, a student has acted out in completely unacceptable ways in my classroom. In these situations, my strategy was—and still is—to quietly ask the student to come out to the hallway so we can talk. I then walk out the door—*never looking back*—and wait for the student to join me in the hallway where we can have a private conversation. I speak softly, using my DJ voice, in a very nonaccusatory tone, and say something like, "Taylor, you seem really upset today . . ." And then I wait . . . in silence.

Over the years, I have had dozens of students from elementary to high school simply begin to cry when I started the conversation with that statement and then just listened. Through their tears, they would often tell me about how their dog died, or their grandmother passed, or how their boyfriend or girlfriend cheated on them, or that dad had just been sent to jail. These are some of the myriad examples of how emotions drive student behaviors. If you don't get to the emotions and instead simply deal with the presenting behaviors, you have little chance of understanding why the student is behaving the way he or she is and then working with him or her to effect some kind of positive change.

Game theory helps us view students' presenting behaviors from the perspective of payoffs. We may see their behaviors as negative, and these behaviors may well be negative in terms of the effect they have on us or on the class as a whole—even on the students themselves. However, if the student continues with these particular behaviors over time, know for certain that there is some kind of payoff the student is obtaining by behaving in this manner, even if it is as simple as venting a whole lot of negative emotion.

You need to work with students to first understand the payoff; then you can begin to work with them to help them achieve a *better* payoff—one that is more gratifying, one that they are more interested in obtaining, and one that works for you as well. Then—and only then—will you see their behaviors change for the better.

TACTIC: GIVE YOUR STUDENTS THE ILLUSION OF CONTROL

It is a basic human need to want to have some control over our lives and our environment. We want control so we can achieve our goals and get what we want. Psychology calls this *agency*, and every student in every classroom wants to feel some degree of control over what happens to them in school (Jensen, 2019). But it's not necessarily important for that sense of control to be real. Consider the following story from *The 48 Laws of Power* (Greene, 1998):

> Sir Christopher Wren was England's version of the Renaissance man. He had mastered the sciences of mathematics, astronomy, physics, and

physiology. Yet during his extremely long career as England's most celebrated architect he was often told by his patrons to make impractical changes in his designs. Never once did he argue or offend. He had other ways of proving his point.

In 1688 Wren designed a magnificent town hall for the city of Westminster. The mayor, however, was not satisfied; in fact he was nervous. He told Wren he was afraid the second floor was not secure, and that it could all come crashing down on his office on the first floor. He demanded that Wren add two stone columns for extra support. Wren, the consummate engineer, knew that these columns would serve no purpose, and that the mayor's fears were baseless. But build them he did, and the mayor was grateful. It was only years later that workmen on a high scaffold saw that the columns stopped just short of the ceiling. (pp. 72–73)

The mayor needed to feel that he had some control over the building of the town hall. Wren needed to feel that he had some control over both the building of the town hall and his reputation as an engineer. Wren's mastery of the illusion of control ensured both men got what they wanted. The mayor got his columns, and Wren knew that posterity would realize that the two additional columns were unnecessary, and his reputation as a master engineer and architect would remain intact.

The need for some sense of control in our lives is primal (Ariely, 2016). Every parent who has ever asked their young children, "Do you want white milk or chocolate milk?" already knows the answer. However, their children feel some sense of control when asked questions such as these, and the parents are happy that the children are drinking milk. (Please note, soda pop or juice were not among the options. This is an influence strategy called *choice architecture*, something we will explore in more detail in chapter 9, page 115.)

Why is it so critical for students to feel like you've given away some sense of control over a situation, even if it is, in fact, an illusion? Voss (2016) explains:

> It comes down to the deep and universal human need for autonomy. People need to feel in control. When you preserve a person's autonomy by clearly giving them permission to say "No" to your ideas, the emotions calm, the effectiveness of the decisions go up, and the other party can really look at your proposal. . . . Great negotiators seek "No" because they know that's often when the real negotiation begins. (p. 78)

Voss (2016, 2018) describes how he actually encourages his opponents to say "No" at times. He feels that asking a question to which the obvious answer would be "No" helps to give the person with whom he is negotiating a greater sense of control. However, Voss uses the "No" response as a way to open the door a crack and stick his foot in. He writes:

> You have to train yourself to hear "No" as something other than rejection and respond accordingly. When someone tells you "No" you need to rethink the word in one of its alternative—and much more real—meanings: I am not yet ready to agree; you are making me feel uncomfortable; I do not understand; I don't think I can afford it; I want something else; I need more information; or I want to talk it over with someone else. Then, after pausing, ask solution-based questions or simply label the effect: What about this doesn't work for you? (Voss, 2016, p. 79)

As an educator, I advise you not to fight this need for some degree of control that all of your students possess because it is simply part of them being human. We see this need for some sense of control in our colleagues, in our students, and in their parents.

As a school principal, I often have some caregivers (usually at the urging of their children) come to me at the beginning of the school year and ask that their child be moved to another classroom. Typically this was because the student wanted to be with their friends. Given what we know about natural selection and the need we all have for belonging to a group, this desire on the part of the student was understandable.

Yet, the teachers had gone to a great deal of work in determining who was in which class. Factors such as class size, educational needs, gender balance, and the like all factored into the making of class groupings. I was always reluctant to second-guess the teachers' work and move these students. Yet, an outright "No" to the caregivers' request was not going to be helpful either.

Instead of refusing the request to move the student to a class with their friends, I would negotiate an agreement. I would explain to the student and their caregivers the criteria that the teachers had used to generate the class groupings. I would then say, "However, it is very understandable that _____ wants to be with [his or her] friends. I get that. Here's what I am prepared to do. You spend the month of September with your new class, the one to which the teachers have assigned you. If, on October 1st, you are not happy there and want to move, I will move you to the class where you want to go on that day. Guaranteed! Agreed?"

This arrangement gave the student and their caregivers a sense of control. The student left that discussion knowing they could get what they wanted if they just toughed out a month with the current class assignment. The caregivers felt they had advocated successfully for their child, enabling both to feel understood and in control.

Not once in over twenty-five years as a school administrator did I have a student come to me on October 1st and ask to move classes. Why? Because over the month of September, they had developed new friendships with some of the students in the class to which they had originally been assigned. In the words of the students, "I don't want to move classes anymore because I made new friends." This was inevitable, and I knew it, just as I knew that an outright "No" to the initial request to move classes was not a great relationship builder with the students or their caregivers. The caregivers and the

students both needed to feel some sense of control over the situation, and I needed to understand and show respect for those feelings just as Voss (2016) suggests.

How do we give extremely challenging students a sense of control? Part of that answer lies in the very word *how*. Asking *how* questions means you are asking for help *from the student*, and when you do this, they may volunteer to help you. *How* questions give the illusion of control. Picture this dialogue:

> Teacher: "Alex, it seems you don't want to do any work in my class." (Pause, wait for the response, listen carefully, and respond in a way that gets you more information.)
>
> Teacher: "Alex, how can I let you not do any work in my class when I insist that all of the other students have to do the required work? How can I do that?"
>
> Alex: "I don't know."
>
> Teacher: "Let me ask you again. How can I let you not do any work in my class when I insist that all of the other students have to do the required work? How can I do that?"
>
> Alex: "I guess you can't."

However the dialogue proceeds, no student wants to be singled out as being exempt from schoolwork in front of their peers. That is embarrassing and leads to teasing and their being shunned. Alex doesn't want that, and neither will your students.

TACTIC: USE THE F WORD

All students need to feel their teachers treat them fairly. Voss (2016) writes, "The most powerful word in negotiations is 'Fair.' As human beings, we are mightily swayed by how much we feel we have been respected. People comply with agreements if they feel they have been treated fairly and lash out if they don't" (Voss, 2016, p. 122). While it's understandable students want to feel fairly treated, it will be very hard for you to achieve, since each student has his or her own conceptions as to what fairness actually looks and feels like.

I once had a group of eleventh-grade girls approach me between classes, and one of them blurted out, "Ms. Myron favors the boys over the girls, and we don't like it. It's not fair!" There it was, out in the open before I had any chance to stop it—criticism of a colleague.

I asked them in a calm and quiet voice if they could give me some examples from their perspective of this teacher favoring the boys, which they did. I met with Ms. Myron later that day, and without naming these girls, I told her what had happened. I informed her that while I had no idea whether or not these students' concerns were valid, the important thing was that these girls *believed* she favored the boys and that she was treating the girls unfairly. Unless she dealt with that in some way, she was bound to have problems with the girls in her classroom. In this case, she chose not to address the *F word* and spent the entire year in conflict with the girls in her class.

One way to be proactive in this regard is to say to your classes at the beginning of the year:

> *I want you to feel like I am treating you fairly at all times. This is very important to me. So please tell me if you feel I am acting unfairly, and we will discuss it. We may or may not come to an agreement, but I promise you I will listen carefully to what you are saying and that you will be heard.*

Simply saying that to your students will go a long way in terms of them recognizing that you are committed to working with them to create an environment that treats them fairly.

This sounds simple, but having your students perceive you as being fair can be very difficult to implement effectively in the classroom. Why? Because as a teacher, you are required to treat each student differently, based on his or her individual needs and academic abilities. Treating students differently and having your students perceive you as treating them fairly is one of teaching's most challenging balancing acts.

TACTIC: FIND THE BLACK SWANS

Up until the late 1600s, Europeans thought that all swans were white (Taleb, 2008). They believed this because they had only ever observed white swans. That all changed in 1697. While exploring Australia, Willem de Vlamingh discovered something never before seen by European eyes—black swans. Now, what was previously unthinkable became real.

Today, *black swan* is a term people use to describe something that is unprecedented or unexpected. Nassim Taleb (2008) coined it to describe events in human history that no one foresaw but which seemed predictable and inevitable in hindsight. In other words, black swans are hidden, but real. Just because we have yet to see one doesn't mean there aren't any around.

What does this have to do with your students and influencing their behaviors? Voss (2016) writes:

> In every negotiation each side is in possession of at least three Black Swans, three pieces of information that, were they to be discovered by the other side, would change everything. . . . Finding and acting on Black Swans mandates a shift in your mindset. It takes negotiations from being a one-dimensional move-countermove game of checkers to a three-dimensional game that's more emotional, adaptive, intuitive . . . and truly effective. (p. 208)

Voss (2016) suggests two strategies you can apply when trying to unearth the black swans of your most challenging students.

1. **Get face time:** There is nothing like a face-to-face conversation where you can read body language, eye contact, tone and pace of voice, and so on. The written word gives you none of that, so asking misbehaving students to write down the reasons for their misdeeds is not effective unless it is followed up with a conversation. As well, this face time must take place in a one-on-one setting. As we discussed earlier, students can act quite differently when

in the presence of their peers than they do when they are alone.

2. **Observe the students you want to win over in unguarded moments:** Watch them in the hallways, in the gym, in the cafeteria or lunchroom, before and after school, and at their lockers. What are they doing? Whom are they hanging out with? What are they talking about?

These kinds of observations are a gold mine of information for you, information you can use in your conversations and negotiations with students to help you to first understand them and determine why they think and behave the way they do. You can then begin to develop effective strategies that will help you influence them to change these behaviors.

This kind of work has a kind of triage component for teachers. Because you likely teach many students, you simply cannot implement these kinds of strategies for all of your students, all of the time. The good news is that you don't need to. What you may need to do, however, is choose the student who is both negative and influential or the student who has much greater potential than they see in themself. You will likely only be able to carry out these kinds of strategies with one or two students at a time, as working with students at this kind of depth takes a great deal of time, focus, and energy. And that's just fine. Choose those students who most need this kind of help, and then begin. Once they are on track, you move on to the next one or two. Do you remember the starfish story from the book introduction (page 1)? Make a difference to that one, and then the next, and the next . . . .

TACTIC: PERSIST UNTIL YOU ARE SUCCESSFUL

Have you tried the same tactics and approaches over and over again with your most challenging students throughout the years but haven't really made much progress in changing their behaviors and helping them be successful in school? And yet, do you keep using the same strategies over and over again? As you reflect on these questions, consider: Does the following description of Sisyphus apply to you? "If Sisyphus were pushing his rock up a new hill every time, he would have a sense of progress. But because he keeps pushing the same rock up the same hill over and over, his work is completely meaningless" (Ariely, 2016, p. 24).

In talking about the importance of persistence, I often think about the story behind the development of WD-40. The WD-40 Company (n.d.) credits the invention of WD-40 to Norman Larsen, founder of the Rocket Chemical Company. Larsen was attempting to create a water displacement chemical and supposedly took forty attempts to get it just right, hence the name WD-40.

The lesson here is clear: very few teachers get things right the first time they try. We all need to recognize and accept that we are going to fail from time to time in our efforts to change student behavior. We are going to get frustrated, and we are going to have to keep trying over and over again until we get it right—perhaps even as many as forty times. With that understanding in mind, I highly recommend you try the processes and strategies described in this chapter with some of your challenging students.

Please understand, however, there are no guarantees that these strategies will work on all of your students all of the time. Why? Because each student and each event and each context are different. There is no formula to be found for motivating and persuading all students all of the time. All teaching takes place in a specific context. You teach certain students at certain places during certain times in their lives within a certain cultural context. Despite your best intentions or use of the "right" tactic, you might also make different mistakes that inhibit your success with using it. *Everything in teaching is contextual.* You have to take a read on the student, the situation, the timing, and the context, and then proceed in the best way you know how.

Although you cannot have a single plan that you are going to utilize for all students, you can have a process in mind and a goal you want to achieve to motivate and persuade your students to become more knowledgeable and to become better human beings. Focus on the process, be patient, and develop your influence plan on a case-by-case, student-by-student basis while taking into account all of the cues and context around you. Remember, when you are working with some of your most challenging students, this will be a one-step-at-a-time long-haul process, and you cannot be in a great hurry for these kinds of students to make substantial changes. You need to remember, "When it comes to negotiations, amateurs talk about outcomes, professionals talk about process" (Reiss, 2010, p. 235).

As you implement these strategies and refine them over time, I am certain that you will see some significant and positive changes in many of your students. And at the end of the day, isn't that why you became a teacher?

SUMMARY

This chapter explored a number of negotiation tactics, such as using open-ended questions, empathetic listening, using payoffs effectively, and giving your students a feeling that they have some control. At the same time, don't lose sight of the aspects of life in a classroom, such as the procedures and routines that work for you, that are nonnegotiable. As you reflect on this chapter, make sure to remember the following.

- It is a universal principle that people want to be understood and accepted. This applies to both you and to the students in your classroom.

- Tactical or empathetic listening requires that you listen with the intent to understand, not react. This involves listening to the words students use, the pace and the tone of the speaker, and the possible implications behind the words the student uses. Using the six aspects of tactical listening is an effective strategy to gather information and to make the student feel they are being heard.

- Setting the stage is important when negotiating with a student. The room, the tone, and the seating all have an impact on the outcome of your conversations. Teachers need to enter these kinds of conversations with a discovery mindset—a scout mindset—genuinely seeking to discover what is going on in the student's mind.

- Substantial behavioral changes will usually not take place quickly. Teachers have to work with students for a significant period of time in order for this to happen.

- Game theory teaches us to think about payoffs (rewards). Students often behave in certain ways because of the payoff they obtain from these behaviors. If teachers are to change the behaviors, they need to understand the payoffs and give students a more attractive payoff.

- All students and teachers have a fundamental need to feel some degree of control over their lives and to feel that teachers treat them fairly. Teachers need to be fair and give students some degree of control (or the illusion of control) in their classrooms in order to meet this need.

- Many students will not understand the motives for their negative behaviors. These are the black swans of behavioral motivation, and they are often difficult to discover. You need to discover them if you are going to be successful in changing student behaviors.

Reflective Practice

This chapter focused extensively on how to negotiate with students. However, I also recommended that you have certain classroom routines that are nonnegotiable because they work for you and your students. Use the steps in this exercise to develop these routines.

1. In the following chart, list the nonnegotiable routines and rules of your classroom, then describe how you have communicated these to your students. Think about when you communicated each routine to your class and how effective your communication has been. As well, describe the consequences you have communicated to your students in regard to what happens if they do not adhere to your nonnegotiable rules and routines.

My nonnegotiable rules and routines	How and when I communicated these to my students	The consequences for choosing not to adhere to my rules and routines

2. The section Practice Tactical or Empathetic Listening (page 97) asks you to think about reframing a student's behavior. For example, if an elementary student who is normally outgoing is suddenly acting sullen and snaps at you, instead of seeing this as rude or defiant, you can reframe their behavior as a sign that possibly there has been a very upsetting event in this child's life.

Use the following chart to describe an incident where a student acted out of character. Then describe how you interpreted their behaviors at the time, and determine how you could have reframed that behavior. (The chart includes an example.) Make a commitment to attempt this strategy the next time a student acts out of character in your class.

Incident description	How you interpreted the student's behavior at the time	How you could reframe your understanding of the student's behavior
Example: Ray, who is usually a very happy, energetic, and engaged student, was sullen and withdrawn throughout the entire class.	Ray is in a bad mood, so I just left him alone and didn't ask him any questions or force him to be involved.	Perhaps Ray is simply not feeling well and should go home. Or maybe something bad has happened, and he is emotionally upset?

The Tactical Teacher © 2022 Solution Tree Press • SolutionTree.com
Visit **go.SolutionTree.com/behavior** to download this free reproducible.

3. This chapter discussed Lambert's (2018) six listening skills. For this practice exercise, choose a student whose behavior you want to change. Be sure to focus on one specific behavior for this exercise. It may deal with academic performance (homework, test preparation, assignments in on time, and so on), or it may focus on a particular classroom misbehavior that is at issue. Using Lambert's (2018) six steps, talk to the student in a private, one-on-one conversation, and follow the six steps using the following chart. Make note of the student's responses in the space provided.

Lambert's (2018) Six Steps	Student's Responses
1. **Effective pauses:** Ask the student an open-ended question, then pause. Be silent. Do not be in a rush to fill the silence. For example: "Janessa, it seems to me that you are really angry today and that you are not your normal self in class. Can you tell me what's going on?" Now, wait . . . and wait . . .	
2. **Minimal encouragers:** Minimal encouragers are the small phrases like *OK, I see, yup, uh huh,* and *yeah* that you say to the student as he or she is speaking to let the student know you are really listening.	
3. **Mirroring:** Mirroring is when you repeat the last few words the other person has said, exactly as he or she said them.	
4. **Paraphrasing:** Paraphrasing is when you repeat the meaning of what you think the student is saying to you, but unlike mirroring, you use your own words, not the student's exact words.	
5. **Labeling:** When you label, you are naming the student's feelings. Don't hesitate to do this for fear of getting it wrong. Even if you get it wrong, the student will know that you are trying and will likely correct you if necessary.	
6. **Summarizing:** Summarizing is when you recap what you heard them say in its entirety once you feel that the student has said all he or she wants to say. The goal here is to get the student to eventually say, "That's right!" When the student says that, you know he or she feels heard and understood.	

After the conversation is over and the student has left, reflect on: (1) what you learned, and (2) how the process worked for you and what you would do again in the future or what you might change.

Source: Lambert, B. (2018, November 19). Chris Voss's tactical empathy: 6 reflective listening skills combined [Video file]. Accessed at www.youtube.com/watch?v=wQwP4j0AqmU on June 9, 2021.

The Tactical Teacher © 2022 Solution Tree Press • SolutionTree.com
Visit **go.SolutionTree.com/behavior** to download this free reproducible.

CHAPTER 9

SOFT TACTICS FOR YOUR CLASSROOM'S PHYSICAL ENVIRONMENT

In *Pre-Suasion: A Revolutionary Way to Influence and Persuade*, Cialdini (2016) describes a trait common to people who are highly effective persuaders:

> The highest achievers spend more time crafting what they did and said before making a request. They set about their mission as skilled gardeners who know that even the finest seeds will not take root in stony soil or bear fullest fruit in poorly prepared ground. They spent much of their time toiling in the fields of influence thinking about and engaging in cultivation—in ensuring that the situations they were facing had been pre-treated and readied for growth. . . . But much more than their less effective colleagues, they didn't rely on the legitimate merits of an offer to get it accepted; they recognized that the psychological frame in which an appeal is first placed can carry equal or even greater weight . . . before introducing their message, they arranged to make their audience sympathetic to it. . . . The best persuaders become the best through pre-suasion—the process of arranging for recipients to be receptive to a message before they encounter it. (p. 4)

Cialdini (2016) also makes the argument that what we present *first* changes the way people experience what we present to them *next*: "The basic idea of pre-suasion is that by guiding preliminary attention strategically, it's possible for a communicator to move recipients into agreement with a message *before* they experience it" (p. 132; emphasis added). Another name for this is *priming*. You could also call it *setting the stage*.

As an example of pre-suasion at work in a classroom all teachers have experienced, imagine you are passing back an assignment or an exam that you have just marked. Often, teachers simply walk around the class and place these exams or assignments on students' desks or they call out students' names, and the students come up to get their papers. Students then look at their results, and what often happens next? Hands shoot up. They have questions or complaints about their marks. "How come you only gave me a 65 percent? Joyce got a 75 percent, and mine is better than hers!" Anyone who has taught K–12 students will have had experiences such as this.

The problem in this example is one of pre-suasion—it is completely lacking. The teacher hasn't properly set the stage. To pre-suade your students—and thus avoid these kinds of situations—you need to do two things:

(1) tell your students *before* the first assessment of the year that you do not give marks—they are *achieved, not received*, and (2) show them exemplar responses *before* passing back their assessments. Let's dig deeper.

In assessing students' work, every teacher must answer this fundamental question: Are you going to give every student 100 percent automatically for each assessment and then deduct for errors and omissions? Or are you going to start by giving every student 0 percent, adding marks for everything they produce on the assessment that meets the assessment's requirements? This is a fundamental assessment question that you need to answer. If you choose to start by *giving* each student 100 percent and then deducting for errors and omissions, you have set the stage to invite students to challenge your assessments and for them to ask the question, "Why did you only *give* me 65 percent?" If you use this model of assessment, the marks your students get are *received*. However, if you tell students prior to the first assessment of the term that you start by awarding a mark of 0 percent, and then you *add marks* based on the work the students have produced in their assessments, students can no longer ask why you only *gave* them such and such a mark, because you don't give any marks at all. Marks using this model of assessment are *achieved*, not received.

The purpose of exemplar responses as a method to pre-suade your students not to clamor and complain upon receiving their assessments is to ensure they see—in detail—what an assessment that received a 95 percent looks like *prior* to getting their own assessment back. They then have the opportunity to compare what they produced in relation to what the 95 percent assessment looked like. The similarities and differences will now be much more evident to them, and the likelihood of confusion and complaints will diminish accordingly.

In this chapter, we explore a number of ways that you can pre-suade your students by what you do with both the physical and the psychological environment of your classroom. This chapter explores ways in which you can plant the seeds of influence, then watch them develop roots and grow in the choices your students make and the ways in which they choose to conduct themselves in your classroom. The specific strategies you'll learn about include the following.

- Plan what your students hear.
- Plan what your students smell.
- Plan what your students see.
- Plan for sights, sounds, and smells.
- Use choice architecture.

TACTIC: PLAN WHAT YOUR STUDENTS HEAR

There are a lot of sounds in a typical classroom, students talking to one another, teachers giving instruction and directions, laughter, video narrations, and so on. Some types of sounds cause anxiety and tension, such as when a teacher yells at a student. But there are specific ways to use sound to establish certain moods in your classroom. The following sections detail tactics for instilling motivation and calm and for using music as a deterrent.

Music for Motivation and Calm

Music has significant power for you to influence how your students feel in your classroom. Think of the common saying, "Music has charms to soothe a savage beast." Since the broadcast of the first radio waves, students the world over have wanted teachers to allow them to listen to music as they did their schoolwork. And while many students will argue that listening to music helps them learn, just as many teachers likely remain suspect of this claim, but there is research to support students for this one, although perhaps not as they would prefer.

In a 2015 study, researchers Laura Ferreri, Emmanuel Bigand, and Aurelia Bugaiska found that when students were exposed to *background instrumental music*, their ability to store new learnings in memory improved. While studies like this suggest that listening to music can be helpful, they are also very specific as to the kind of music that is helpful: music that is *instrumental, soft, calming,* and *pleasant to the ear* (Kang & Williamson, 2014). Pachelbel's *Canon* and Bach's *Air on the G String* are good examples of this kind of music.

Given this, what role might music play in your classroom? How can you use music to improve classroom behaviors and increase learning? We all know—simply from personal experience and observation—that music can have a tremendous impact on our mood and feelings. Play Beethoven's *Sonata Pathetique,* Eric Clapton's "Tears in Heaven," or "Jealous" by Labrinth in your classroom, and watch the room go quiet. On the other hand, play "Wake Me Up Before You Go-Go" (also known as "TheJitterbug Song") by Wham! or Rick Astley's "Never Gonna Give You Up" or "Together Forever," and watch the energy in the room go way up.

You might be thinking, "This author is stuck in the '80s. He's still listening to Wham! and Rick Astley in his classes." You would be wrong. (See my current playlist in table 9.1, page 118.) For years, I have played these songs and others like them (bouncy, upbeat, full of energy—songs from many different decades) before the start of my morning classes. I remember watching the mood in the room change from sleepy and low-key for an 8:00 a.m. class to energy on the rise, with students smiling and interacting with one another far more than they had before the music started to play.

It's also common knowledge that people in the movie and television industries use music to influence how they want audiences to feel, even dating back to the silent film era, which featured live musicians playing sound to the soundless visuals (Paris, 2021). There is something here for you as a teacher that will significantly influence your classroom's mood. And if you're not sure what music your students find calming or upbeat, simply ask them for some recommendations. Knowing that you are going to play "their music" in class will most certainly get their attention and their recommendations. A caution here: be sure to listen closely to the lyrics prior to playing any student-recommended songs.

However, it's important to play the kind of music that evokes the behaviors you want to influence. If you want students to work quietly, then play some soft instrumental background music. If you find their energy is low, play something bouncy and upbeat prior to class. However you choose to use music, whenever you choose to use it, music can be an extremely effective tool for helping your students achieve the learning goals you set out for them. Used wisely, used well, and used at the appropriate times, music can be a powerful addition to your teaching repertoire.

Table 9.1 shows the playlist I use in my classroom. You will see that some are new; some are old; some are well-known, while others are more obscure. I do not include this listing as any kind of scientific proof that these songs will work in your classroom; I just know that they work in mine. As a little experiment, play any two or three of these songs in a row to yourself, and then check to see if your feet are tapping or your body is moving to the beat. Did your energy level go up a bit? How is your mood now? Don't be surprised if that same music results in an enthusiastic conversation, like the one I had with a student before a morning class as I was completing this book. She greeted me with an enthusiastic, "Good morning, Dr. Ripley!" one morning before class began. I responded, "That's a lot of positive energy for this early in the morning." She answered with a big smile, "It's the music."

Music as a Deterrent

Thus far, we have been exploring ways to infuse more energy and improve learning in your classroom through the use of music. However, you can also use music to achieve other ends. Research confirms music's effect on the physiological systems that affect stress (Thoma et al., 2013), and there are numerous historical examples of music used as an implement of torture (Papaeti, 2020). While such extreme examples are deeply unethical, this knowledge points to how you can use music to more subtly demotivate undesirable behavior in ways that benefit both students and your classroom environment.

Table 9.1: Dale's Go-To Classroom Playlist

Title	Artist	Title	Artist	Title	Artist
"Rollercoaster"	Bleachers	"Hot N Cold"	Katy Perry	"That Thing You Do"	The Wonders
"Keep the Car Running"	Arcade Fire	"Waking Up in Vegas"	Katy Perry	"Shut Up and Dance"	Walk the Moon
"Livin' on a Prayer"	Bon Jovi	"Brandy (You're a Fine Girl)"	Looking Glass	"Dynamite"	Taio Cruz
"Born This Way"	Lady Gaga	"Don't Stop Me Now"	Queen	"Waka Waka (This Time for Africa)"	Shakira
"Carry On"	Fun	"Come and Get Your Love"	Redbone	"Wake Me Up Before You Go-Go"	Wham!
"Tubthumping (I Get Knocked Down)"	Chumbawamba	"Never Going to Give You Up"	Rick Astley	"You're So Beautiful"	Jussie Smollett and Yazz
"Heaven Is a Place on Earth"	Belinda Carlisle	"Together Forever"	Rick Astley	"Bang Bang"	Ariana Grande, Jessie J, and Nicki Minaj
"I Don't Want to Go Home"	Southside Johnny and the Asbury Jukes	"Disturbia"	Rihanna	"Kings & Queens"	Ava Max
"Don't Stop Believin'"	Journey	"Run Runaway"	Slade	"OMG What's Happening"	Ava Max

While I was serving as a principal at a junior high school, a man who lived close to the school came to see me with a complaint. He informed me that a group of students was smoking in the alley behind his garage at noon hours. He didn't mind the students so much as he minded the cigarette butts they left on his driveway. He was reluctant to confront this group of boys because, in his mind, they knew where he lived, and "they might come back late at night and throw eggs at my house." Therefore, he wanted me to solve the problem.

He was a pleasant man with a valid concern. My problem was that he couldn't identify any of these students, even after being offered a chance to look at a yearbook, as he had never gone out to take a close look at these boys. While I could have gone for a drive, found these students myself, and asked them not to smoke there, I was concerned that these students might comply with my request for a day or two and then simply return. I wanted something more permanent.

"Do you have any Barry Manilow music?" I asked this neighbor, guessing by his age that he might be a fan.

"I love Barry Manilow," he replied immediately. "I have lots of his music. Why do you ask?"

"Here's my suggestion," I told him. "Make sure your garage door is open about an inch or so at the bottom, just enough to let sound out. Then every school day before the noon hour, play Barry Manilow on a player in the garage, and turn up the volume to maximum. I will check with you next week to see how things are going."

He thought this was very funny and promised to try my strategy. When I called him the following week, he said he never saw the students or their cigarette butts after the third day. He played Manilow's *This One's For You* album over and over for three days. Apparently, these students didn't have the same taste in music as he did.

At this point, you may think, "That's great, but I can't blare loud music in my classroom." No, you can't. But there are many additional ways to apply this example, utilizing music in ways practical for the classroom to influence students' behaviors in a productive direction. For example, on one occasion, when my students were working in groups on a class project, and they were not as focused as I felt they ought to be, they asked me if I would play some music while they worked. "Sure, I would be happy to." On came Barry Manilow, followed by a chorus of moans and groans from the students. We cut a deal where they agreed to work harder, and I agreed to play the kind of music they wanted. After that, if things in the classroom were starting to move slightly off track, I would sometimes simply say (with a big grin on my face), "You need to get a little more focused, dear students. Otherwise, it's Barry Manilow time." It usually worked.

TACTIC: PLAN WHAT YOUR STUDENTS SMELL

As a teacher, you must often work closely with students; thus, the importance of personal hygiene cannot be overstated. Most of us have heard students complain about "that teacher"—the one with the bad breath. I have had students come to me for help in subjects that I don't teach them, and when I have asked them why

they don't get help from the teacher that teaches that subject, the reply is sometimes, "I did once, but [his or her] breath is just awful, and I don't want to get that close ever again."

Not many teachers pay close attention to the power of smells, but as Ackerman (1990) reminds us, odor can have a powerful effect on our perceptions of the world:

> As has been proven in many experiments, if you hand people two cans of identical furniture polish, one of which has a pleasant odor, they will swear that the pleasantly scented one works better. Odor greatly affects our evaluation of things, and our evaluation of people. (p. 39)

Odor can impact (most often at the subconscious level) what we are attracted to or repelled from, how we judge the efficacy of something, and how we judge people. Some teachers use scented wax cubes in their classrooms on occasion so that their classroom smells pleasant and inviting. This can be especially effective for interior classrooms without windows or during winter months when it is challenging to get fresh air into the classroom. It is difficult for people not to feel positively affected by smells like apple pie, cheesecake, cinnamon, and cedar wafting through the air. Of course, it is prudent to check with your students and their caregivers about any scent or chemical sensitivities before using a strategy such as this.

Whether it's the scent of your classroom or the bad breath and body odor of a teacher or student, smell can be a significant impediment to teacher effectiveness. On the flip side, fresh breath and clean clothes will mostly go unnoticed by your students, but these pleasant smells (or simply the absence of bad smells) can enhance your effectiveness.

TACTIC: PLAN WHAT YOUR STUDENTS SEE

A classroom, by its very nature, usually has plenty of visual stimuli: students engaging in group work, a teacher or two up front or moving among student groups, wall displays, smartboards, and so on. In this section, we will explore how you can effectively use the visuals in your classroom to positively influence your students. Specifically, you'll learn about the impact of color, grayscale, and images.

The Impact of Color

In episode 1, season 2 of *Abstract: The Art of Design* (Dadich, 2019), artist and sculptor Olafur Eliasson begins by placing different colored sheets of paper directly up to the camera lens, thus transforming the entire TV screen of anyone viewing into the color of the sheet of paper he holds up to the camera lens. As Eliasson does this, he tells viewers, "Think of the (TV) screen as a lamp . . ." (as cited in Dadich, 2019). He then places a yellow sheet, then a pinkish-red sheet, then a blue sheet in front of the camera lens, which transforms the entire screen into the color of the paper, bathing the viewer's room in that particular color. "Red light makes you more calm; it makes you tired; it relaxes you. Where with a certain blue color, you stay awake. So, every color has a sort of different way of influencing us" (Eliasson, as cited in Dadich, 2019).

Others are less sure about the effect of color on people. Psychology researchers Andrew J. Elliot, Markus A. Maier, Arlen C. Moller, Ron Friedman, and Jörg Meinhardt (2007) argue, "Little is known, at present, regarding the effect of color on psychological functioning. . . . In the literature at present, there is no clear evidence for a color effect on performance attainment" (pp. 154–155). Even after an additional eight years of research into the possible influence of color on human behavior and mood, Elliot (2015) still says, "Theory in this area remains at a nascent level of development" (p. 2).

Of these differing views, the first (Eliasson) is an artist; the second (Elliot) is a psychologist. Perhaps we can learn something from both perspectives that we can put to use in our classrooms?

In experiments to determine the effect—if any—of color on performance by high school students, Elliot and colleagues (2007) find:

> Strong support for our hypothesized effect of red on performance. . . . The perception of red *prior* to an achievement task *impairs* performance relative to the perception of green or an achromatic color. . . . The present findings represent the first demonstration of a direct, replicable effect of color on performance using rigorous experimental methods. (p. 165; emphasis added)

The lesson for teachers is: please do *not* use red paper for exams, and please do *not* use red paper for things like art projects or classroom decorations *prior to* performance assessments. As Elliot (2015) says in his later work, "Viewing red prior to a challenging cognitive task has been shown to undermine performance" (p. 3).

If it is unwise to use red as a color for exam papers, we must ask: Is there a color teachers should use to print exams that enhances student performance? In 2009, researchers David R. Fordham and David C. Hayes concluded a ten-year study that explored this question. They utilized different colored paper for exams (yellow, green, blue, and pink) as well as white. They find:

> Paper color did have a *significant effect on student performance.* Students with white and yellow colored paper performed significantly better than students with either blue or pink colored paper. Students with green colored paper performed somewhere in the middle of the other four colors. (Fordham & Hayes, 2009, p. 187; emphasis added)

The lesson for teachers? Perhaps we should simply *leave the white paper in the photocopier* after all.

There is an interesting cultural element to the effect of color on people, given that different colors can have different meanings in various cultures. For example, red generally has a positive connotation for the Chinese. Yet, in an experiment (Shi, Zhang, & Jiang, 2014) where fifty-eight Chinese undergrads received problem-solving idioms, and the letters were given in either red or blue, participants who received the red letters performed *worse* than did participants with the blue letters.

As teachers, we should not only be careful of the color of the paper we use or the color of the lettering, we also need to be mindful of the color of our clothing. Elliot (2015) finds "Viewing red on self or other has been shown to increase appraisals of aggressiveness/dominance" (p. 4). Thus, according to Elliot's (2015) research, if you wear a bold red color, this has the potential for students to perceive you as being more aggressive or attempting to display dominance in the classroom. In general, most see red as a "power color," making such findings unsurprising. Richard L. Dukes and Heather Albanesi (2013), from the University of Colorado, tell us that red is also associated with "notions of hot, stop, warning, prohibition, caution, anger, embarrassment . . ." (p. 96). Even the phrase *seeing red* is something we all immediately associate with feeling angry.

The considerations for teachers don't end with red, however. What about the color of the pen you use to mark students' assignments? Does that matter, given we naturally associate colors with their respective places in the natural world? Green is the color of trees and grass and is thus associated with nature, growth, and fertility. Blue is the color of the sky, and yellow the color of the sun; thus, these colors evoke in us an automatic subconscious association with the equivalent colors found in the natural world. According to Dukes and Albanesi (2013), the answer about whether your pen's color matters is, "Yes!" In the study, "Seeing Red: Quality of an Essay, Color of the Grading Pen, and Student Reactions to the Grading Process" (Dukes & Albanesi, 2013), participants received four versions of an already-graded essay. Researchers then asked the participants how they felt about the comments the grader made. Some of the comments were in red pen, others in blue. The participants exhibited greater negative feelings toward the graders when the comments were written in red rather than blue. Dukes and Albanesi (2013) determine:

> In the context of communication, *writing in red seems to shout in the same way as writing in all caps* or writing which is underscored. That is,

writing in the color red is loaded with emotion, and this additional emotional loading of messages on the grading of student assignments may not be a tactic that teachers should use to convey constructive, critical comments to students. (p. 96; emphasis added)

They further conclude: "If red writing on a student's paper adds emotional loading that the teacher does not intend to be part of the content of the communication with the student, the rethinking of the choice of pen color is worthwhile" (p. 99).

Given this research, you may want to consider using purple or green pens for marking rather than traditional red. They serve the dual purpose of standing out from the blue or black ink most students use—so your comments will be easy to see—and these colors are pleasant and non-aggressive.

While teachers can certainly choose which color pen they use to mark student products, they have little control over the type and color of the lighting in their classrooms. Still, it is interesting to note what studies show about the effect of lighting on student performance. Can fluorescent lights—the kind used in many classrooms—with different color temperatures impact alertness and cognitive performance of students? Yes, they can. Researchers Sarah L. Chellappa, Roland Steiner, Peter Blattner, Peter Oelhafen, Thomas Götz, and Christian Cajochen (2011) find that exposure to blue light leads to *significantly faster reaction times* in tasks associated with sustained attention but not in tasks associated with executive function. They describe this as an effective tool for improving cognitive performance.

How can you use the effects of images and color in your classroom to subtly influence your students? Besides avoiding red prior to assessments and marking with a green or purple pen, there are a number of other strategies that may work for you, such as using grayscale.

The Impact of Grayscale

We are aware of optical illusions, how our brains sometimes play tricks on us with visual images. Our brains also play tricks on us via our cognitive biases. Researchers Shana Lebowitz, Allana Akhtar, and Marguerite Ward (2020) describe sixty-one such cognitive biases that all humans are prone to, some of which have undesirable impacts in your classroom. However, you can use these cognitive biases with great effect to positively influence your students as well, if you do so properly.

One such cognitive bias is the *focusing illusion*, which can victimize both teachers and students. Kahneman (2011b) tells us:

> Any aspect of life to which attention is directed will loom large in a global evaluation. This is the essence of the *focusing illusion*, which can be described in a single sentence: Nothing in life is as important as you think it is when you are thinking about it. (p. 402)

In other words, what we focus on at any particular moment becomes disproportionately important relative to the rest of our priorities because our other priorities are not even present in our minds at that moment.

Kahneman (2011b) says most of us make decisions based on the *what you see is all there is* (WYSIATI) principle. In other words, we form impressions and make decisions based *only on the information we have available*. This makes sense. WYSIATI is a quick and efficient way to judge people, make decisions, and move forward quickly—except when we step back and realize that we are likely missing a great deal of additional information that may help us make more informed, and perhaps better, decisions. Nonetheless, we only have so much time and energy to spend; we can't research everything to the *n*th degree, so WYSIATI kicks in (an automatic part of our thinking-fast system), we decide and act, and then move on.

You can use the WYSIATI principle as a powerful motivator in your classroom. If you can get your students to really focus on something—to the exclusion of all else—then that something will become exceptionally important to them at that time. In *Thinking, Fast and Slow*, Kahneman (2011b) describes Shane Frederick's Cognitive Reflection Test, which asks two particular kinds of questions designed to evoke an immediate and intuitive answer that is ultimately incorrect. Have some fun with this and answer the following two questions below before reading further (Kahneman, 2011b). (You will find the correct answers at the end of this chapter, on page 127.)

1. If it takes five machines five minutes to make five widgets, how long would it take one hundred machines to make one hundred widgets? One hundred minutes *or* five minutes?

2. In a lake, there is a patch of lily pads. Every day, the patch doubles in size. If it takes forty-eight days for the patch to cover the entire lake, how long would it take for the patch to cover half of the lake? Twenty-four days *or* forty-seven days?

What is important about these questions is how the experimenters used the focusing illusion to improve student performance in responding to them. In conducting this test with forty college students, half of these students received these two problems in a font that was both small and used washed-out gray print. They were legible but caused cognitive strain for participants (Kahneman, 2011b). In other words, because the font was faint and small, the students had to really focus in order to read the problems. In scoring the results, 90 percent of the students who saw the problems in normal font made at least one mistake, while the number of mistakes among students who received the small gray font dropped to only 35 percent. Why? Because the font forced them to focus.

You may want to utilize this strategy on occasion by writing particular exam questions in smaller font sizes or printing your master copy in grayscale rather than black. Doing so will likely force your students to focus more intensely, and achievement should increase as a result.

The Impact of Images

Color isn't the only aspect of what students see that influences their behavior. I know a teacher who posted a classroom sign reading, "You don't have to study for this class—only if you want to pass." I had a large banner in my classroom that read, "KNOWLEDGE HAS VALUE!"

If you want to influence your students positively, you need to give some consideration to the images and messages you display in your classroom. These posters, pictures, and signs send messages to your students, and you want those messages to be in harmony with the goals you have for them. For example, Cialdini (2016) tells us that we know people associate fluffy clouds with comfort. You could therefore ensure that the desktop image on your classroom laptops or tablets is a picture of fluffy clouds, or you could put some posters around the room with this image.

A study designed to stimulate helpfulness in people had the subjects in the study look at a number of pictures of people who were standing close together. The hypothesis was that because closeness and helpfulness go together, that the subjects' level of helpfulness would increase, *which it did* (Cialdini, 2016). Might such images increase the level of helpfulness in your classroom as well?

Cialdini (2016) provides us with some additional suggestions. If you want your students to be more achievement oriented, then post pictures of runners winning a race. If you want your students to be more careful and critical thinkers, display a statue or pictures of Rodin's *The Thinker*. For example, when teaching critical thinking, I bring a statue of Rodin's *The Thinker* into the classroom and tell my students to look at it closely. *The Thinker* is depicted as being still; there is no indication of movement or action. All of the action is taking place inside of the mind. The entire time that I am having this discussion with them, I am wearing a tie with the image of *The Thinker*. I encourage my students to emulate *The Thinker* when they are faced with a problem. I tell them not to immediately jump into action at the first solution they come up with. Rather, I suggest they play with the problem in their mind, challenging themselves to come up with multiple ways of addressing the problem, then figuring out which one they want to try first and why.

The message is: "Be still! Emulate *The Thinker*, and spend some time thinking before jumping into action."

TACTIC: PLAN FOR SIGHTS, SOUNDS, AND SMELLS

The preceding tactics all work well in isolation, but it's also possible to bring them all together at once. A district administration team once assigned me to the principalship of a junior high school where enrollments were in steep decline. I received the mandate to try to increase student enrollments; if I could not, the district administration would have no choice but to consider closing the school. While there were many strategies that I used to make the school more appealing to students and their caregivers, several of them focused on the triple play of sights, sounds, and smells together.

In the early spring, we put on an open house, which was an opportunity for caregivers of potential future students to visit the school, meet the staff, and hear about our programs firsthand. Knowing that we would never get a second chance to make a first impression, I thought a great deal about what I wanted these prospective students' caregivers to see, hear, and smell *the moment they walked through our school's front doors.*

The following details what caregivers saw, heard, and smelled when they first walked into our grades 7–9 school (U.S. grades 6–8).

- **Sights:** I chose a number of our most charismatic ninth-grade students to act as hosts. Dressed in a T-shirt with the school logo prominently displayed on the front, the first contact these caregivers had was with a very polite and charming student who welcomed them to our school with a big smile and showed them where to proceed for the introductory part of the evening. Later in the program, these same students acted as tour guides, showing the adults around the school and demonstrating some of our programs. What I wanted these caregivers to think—primarily at the subconscious level—was, "So that's what a student turns out to be like after three years at this school. I want that for my child."

- **Sounds:** Based on the ages of most of the students who might be entering our seventh-grade program, I calculated how old their caregivers likely were. I then determined how old the bulk of these caregivers would have been when they were teenagers. I did some research, and looked up the names of the top hits of that era. That's what these caregivers heard when they walked through the doors of our school, the music from their teenage years: songs from when they were in high school, songs they listened to and danced to when they were young and perhaps fell in love for the first time, and so on. I wanted to tap into those feelings of youth and energy and good times, albeit at a subconscious level.

- **Smells:** To evoke pleasant odors, I had the home economics teacher—whose classroom was close to the main entrance of the school—begin baking chocolate chip cookies an hour before we opened our doors. Not only were the hallways filled with the smell of freshly baked chocolate chip cookies, but these very pleasant ninth-grade students offered these cookies as a snack when they greeted the caregivers at the door. The next year, we popped popcorn and gave that away.

The smell of chocolate chip cookies, the warm welcome from a polite and smiling ninth-grade student, and the sounds of music from their teenage years all worked together in harmony to plant a seed in the subconscious mind of the caregivers who attended. This place *feels* great! This is a place that *feels* homey, welcoming,

happy, and safe. This is a school that I would *feel* good sending my son or daughter to.

I do not want to downplay how essential it is that a school have strong academic, athletic, and fine arts programs. Our school had some strong teachers in all these areas, and we were getting better as time went on. However, this kind of information appeals to System 2 thinking—the slow, deliberate, rational brain (Kahneman, 2011b). Your first opportunity with caregivers and students alike is to appeal to System 1 thinking—the emotional, reactive, subconscious workings of the brain—the part of the brain that kicks into autopilot and goes by *feel*. In this example, I was convinced these caregivers would make a decision first by how they felt about the school and then rationalize a decision later via the factual information we provided. In other words, *first I talked to the elephant, then I talked to the rider.* (See Speak to the Elephant, Not the Rider, page 53 in chapter 5.)

Enrollments doubled in less than three years. We had to get renovations done to the school in order to accommodate the number of students wanting to attend our school. Never underestimate the power of an appeal to the senses. It taps into System 1 thinking, and when done well, it *feels* very, very good.

While this section's example focuses on an appeal to parents, I invite you to take a look at your classroom as if you were entering it for the first time as a student. Stand in the doorway, looking around slowly and deliberately, and ask yourself these questions.

- What do you see?
- What do you hear?
- What do you smell?
- What do you feel?

Now, proceed accordingly.

TACTIC: USE CHOICE ARCHITECTURE

A powerful way to positively manage students' behavior in the classroom is to use the principles of *choice architecture*, which is when the person endeavoring to influence (the teacher) attempts to give the person being influenced (the students) some degree of choice. However, the way you present these choices is specifically designed to lead the students to the choice you want them to make. This is sometimes called *coloring the choices*—making the option you want the students to choose stand out as the most preferable.

Richard Thaler from the University of Chicago and Cass Sunstein (2008) from Harvard University highlight how seemingly small details influence how people make decisions:

> As we shall see, small and apparently insignificant details can have major impacts on people's behavior. A good rule of thumb is to assume that "everything matters." In many cases, the power of these small details comes from focusing the attention of users in a particular direction. A wonderful example of this principle comes from, of all places, the men's room at Schiphol Airport in Amsterdam. There the authorities have etched the image of a black housefly into each urinal. It seems that men usually do not pay much attention to where they aim . . . but if they see a target, attention and therefore accuracy are much increased. According to the man who came up with the idea, it works wonders. "It improves the aim," says Aad Kieboom. "If a man sees a fly, he aims at it." Kieboom, an economist, directs Schiphol's building expansion. His staff conducted fly-in-urinal trials and found that etchings reduce spillage by 80 percent. (pp. 3–4)

An excellent example of choice architecture in action involves an experiment Thaler and Sunstein (2008) conducted in high school cafeterias. The director of food services (Carolyn) for a large city school system conducted an experiment regarding the kinds of food choices high school students made for lunch. In some of the cafeterias, staff placed desserts first in the line, while in other cafeterias, they placed desserts last. In some of the schools, staff put carrot sticks at eye level, while at others, it was french fries. The results were significant:

> Simply by rearranging the cafeteria, Carolyn was able to increase or decrease the consumption of many food items by as much as 25 percent. Carolyn learned a big lesson: school children, like adults, can be greatly influenced by small changes in the context. (pp. 1–2)

You are responsible for organizing the classroom environment in which your students will make decisions and choices about their learning and their behavior. The goal is to help you create a choice environment in your classroom that makes it *easier* and *more likely* for students to choose what is best for themselves, for their classmates, and for you. The following sections outline two approaches to choice architecture: planning where your students sit and being prepared when they lack supplies.

Planning Where Your Students Sit

There are two factors for you to consider in regard to the seating arrangement in your classroom: (1) How do you have the desks or tables and chairs arranged? and (2) How much freedom do students have to choose—given the arrangement of the desks or tables that you have created—where they can sit? By making careful decisions with the first of these factors, you can give students more freedom with the second.

By determining classroom seating arrangements *prior* to the first day of classes each year, you can ensure the arrangement you determine will have a positive influence on your students. However, the furniture you have access to will partially determine the range of decisions you have to make. Do the students sit at desks? At small individual tables? At larger tables? All of these types of furniture will present both possibilities and limitations as to how you can arrange your classroom seating plan.

You will need to *maximize your physical proximity* to your students. A great deal of research (Martin, 2015; Weaver, Scherer, Hengen, & Shriver, 2020; Wehby & Lane, 2009), as well as decades of teaching experience, tell us of this unwavering relationship between student misbehavior and where the teacher is physically in the classroom. The proximity rule goes like this: *The closer you are to any student or group of students in your classroom, the less likely they are to be off-task or misbehaving.*

All good teachers know this great truth and use it in their teaching practices and in the ways in which they arrange where students sit in their classrooms. However big your classroom is, and no matter what furniture your students have (desks, tables, and so on), you will want to arrange these so that you optimize sightlines and physical proximity to all of your students.

If you have students sitting at individual desks, a horseshoe-shaped configuration (with either one row of students or two rows if necessary) works really well in order to maximize your proximity. To do this, you simply place the student desks or tables around the perimeter of the room, and you then direct activities and teach from the open part of the horseshoe. This way, you are never more than three or four steps away from any student, and your sightlines are unobstructed.

In addition to factoring in proximity, you want to configure students' desks in ways that support the specific kinds of learning activities that you will have them engaged in. Sometimes you may want them in groups of two, other times in groups of four, and still other times, you want them to work individually.

Finally, your movement around the classroom matters: "You need to *move around the classroom constantly*. Teach from the front, the back, the sides, and the center. Remember, the physically closer you are to your students, the more on task they are likely to be" (Ripley, 2019, p. 16).

Some teachers have alternative kinds of seating besides desks or traditional chairs available to students, such as bean bag chairs, couches, exercise bikes, carpet areas, and so on. Make adjustments to your plan based on how you can best use these types of furniture to enhance the classroom experience and influence students to make good choices for their own learning. This is a wonderful example of choice architecture in practice. You choose where the desks or tables are in the classroom, while you may then allow the students to choose where they can sit.

Being Prepared When Students Lack Supplies

We have all seen this happen in schools many times: a student walks into a classroom and says to the teacher, "I don't have a pen," "I forgot my tablet," and so on. The student does not have the supplies that are necessary to do the required work. Some teachers get upset at this and spend time chastising the student. This wastes precious class time and often does little or nothing to change the student's behavior. Effective teachers use a different approach—they use *choice architecture* to deal with the problem of students coming to class without supplies or their texts.

In setting up their classrooms *before* the beginning of the school year, effective teachers *set up a student supply section* somewhere in the room. This could be a shelf in the classroom that might have a coffee can filled with pens and paper, a stack of both lined and plain paper, a stapler, a three-hole punch, a roll of tape, or any other kinds of supplies that the students will need.

On the first day of classes, tell your students about the procedures that are in place in your classroom. One of these procedures is to tell the students what to do if they come to class without pens, paper, laptops, textbooks, and so on. Then, instruct students that when they come to class without the necessary supplies, they simply go to the student supply shelf, take whatever they need to do their work, then take their seat. There is no need for discussion with you, and there is no need to waste any class time. Students simply get what they need, go to their desks, and get ready to work.

This simple strategy is extremely effective. First, let's be honest—we all forget things from time to time. Students are entitled to do this as well, and teachers should be understanding when this happens to them. Second, class time is precious, so don't waste it discussing what to do about the absence of supplies after the first day. After that first class, they know what to do.

If your school will not supply you with pens and pencils in order for you to implement this strategy, all you need to do is walk down the hallways of your school and look at the floor. Over the course of a few days, you will be able to collect more than enough pens and pencils. Inexpensive golf pencils work well also. For more expensive items, like tablets or textbooks, you will want to ensure students return these items to you at the end of class.

If you're concerned about getting such items back, you have options well-aligned to choice architecture. To ensure this happens, I used a simple yet effective strategy: rather than leave the more expensive supplies on the student supply shelf, I kept these by my desk. If a student needed to borrow a tablet, laptop, or textbook for the class because they had forgotten theirs, I would make a trade. They could get the laptop or textbook in exchange for *one shoe*—a shoe which they could get back when they returned what they borrowed at the end of the class. This strategy worked wonderfully, as students seemed to always remember to return the borrowed item when they started walking out of class with a limp and suddenly remembered, "Oh yeah, my shoe!"

Take special note of the extensive use of choice architecture in this strategy. A student can choose to come to class with or without supplies, but they cannot choose not to do the work because they don't have the necessary supplies. These are readily available for them. As well, students who are disorganized or who live in circumstances where school supplies are too costly won't feel singled out or face unjust discipline when you utilize this strategy. Sure, they could choose to leave my classroom with a borrowed textbook or laptop and walk around school for the rest of the day with one shoe on and one shoe off, but in over thirty years of teaching, none of my students ever chose this option. Why? Because no one wants to walk around school all day looking like that. The other students, including members of their own pack, would laugh at them—and they know it.

SUMMARY

In the Use Choice Architecture section (page 124), you learned how the image of a fly etched into the urinals at the Amsterdam airport reduced spillage by 80 percent (Thaler & Sunstein, 2008). There is an important message in this story for you to remember when you set up your classroom environment and when you establish the procedures you want your students to follow in your classrooms: "Small and apparently insignificant details can have major impacts on people's behavior. A good rule of thumb is to assume that *everything matters*" (Thaler & Sunstein, 2008, p. 3; emphasis added).

These people are your students. Please remember: *everything matters!*

As you reflect on this chapter, make sure to remember the following.

- Teachers will be more successful in influencing students' behaviors if they set the stage in ways that support their desired outcomes. This is called *pre-suasion*.

- Sights, sounds, and smells all influence how students feel in your classroom. You can use any one of these tools, or all three in combination, to help move students in the direction you want them to go.

- Music can be an effective tool to set the emotional tone of a classroom. Use it to energize students as well as to calm them down or even deter undesirable behaviors.

- Color can have a very powerful impact on how students feel. There are numerous ways to use color to positively impact how students feel in your classroom and how they perform on your assessments.

- Choice architecture occurs when you give your students some degree of choice. However, you must design the way you present these choices to lead students to the choice you want them to make.

- The correct answers to the two questions from The Impact of Grayscale (page 122) are: *five minutes* and *forty-seven days*.

Reflective Practice

Use the following questions and activities to reflect on and make changes to your practice.

1. In your assessment practices, do you start by assuming each student is at zero and then add marks for the quality of their work as per your assessment criteria? Or, do you start by giving each student 100 percent and then deduct for errors and omissions? Why did you choose the strategy you utilize? Have you clearly communicated your reasons to your students?

2. Consider using music in your classroom in certain circumstances. Survey your students for their top five suggestions, and be sure to use some of their suggestions where appropriate.

3. Spend some time thinking about what your students smell in your classroom. Is there a way you can utilize their sense of smell on certain occasions in order to enhance their positive feelings of being in your classroom?

4. Before or after school, when there is no one around and you are not distracted, stand in the doorway of your classroom. Imagine you are seeing this classroom for the first time. Look carefully at each of the following.

   a. The arrangement of the desks, tables, and other furniture

   b. The wall color

   c. What is displayed on each of the walls

   Next, determine how much of what is on display is teacher driven and how much is student work or student controlled. Consider the following.

   a. How motivated would you feel to learn in a room that looked like this if you were a student?

   b. How would you feel as a student walking into a classroom that looked like yours?

   Based on your answers to these questions, make any changes that you believe would either enhance the learning that goes on in your classroom or that would make students feel better being in that space.

5. Try an experiment on one of your in-class assessments by printing it in grayscale in order to make the students focus more on what the test is asking of them. You might want to do this only with the particularly challenging questions on the exam. Compare both the degree of concentration you see in your students during the assessment and their test results compared to previous assessments. If you notice an improvement, use this strategy on occasion, especially on assessments that have significant weightings.

CHAPTER 10

SOFT TACTICS FOR MOTIVATING STUDENTS BY TAKING SOMETHING AWAY

All of us are familiar with the ways in which advertisers use scarcity to get us to buy certain products. Commercials that tell us that "The sale ends today" are using the strategy of scarcity to motivate us into making a purchase. And while scarcity may most often refer to a limited number of items, it can also refer to a limited amount of time. As a motivational tactic, scarcity triggers in us the idea that if we don't act quickly or in a certain way, we will miss out on something. In the digital world of social media and texting, this is *fear of missing out* (FOMO), which is defined as "a pervasive apprehension that others might be having rewarding experiences from which one is absent" (Przybylski, Murayama, DeHaan, & Gladwell, 2013, p. 1841).

There are many ways you can use scarcity and loss aversion in your classroom as motivators for your students, and in this chapter, we explore the following tactics for creating the kinds of scarcity that will keep your students on track.

- Make things scarce.
- Use loss aversion.
- Soak up extra time with sponge activities.

TACTIC: MAKE THINGS SCARCE

Scarcity is a well-known motivator that Cialdini (2007) suggests is a very effective influence strategy: "Opportunities seem more valuable to us when their availability is limited" (p. 238). Advertisers have long-used the scarcity strategy: "Buy now while quantities last!" and "Limited to the first fifty customers." Sound familiar?

The scarcity principle is a powerful force in our personal lives as well. Think about someone you love—a son or daughter perhaps—who lives far away and only comes home for Christmas. Think about how much you value time with that child because it is so scarce compared to the time you spend with the son or daughter who still lives at or near home. Or maybe you're interested in buying a restored car or renting property where the seller has invited multiple interested individuals at the same time? These scenarios all influence how people assign value.

You can use scarcity in your classroom by limiting the availability of things students value. For example, in one high school where I taught, many students arrived late on Monday mornings. So our humanities department brought in a supply of coffee and donuts for the students every Monday morning, about a half-hour before classes started. Any student who came before classes began could help themselves. Limited supply was key—you had to arrive at school *before* the coffee and donuts ran out if you wanted some for yourself.

Teachers can also create scarcity by limiting the amount of time they give students to complete redo assignments. For example, if a student wants to redo an assessment in order to attempt to improve their mark, you can say, "I will give you two days to redo your work, after which time I will not reassess it."

During exams, you can also make a point of announcing how much time is left. By announcing to the class at the exam's halfway mark, "You only have twenty-five minutes left!" students are reminded of their limited time, which can help some students to increase their focus on the task at hand. However, be mindful that this tactic can increase test anxiety for students predisposed to it. In this case, however, students who experience *diagnosed* text anxiety are typically eligible for extra time when taking tests.

I often use small candies like peppermints as a reward for in-class verbal review activities. I simply ask a review question out loud, and the first person with their hand up gets the chance to answer. If they get the correct answer, they win the candy and sit out answering the next five questions. If they don't get the correct answer, then the student who shot their hand up second gets a chance. There are limited candies and limited questions, thus the value of the prize increases. From first-grade students to twelfth, I've seen both boys and girls focus intently on winning a candy that is worth a grand total of one penny. Why? Because it's not really about the candy. There are only going to be a limited number of winners, and they want to be one of them.

Ultimately, you need to have something that most students want. This could be in the form of prizes—anything from small candies to movie certificates. Or you might provide them with the opportunity to obtain something that is nontangible, such as free time, exemptions from exams, or passes to get out of class early.

Whatever you choose as the giveaway, there must be fewer of these than there are students.

For example, let's say I am going to give away five exemptions to an upcoming exam. Most students like the idea of having free time while their classmates write a test. I am careful to choose an exam that is of lesser consequence, and I tell the students receiving the exemption that I will simply insert their current class average as the mark on that exam, or I can take this exam mark completely out of their grade calculation. While you must be mindful that students' grades ultimately represent the level of learning they've achieved, it's usually possible to use this approach in a targeted way such that students' final marks at the end of the semester or school year are accurate and representative of their learning.

At this point, I am offering the class five things that most of the students in my class want. It is here that I tell them how they can earn—win these exam passes. There are myriad ways you can use something like this to motivate students, and you can connect them to criteria that motivate learning. In my practice, the students I gave exam passes to met criteria such as the following.

- Had the greatest percentage improvement on the next assignment

- Completed and handed in to me a high-value assignment, such as a novel study with a three-page reflection, with the essay achieving a minimum of 75 percent

- Get to participate in a draw if they're at their desks and ready to work when class starts

On occasion, I also used store passes with my classes. I would give these out to select students who accomplished a certain task. Once a week, I would then take them to the nearest convenience store, where they could purchase anything they wanted up to the value of the pass.

Here's another approach that always worked well for me when I had assigned a due date for work that was several days away: tell students that if they complete an assignment sooner than the due date, they don't have to do as much work. For example, if you assign three pages of writing work on a Tuesday, and you tell your class that this is officially due on the following Friday, tell them it only needs to be *two* pages long, *if* they turn it in on Thursday. You can modify this tactic in ways that work across the elementary and secondary grades. Of course, by picking the "reward date" for handing in the assignment that works best for you, you can be certain that's when most students will hand that work in.

Whether you use peppermints, movie passes, exam passes, free-time passes, get-out-of-class-early passes, or store passes is quite irrelevant. You can choose whatever motivates your students the most. You know them best. In chapter 12 (page 151), we will look more closely at the upside and downside of using rewards to motivate students. But for now, know that you can use scarcity very effectively to motivate your students.

TACTIC: USE LOSS AVERSION

Loss aversion is the idea that *losing what we already have* has a much greater negative impact on us than would the positive impact of a similar gain (Kahneman, 2011b). A simple example of the concept of loss aversion is the negative feelings a person would have if they lost $100, which would likely be far more painful than the pleasure they would experience if they found $100. Loss aversion explains why, when people pay for purchases with cash rather than with a credit card, this usually results in them spending less. Why? Because when you pay with cash, you lose something that you already possess, the cash in your wallet or purse. Now you have it, then you don't. When you pay with a credit card, you still have the credit card. There is no immediate and visible loss.

We can see loss aversion at play even in infants. When babies have nothing in their hands, they will often entertain themselves by looking around or waving their hands in the air. Now, give the baby a toy to play with, wait a minute, and take the toy away. Often, the baby will begin to cry. The baby was happy enough without the toy, but when the infant *has* the toy, losing it causes the baby distress.

Kahneman (2011b) views loss aversion as:

> A powerful conservative force that favors minimal changes from the status quo in the lives of both institutions and individuals. This conservatism keeps us stable in our neighborhood, our marriage, and our job; it is the gravitational force that holds our life together near the reference point. (p. 305)

You can use loss aversion in a variety of ways to motivate students. For example, try pointing out to students not *what they gain* by acting in a certain way but rather by pointing out *what the student will lose* if they don't follow a specific request. Telling a student, "You will have to stay in at recess or after school if you don't . . ." threatens students with the loss of something they already have—the freedom to play with their friends at recess or the freedom to go home after school. Telling a student you will remove him or her from the classroom to work alone in some form of an in-school suspension room threatens the student with the loss of his or her group. We know that students are social beings, and prolonged removal from the group is a significant loss for most students. This also often works with students who are chronically late with turning in assignments. For example, if you tell your class they will lose 10 percent on their score for each day the assessment is late, up to a maximum of five days (after which you will no longer accept it at all), students, for the most part, don't want to lose marks for handing in the assessment late.

While it can be effective, use this tactic with caution. It can cause a negative reaction from students toward you as the teacher, which is a particular concern if you're trying to build trust with a student. Further, a student who isn't motivated by losses from late penalties and deadlines, for example, will be no more likely to turn in work on time than without the penalties. At that point, the student's grades are a measure of their promptness and not their learning.

Consider also how loss aversion might impact how students react to your use of other strategies in this book. For example, keep in mind the frequency with which you give students rewards, such as whole-class awards for good behavior: an afternoon movie once a month or extra time in the gymnasium once a week. Properly implemented, these kinds of whole-class rewards can be effective motivators. However, if teachers give these types of rewards out routinely and they become part of the established classroom practices, then students will likely come to expect them without connecting these rewards to appropriate behaviors. Once these types of whole-class rewards enter the domain of student expectations, any teacher attempting to take them away will face significant resentment. Why? Because loss aversion has kicked in. From the students' perspective, you are taking away something they already have and are entitled to.

To help keep this scenario from playing out while still using whole-class rewards as a motivator, do two things.

1. Ensure your students understand the connection between the reward and the behaviors that have earned them the reward.

2. Don't do this routinely. Don't make this such a common practice that your students come to expect it. Ensure the timing you give such rewards feels random to students. For example, avoid daily, weekly, and monthly patterns.

TACTIC: SOAK UP EXTRA TIME WITH SPONGE ACTIVITIES

In *The Successful Teacher's Survival Kit* (Ripley, 2019), I discuss the importance of keeping students productively engaged in the classroom as much as possible. Students who are bored will typically look for something to entertain or occupy themselves. These activities are often not productive and can, in fact, be very disruptive. This is where *sponge activities* come into play. The role of the sponge in a kitchen is to soak up excess spillage. All teachers have excess spillage in their classes. This spillage comes in the form of *time*, and sponge activities soak up that kind of time.

Much as you may never feel you have enough classroom time with students, it is rare that you will ever give a lesson that ends exactly on time, with all of the students in your class finishing their work at precisely the same moment and at exactly the time the class ends. It never happens! Instead, some students finish long before other students. Or, you work your way through your lesson plan faster than you thought you would, and there are five or six minutes of class time left when you have finished. The time isn't long enough for you to start the next lesson, but it's more than enough time for your students to get into mischief if you don't find a way to utilize it. What can you do?

Some examples of sponge activities that you can use, depending on the grade you teach, include the following.

- Have books like the annual *Guinness World Records* and the annual *Ripley's Believe It or Not!* available around the room for the students to browse through when they have a few minutes to kill. These books are perfect for sponge time because students find them colorful and filled with interesting pictures and facts. They are quick to read since each page tells a few stand-alone stories, and the stories are typically very engaging.

- Have short storybooks for younger students, along with a Play-Doh table or drawing table and the like—simple activities that are engaging, fun, and brief.

- Have a variety of magazines available, the kind that your students are interested in. For older students, this may range from *Teen Magazine* to *People Magazine* to *Sports Illustrated* to *Car and Driver Magazine* to *National Geographic*. You can ask your students near the beginning of the year what kinds of magazines they like, and try not to judge them when they answer. Judging their taste in magazines doesn't help—unless they're age-inappropriate, just get the magazines! These magazines do not have to be something you buy off the rack, nor do they need to be current. Check with friends and colleagues if they have months-old issues they're happy to give you.

- Have a computer folder ready with some short, motivational, and inspirational video clips that you can show to the entire class. YouTube, TED Talks, TeacherTube, and so on have many resources that work in situations such as this. Motivational videos about Nick Vujicic, Dr. Seuss stories, and fairy tales on YouTube for younger students—all of these work well to soak up the last few minutes of a class. They engage and teach students while keeping them—*and you*—out of trouble.

The best time to determine sponge activities you want to offer is before the school year. You may want to acquire copies of books and magazines that would be of interest and age-level appropriate for the students you will be teaching. When you set up your classroom for the upcoming school year, have these available for your students when school begins. When you establish your classroom procedures and routines during the first week, teach your students when and how to use them.

Note that it is the *students themselves who get to choose* what they want to do during sponge time. However, they are choosing from an array of options you've already determined. This is choice architecture at work in your classroom (see page 124). And what have you taken away from your students through this strategy? The opportunity to spend the last few minutes of class bothering their classmates, getting into mischief, or simply wasting time.

SUMMARY

This chapter explored various ways in which you can use strategies that create scarcity in your classroom to motivate your students. As well, it examined the psychology of loss aversion and explored ways in which you can use students' desire to keep what they already have to move them in the directions you want them to go. As you reflect on this chapter, make sure to remember the following.

- The scarcity principle tells us that some things typically seem more valuable to people when there is limited availability or limited access to them, which makes them useful motivators in certain situations.

- You can limit the number of rewards available to your students, or you can limit intangibles, such as the amount of time available.

- Customize the rewards you give students based on their grade and what they find desirable.

- Loss aversion tells us that our desire to keep what we already have is stronger than our desire to obtain something of equal value that we do not yet possess. Use it to motivate students by, for example, taking away a recess or access to peers.

- Sponge activities are the options that you give to your students to fill the small bits of free time that often come up in a class, such as when a lesson ends early. They are a form of choice architecture in which you limit the choices available to students to those you've selected ahead of time.

Reflective Practice

Use the three activities in this reproducible—(1) identify scarce rewards, (2) utilize loss aversion, and (3) engage in sponge activities—to reflect on ways to motivate your students.

Identify Scarce Rewards

Think about the students you have in your class. Based on what you know about them, use the following chart to list three types of tangible rewards you are confident they will like and three nontangible rewards you believe they would want. Ensure you create scarcity in issuing these rewards.

Three tangible rewards you believe your students would value	Three nontangible rewards you believe your students would value
Examples: candies, small toys, pizza, movie pass, movie of the month afternoon, store pass	Examples: free class time, exemptions from exams, get-out-of-class early passes
1.	1.
2.	2.
3.	3.

After you complete your list, try implementing some of these strategies in your classroom. Monitor which ones appear to work the best with your particular students, and adjust your implementation strategies accordingly.

Utilize Loss Aversion

Think about what you learned about loss aversion in this chapter. List three ways that you are currently using loss aversion, or three ways that you could use the loss-aversion strategy with your class.

1. _____

2. _____

3. _____

Which of these strategies seems to be the most effective for your particular students? How might you utilize loss aversion more effectively, given the students you have at this time?

The Tactical Teacher © 2022 Solution Tree Press • SolutionTree.com
Visit **go.SolutionTree.com/behavior** to download this free reproducible.

Engage in Sponge Activities

Think about the ideas discussed in the Soak Up Extra Time With Sponge Activities section (page 132). If you currently do not use sponge activities, list five sponge activities that you commit to implementing in your classroom within the next three weeks. Use the space provided to reflect on the outcomes.

1. _____

2. _____

3. _____

4. _____

5. _____

The Tactical Teacher © 2022 Solution Tree Press • SolutionTree.com
Visit **go.SolutionTree.com/behavior** to download this free reproducible.

CHAPTER 11

SOFT TACTICS FOR PERSUADING STUDENTS WITH THE RIGHT WORDS

Positive words, used properly, often yield positive results, far more effectively than do negative words. Consider the following story from business management consultant Eli Amdur (2020), who describes two otherwise very similar municipalities in New Jersey that, in 2004, took two different approaches to proposed open-space initiatives:

> Municipality #1 worded its ballot question like this: "Should the township create a Municipal Trust Fund for land preservation based on a tax of 1 percent per $100 of assessed value?" Note these positive words: create, trust fund, preservation.

> Municipality #2 posed this question: "Should the village impose an additional tax levy of up to 1 percent per $100 of assessed value for its Municipal Trust Fund?" Note the negative words: impose, additional tax levy.

> Do I need to tell you the results? In municipality #1 it passed by a margin of 52–48; in #2 it failed by—oh my!—52–48. And you can look all day long for other differentiating causal factors, but you won't find them. That's how similar the two were. Conclusively, the differentiator was the wording of the ballot questions.

This story illustrates the power of using *words that have a positive tone* rather than a negative one. Positive words speak to the elephant, as in our Speak to the Elephant, Not the Rider tactic (page 53). In this chapter, you will explore how you can use words more effectively to achieve the results you want in your classroom. You'll find the following tactics:

- Increase your influence every time, using rhythm and rhyme (and repetition).
- Use the contrast principle to nudge students in a direction.
- Use the butterfly effect.

TACTIC: INCREASE YOUR INFLUENCE EVERY TIME, USING RHYTHM AND RHYME (AND REPETITION)

Have you ever wondered why so many people can remember the words to songs from years ago, but struggle to remember other events from the same time period? We know the answer to this question. There are two aspects to songs that tend to make them easy to remember.

1. **They use rhythm and rhyme:** We have discovered how rhyming phrases are "mentally processed more easily than nonrhyming

phrases" (Goldstein et al., 2008, p. 164). As a result, they are easier to remember.

2. **We listen to them a lot:** We tend to have heard the songs we remember well over and over and over again. We remember the words to the top ten hits from our teen years because we listened to them repeatedly. They are ingrained in our memories. Such is the power of repetition.

Think of how early childhood teachers do not teach the alphabet by simply verbalizing the twenty-six letters of the alphabet once and then expecting their students to know them. Rather, they *sing* the letters in a way that emphasizes rhyming: A B C D E F *G* . . . H I J K L M N O *P* . . . Q R S T U *V* . . . W X Y and *Zee*. And then they teach this to the children in a song and repeat the song over and over and over again.

The lesson here for you is clear. When you really want your students to learn something, when it is critical for your students' success that they master certain information, then teach it with the three Rs: rhyme, rhythm, and repetition. The following sections explore the thinking behind and tactics for using rhyme and rhythm and then repetition.

Using Rhythm and Rhyme

Philosopher Friedrich Nietzsche (1878/1974) made the following arguments in regard to the power of rhythm:

> What could have been more useful for the ancient, superstitious type of man than rhythm? It enabled one to do anything—to advance some work magically; to force a god to appear, to be near, and to listen; to mold the future in accordance with one's will . . . without verse one was nothing; by means of verse one almost became a god. Such a fundamental feeling can never be erased entirely; and even now, after men have fought against such superstitions for thousands of years, the wisest among us are still occasionally fooled by rhythm—if only insofar

as we sometimes consider an idea truer simply because it has a metrical form and presents itself with a divine skip and jump. (p. 140)

Nietzsche (1878/1974) makes two arguments here.

1. Since ancient times, humans have seen words spoken with rhythm and rhyme as having more power than words spoken in plain prose. William Shakespeare (1606/2005) used this technique in *Macbeth* when he had the witches sing and rhyme as they brewed their potion: "Double, double, toil and trouble, fire burn and cauldron bubble." Stage magicians similarly use the phrase *hocus pocus* when performing magic tricks. Both Shakespeare and the magicians of that era were using the power of words that rhymed.

2. In spite of thousands of years of advancements in human history, people will still sometimes consider an idea as valid simply because it was presented to them with rhythm and rhyme. We, of course, are far too sophisticated and advanced for such nonsense in the 21st century.

Or are we? In a study conducted in 2000, researchers Matthew S. McGlone and Jessica Tofighbakhsh from Lafayette College attempted to determine whether stating a phrase in poetic form as compared to stating the same phrase in prose form would be a factor in participants' perceptions of the truthfulness of the statement. They used commonly known *aphorisms* for their experiment, stating:

> Aphorisms are succinct statements that offer observations and advice about universal human concerns such as . . . health ("An apple a day keeps the doctor away") and friendship ("Birds of a feather flock together"). Although they enjoy a reputation among laypeople as distillations of age-old psychological wisdom, aphorisms are commonly characterized by psychologists as dubious generalizations. (p. 424)

McGlone and Tofighbakhsh (2000) took aphorisms and altered the wording, but not the meaning. For example, *woes unite foes* became *woes unite enemies*; *what sobriety conceals, alcohol reveals* became *what sobriety conceals, alcohol unmasks*; and *caution and measure will win you treasure* became *caution and measure will win you riches*. They then tested participants for their views on how truthful the statements were when presented in these two forms, one rhyming and the other not. The results showed: "Extant rhyming aphorisms in their *original form* (e.g., 'What sobriety conceals, alcohol reveals') *were judged to be more accurate* than modified versions that did not preserve rhyme ('What sobriety conceals, alcohol unmasks')" (McGlone & Tofighbakhsh, 2000, p. 424; emphasis added).

It appears that what Nietzsche (1878/1974) said in the late 1800s still holds true, even today: "We sometimes consider an idea truer simply because it has a metrical form and presents itself with a divine skip and jump" (p. 140).

In addition to knowing that information presented in rhyming form can give that information the appearance of being more valid, most teachers also believe that information presented with rhyme and rhythm is easier for students to remember. Why is this? In a seminal study conducted in 1969, Gordon H. Bower and Laura S. Bolton argue:

> The hypothesis is that rhymes are normally easily learned because knowledge of the rhyming relation considerably restricts the range of response alternatives that need be considered for a given stimulus. That is, knowing the stimulus term and knowing that the correct response rhymes with the stimulus, one is able to exclude many list responses from consideration, restricting consideration to only the rhyming candidates. (pp. 453–454)

To show these conclusions remained valid forty years later, researchers Barbara Tillmann and W. Jay Dowling (2007) conducted experiments in which participants received the same information but in two different forms, one being prose and the other poetry. They find that when the information was presented in poetic form, participants remembered it longer than did those participants who were presented with the same information in prose form. Further, researchers Kirsten Read, Megan Macauley, and Erin Furay (2014) describe their experiments with children between ages 2–4 in which parents read either a rhymed or nonrhymed version of the same animal story to their children. When tested for word retention, "Children performed better in the rhyme condition across the age range despite differing levels of word familiarity" (Read et al., 2014, p. 354).

Advertisers have used rhyming with great effect to help consumers remember the names of their products with slogans such as "It takes a licking and keeps on ticking," and "Nothin' says lovin' like something from the oven." Protesters also understood the power of rhyming. In the 1960s, anti-Vietnam protesters didn't chant, "Hell no, we refuse to go to Vietnam!" Instead, they chanted, "Hell no, we won't go!" (MyFootage.com, 2018). On September 17, 2011, demonstrators gathered in Zuccotti Park in New York's financial district in what came to be known as the Occupy Wall Street protest (Cohen, 2015). They chanted slogans such as, "All day, all week, occupy Wall Street!" (it sounds much more rhythmic when fifty people are yelling it).

You can use rhyming with students in these same ways, regardless of subject. For example, teacher Alex Kajitani, also known online as the Rappin' Mathematician, has a series of videos demonstrating how he uses rhyming and rap to teach students mathematics concepts like multiplication tables and how to add numbers that have a decimal point (MathRaps, n.d.). These videos are fun, high energy, and through repetition and rhyme, help students to remember basic mathematics concepts. I highly recommend watching these videos, even just for fun.

The lesson here for you is simple. If you really want to influence your students to help them remember something important, find a way to make it rhyme.

Using Repetition

Learning and repeating acronyms is another very effective tool to help students memorize essential information. This can be particularly helpful when students need to learn sequences; for example, in solving equations, students learn the acronym BEDMAS (brackets, exponents, division, multiplication, addition, subtraction) as the proper order of operations. "My very elegant mother just served us nachos" is a sentence teachers can use to help students learn the order of the planets moving outward from the sun. By having students repeat this sentence multiple times until they learn it, it becomes quite easy for them to write that sentence, and then take the first letter of each word and sequence the planets accordingly (Mercury, Venus, Earth, Mars, Jupiter, Saturn, Uranus, Neptune).

In Alberta (where I teach), the province requires students to write diploma exams at the end of their twelfth-grade year. Post-secondary institutes use these exams as criteria for admission, so they are of significant importance to any student seeking university or college admission. Because of this, there is a great deal of pressure on teachers who teach these diploma exam courses to ensure that most of their students pass these exams. This is important to the students, to their parents, and to the school administration.

After the province scores the exams, it provides schools with an exam analysis. This report shows how each student responded to each of the exam items, and then provides an overall analysis. From this information, it is very easy to determine how students in various teachers' classes performed on each item of the exam.

I once met with my colleagues in the social studies department of the high school where I taught to review how our students performed on the diploma exams. One teacher—whose students had not done well on this particular diploma exam—kept repeating, "I taught that. I don't know why they did so poorly on that question. I taught that!"

"How many times?" I asked.

"Once!" he replied, looking puzzled at my question.

John Wooden would not have approved of that response. Wooden coached basketball at the University of California, Los Angeles, from 1948 to 1975. Over a twelve-year period during that time, Wooden and his UCLA team won ten NCAA national championships (Wooden, 1997). At the time, no other team had ever won more than two in a row. Wooden's players revered him, not only for his ability to teach them about basketball but also for his ability to teach them about life. Wooden was a master teacher, a specific highlight of which are his *laws of learning*. According to Wooden (1997):

> The four laws of learning are explanation, demonstration, imitation, and repetition. The goal is to create a correct habit that can be produced instinctively under great pressure. To make sure this goal was achieved, I created eight laws of learning; namely, explanation, demonstration, imitation, repetition, repetition, repetition, repetition, repetition. (p. 144)

While you may not have the time in your classroom to repeat everything you teach several times as Wooden suggests, avoid my colleague's mistake of believing that because you have taught something *once*, your students have learned it. In addition to increasing the potential of students to remember information by repeating it, repetition also has the power to increase the perceived veracity of that information. In other words, information that is repeated is often perceived as being more truthful (McGlone & Tofighbakhsh, 2000, p. 424).

Repetition is a powerful teaching tool, one that good teachers use with remarkable effectiveness. Know that if you really want your students to learn something—a piece of information or a skill that is foundational and essential to what they will be learning later—you are likely going to have to teach it more than once.

TACTIC: USE THE CONTRAST PRINCIPLE TO NUDGE STUDENTS IN A DIRECTION

You will recall the story from the introduction of this book about Rosser Reeves, the American advertising executive who changed the blind beggar's sign from *I AM BLIND* to *IT IS SPRINGTIME, AND I AM BLIND*. Donations increased dramatically.

What happened here? Why did those four words (*It is springtime, and*) cause more people passing by to give money to the blind man? These four words resulted in passersby subconsciously *comparing their reality with his*. It was springtime, and they could see all the signs of new life. The blind man could not. This story is an example of the *contrast principle* in action, which Cialdini (2007) tells us:

> Affects the way we see the difference between two things that are presented one after another. Simply put, if the second item is fairly different from the first, we will tend to see it as *more different* than it actually is. (pp. 11–12; emphasis added)

For example, there is an old story about a poor farmer who lived in a small house with his wife, his many children, and his mother-in-law. He went to his rabbi to complain about the crowding and the arguing that were a large part of his daily life. He asked the rabbi for advice. The rabbi told him to bring all of the farm animals into the house to live, and if he did, God would bless him. Bewildered but obedient, the farmer did what the rabbi recommended. Two days later, the farmer was back to see the rabbi. He said, "My life is horrible. The animals defecate everywhere, they smell, my family is miserable, and my house is more crowded than ever!" The rabbi told him to go home and put all of the animals out of the house, and then God would bless him for sure. Two days later, the rabbi passed the man on the street. "How are things at home?" he asked the farmer. The farmer smiled, "Things at home are wonderful!"

At some point, the contrast principle has affected most of us without our being aware of it, because it is often virtually invisible. Imagine you have a mechanic give you an estimate of $1,400 to repair your car (ouch!), but when you arrive to pick up your vehicle, the bill is only $1,100. You're happy because you "saved" $300. Now imagine the reverse, where you are told the estimate is $800, but the bill turns out to be $1,100. In your mind, you just paid $300 more than you expected. This doesn't feel good—even though in both cases, your repair bill was $1,100. The same thing occurs when a car salesperson tries to change how you perceive the cost of a car or a clothing salesperson the cost of an expensive shirt by comparing your potential purchase to a more expensive item.

The contrast principle occurs in schools in many ways. Think about how many times you and your colleagues have talked about how this year's class compares to last year's class. "Oh, the class I had last year was so much easier to handle," or "Last year's class was not as academic as the group I have now." Unfortunately, the students in the first class in this example likely are not as poorly behaved as this teacher perceives them to be. And the students in the second class are probably not quite as bright as this teacher thinks they are. The contrast principle is distorting these teachers' perceptions of each year's students.

I find this happens most often in grading practices. If you are marking a class set of student assessments, and you mark two or three in a row that are particularly poor, the next student's assessment—which may simply be average—will tend to appear *better* than it actually is because of how it compares to the preceding ones. The opposite can also happen when you mark one or two exceptional assessments and then unconsciously penalize the next one because it appears to be *weaker* than it actually is.

However, it's also possible to use the contrast principle to great effect with students by coloring the choices you give them. Give students two choices, but make the option you want students to choose the more attractive choice. Ask a class if they want to write a one thousand–word persuasive essay or a five hundred–word persuasive essay, and guess which option they will choose. Remember this the next time you want your students to write a five hundred–word essay without complaint. Start with the one thousand–word essay assignment, and then compromise down to the five hundred words that you really wanted in the first place.

You can also use the contrast principle to motivate your students to increase the value of their work, a strategy that works well with underachieving students. You tell the student something to this effect: "Look, Dave, you and I both know you can do well on the upcoming unit test. Tell you what. If you get any mark under 70 percent, it is what it is. But, if you get a mark *over* 70 percent, I will add a bonus of 15 percent to your mark."

Remember, as a teacher, if you issue twenty to thirty assessments over a term, a single bonus of 15 percent will make no significant mathematical difference in the final outcome. It will, however, show a student he or she is capable of achieving a minimum of 70 percent if the student applies him- or herself. This goes back to chapter 6's tactic of starting with small commitments focused on self-identity (page 65). Your goal is to show students what they can do, transforming their self-identity in the process.

You can use this same value-added strategy with an entire class by offering the 15 percent to everyone who achieves a mark of over 70 percent. If you want to increase your incentive, you can add even more value by saying something to the effect that "If the class average is 70 percent or over, I will give you thirty minutes of free time on Friday, or you can watch a movie on Friday afternoon"—whatever you think will be an effective class motivator. The contrast principle is in action here—the students have the choice of regular work on Friday afternoon or something they likely want more.

The contrast principle is another reason why it is so important for you to start the school year by making a positive first impression on your students. On their first day in your class, your students will subconsciously compare you with their previous teachers. Students, like all of us, make snap judgments based on comparisons.

Do you seem nicer or not as nice as their other teachers? Is your class going to be as much fun as was Mr. Jones's or Ms. Smith's class last year, or will it be boring? Knowing that your students will be making these comparisons allows you to carefully determine how you want to be perceived at the outset of the school year and then prepare and present yourself accordingly. You will explore effective ways to accomplish this in chapter 13 (page 163). There are many variations and applications of this strategy, and you can use all of them to great effect with particular students or classes.

The following sections each explore an application of using the contrast principle in your classroom: using images and metaphors your students understand, shifting and reframing the focus, overcoming negativity bias, and adopting the *door in the face* strategy.

Using Images and Metaphors Your Students Understand

New and complex concepts can be difficult for your students to understand. What you are trying to teach may be out of reach for them—they just can't get it. If you want your students to understand new ideas, especially abstract and complex ideas, you must present these new learnings using language and images that your students *can* relate to, either based on what they already know (scaffolding) or by using images and metaphors that link to what they are already familiar with.

For example, if you are attempting to get the concept of feminism across to elementary students, I wouldn't advise having them read the works of Germaine Greer or Gloria Steinem. Instead, consider sources that your students are interested in. If a significant number of your students watch *The Simpsons*, you could show them YouTube clips and examples from the series where Lisa Simpson celebrates the virtues of feminism. Now they will likely get it! This approach can also serve as your gateway to get students more interested in the deeper explorations.

You can also use the power of imagery and metaphor to influence how students make choices about their approach to learning. All teachers have at least some concern about students cheating on assessments. Curious about this, Ariely (2008b) conducted a series of experiments designed to see how fundamentally honest people were. He wanted to look at questions that explored the kinds of circumstances under which normally honest people would cheat and what might motivate them to be more honest. Researchers asked one of two groups to write down the names of ten books they read in high school. They asked the other group to write down as many of the Ten Commandments as they could remember (Ariely, 2008b). They ensured that each group had the opportunity to cheat in a way that precluded them being caught. About the outcome, Ariely (2008b) writes: "The result surprised even us: the students who had been asked to recall the Ten Commandments had not cheated at all" (p. 284). The other group did cheat when relating the books they read in high school. Ariely (2008b) concludes:

> What especially impressed me about the experiment with the Ten Commandments was that the students who could remember only one or two Commandments were as affected by them as the students who remembered nearly all ten. This indicated that it was not the Commandments themselves that encouraged honesty, but the mere contemplation of a moral benchmark of some kind. (pp. 284–285)

The take-home from this study is that if you want to encourage students to be more honest, *prime them* to do so. Conduct a reading about a child who is honest or an exercise that asks students to think about or write down what their spiritual beliefs tell them about being honest. These kinds of classroom activities take the students to a place where they must think about what it looks like when a person behaves in an honest manner. That is a powerful and effective use of imagery.

Let's consider another example. In "Nobody's Watching?" researchers Kevin J. Haley and Daniel M. T. Fessler (2005) placed different images on a computer screen while asking people for donations. For one of the participant groups, the image was a pair of eyes. The participants who were being "watched" by the eye images donated a whopping 31.4 percent more than did the other participants (Haley & Fessler, 2005). Consider also an example from "Good Lamps Are the Best Police" (Zhong, Bohns, & Gino, 2010), which finds that participants in a room with the lights only slightly dimmed cheated more than their counterparts in a well-lit room. As teachers, we know from classroom experience that students behave differently when they are aware teachers are watching them, but these findings suggest just the feeling of being watched is as likely to alter student behavior as actually devoting the time and energy needed to watch all students closely.

You can also use this thinking with other teachers as part of professional learning. In "The Difference Is Great Teachers," Eric Hanushek (2010) from Stanford says, "In a single academic year, a good teacher will get a gain of one and a half grade-level equivalents, while a bad teacher will get a gain equivalent of just half a year" (p. 84). To demonstrate the impact of this idea in a visual way to the preservice teachers I teach, I have two of them line up side-by-side at one end of our classroom. Teacher A takes six small half-steps forward (one for each year of elementary school) to represent a student who had poor teachers throughout elementary school. Teacher B takes six giant steps forward—three times the size of Teacher A's steps—to show the progress of a student who had good teachers for all six years of elementary school. What was once simply a concept is now a very powerful visual: the gap between these two students, represented by where each preservice teacher is standing relative to one another, is huge. In this way, the whole class of preservice teachers can readily *see* that a student who had poor teachers ends up at a third-grade level, while the student who had good teachers all the way through ends up at the ninth-grade level—a six-year gap that is now visible with a powerful impact. How might you use this approach of making concepts visual to teach essential learning for the students in your classroom?

Shifting and Reframing the Focus

Another way to use the contrast principle to motivate your students is by *changing the focus*. In her TED Talk "Every Kid Needs a Champion," Rita Pierson (2013) tells the story of giving a test with twenty questions with one student who got eighteen of the questions wrong. She put a *+2* on his paper and a big smiley face. The following paraphrases Pierson's (2013) telling of her conversation with the student that followed:

> Student: *"Ms. Pierson, is this an F?"*
>
> Pierson: *"Yes."*
>
> Student: *"Then why did you put a smiley face?"*
>
> Pierson: *"Because you're on a roll. You got two right; you didn't miss them all. And when we review this, won't you do better?"*
>
> Student: *"Yes ma'am, I can do better!"*

Pierson (2013) goes on to tell her audience why she did this: "You see, minus-eighteen sucks all the life out of you. Plus-two said, 'I ain't all bad!'" This is an excellent example of using the contrast principle to change the student's focus. This student was focused on the failure, the minus eighteen. And while telling a student to focus on the plus two isn't going to change the reality, notice how she paired that plus two to an offer of hope and encouragement that the student could and would do better in the future. This strategy is also known as *reframing*, and it is a powerful tool that you can use to motivate your students.

Let me tell you about an example of reframing from antiquity. The Battle of Hydaspes was fought in 326 BCE between the armies of Alexander the Great and King Porus of Paurava in what is now the Punjab region of Pakistan (Kurke, 2004). While Alexander was very adept at winning battles through the brilliant utilization of his calvary, he now faced what seemed an insurmountable problem: the Indian army of King Porus had some two hundred heavily armored war elephants stationed every fifty feet in front of his soldiers. Horses have an instinctual fear of elephants, and Alexander knew that if he tried to utilize his calvary horses, they would run away in terror as soon as they saw or smelled the elephants. So what did he do?

Historian and author Lance B. Kurke (2004) tells us, "Alexander reframed the problem. Instead of relying on military might, the solution rested on an elegantly choreographed use of the enemy's very strengths against them" (p. 11). Elephants can be trained, but only if they establish a special relationship with their trainer from birth. At birth, these war elephants had been taken away from their mothers and trained by young boys called mahouts (Kurke, 2004). These boys fed, bathed, brushed, rode, and trained their elephants for many years, and the elephants remained very obedient to their particular trainer but only to that one person. Knowing this, Alexander chose to *ignore the war elephants altogether*. He recognized that the elephants were not the primary problem; their trainers were. Consequently, he had his archers focus not on the elephants, not on the soldiers, but on the mahouts. Without them, no one else could control the elephants. Alexander then targeted the elephants' eyes to blind them and followed this by having his javelin throwers spear them. The elephants stampeded into the Indian army, causing extensive death and disarray (Kurke, 2004). By reframing the problem from one of how to utilize horses against elephants to a problem of how to disable the elephants, Alexander was able to win this decisive battle.

If you take nothing else from this example, be sure to remember this: *Alexander recognized that the elephants were not the primary problem*. I shudder to think of the many times I tried to solve a problem with a student or group of students, and all the while, I was not focused on the primary problem but rather a symptom. Has that ever happened to you?

What can reframing look like in schools? During my first year teaching at a junior high school, I took on the task of coaching the senior boys' basketball team. The school had a very rudimentary athletic program, so I knew that I was starting to build the team essentially from scratch. In order to build for the future, I chose to have mostly seventh- and eighth-grade boys on the team, even though I knew they would be playing against boys who were two years older than them, two years bigger than them, and with two years more experience than them. It was highly unlikely that we would win many, if any, games.

I had a problem. I knew I couldn't keep these boys motivated by promises of future basketball glory two years down the road when we had worked together as a team for two years and they would then be in ninth grade. I needed something much more immediate. Remembering the notion of reframing, before every game, I gave my players a goal focused on what they *could* achieve. (Recall our discussion of SMART goals in chapter 7, page 73.) So, depending on the quality of the opposing team, I would set one offensive goal and one defensive goal:

> *OK guys, the team we are about to play is really good. We are not going to win this game by scoring more baskets than they do. Two years from now, we will teach this school a lesson or two about what great basketball looks like, but not today. Today your goal is to score at least ten points, and to keep them from scoring more than sixty points. Got that? Defensively, your goal is to keep them below sixty points, and offensively, you are to score at least ten points. Now, let's get out there and make this happen. I know you can do it!*

It was really quite an amazing thing to watch this group of twelve- and thirteen-year-old boys working hard until the final buzzer and cheering as they walked off the court after losing fifty-six to thirteen. By reframing the problem, in their eyes, they had won! And yes, they did teach that team a few lessons about basketball two years later.

Reframing can also work in situations that involve student discipline. For example, I once had to discipline a ninth-grade student for a serious breach of school policy. She was an honor student who had, up until that point, an unblemished record in terms of disciplinary offenses in her three years at the school. I told

her that I had no choice but to suspend her for three days. She broke down crying and begged me not to suspend her. So, I gently told her that she ought to look at this another way. If I didn't suspend her but suspended all of the other students who were involved, others would see her as unfairly receiving preferential treatment compared to other students. On the other hand, if she, "the perfect student who never gets in trouble," got suspended just like everyone else in the same circumstances, those same students would look at her more as one of their own. She thought about this, the tears stopped, and she said that she would be fine with the suspension.

Overcoming Negativity Bias

Helping students shift from the negative to the positive is especially important when you consider *negativity bias*, which psychology teacher and education consultant Kendra Cherry (2019) describes as "our tendency not only to register negative stimuli more readily but also to dwell on these events." Also known as *positive-negative asymmetry*, this negativity bias means that we feel the sting of a rebuke more powerfully than we feel the joy of praise. In almost any interaction, we are more likely to notice negative things and more vividly remember them later (Cherry, 2019).

Why do we do this? Think about our exploration in chapter 1 (page 9) and chapter 2 (page 17) of natural selection and our need to survive and reproduce that necessitated humans living in groups. To live in a group and to have yourself matter to the group were essential to your survival. Humans are hardwired to pay special attention to things we see as negative because doing so helped our ancestors survive (Schenk, 2012). As a result, we often perceive potential threats as being far more dangerous and much more likely to occur than what is actually real.

We also tend to have a strong desire to find causes behind the experiences that happen in our lives. Cognitive theorists call our tendency to detect agency or cause behind events that happen to us Hypersensitive or Hyperactive Agency Detection Device (HADD). In

God: A Human History, Aslan (2017) argues that HADD—like our negativity bias—promoted human survival:

> HADD explains why we assume every bump in the night is caused by someone doing the bumping. . . . There is no harm in mistaking a tree for a predator, but there certainly would be in mistaking a predator for a tree. Better to guess wrong than to be eaten. (p. 38)

In our hunter-gatherer past, it was safe to ignore or minimize those things around us that were either pleasant or non-threatening (the positive things). To disregard those things around us that were dangerous (the negative things) could be fatal and often was. We—you and me—are alive today because our ancestors knew how to read the signs properly. Our *actual* ancestors—the ones who mistook a bush for a lion and ran away—may have been mistaken, but in spite of this error, they survived and reproduced. However, our *potential* ancestors—the ones who mistook a lion for a bush and didn't run away—well, they didn't make the cut. As a consequence, we are hardwired to focus more on the negative than the positive. Although this mindset helped early humans survive, this negativity bias has consequences in your classroom.

Researchers Tiffany Ito and John T. Cacioppo (2005) from the University of Chicago showed participants one hundred pictures designed to evoke either positive feelings (happy people, a beautiful day, a new car) or negative feelings (a mutilated body, a dead animal, and so on); still other images were neutral (a plate, a toaster, and so on). They asked participants to rate the degree of their positive or negative reactions to the images, and the results showed that the brain reacts more strongly to the negative imagery than it does to the positive or neutral imagery. This should not come as a complete surprise to us. As Steven D. Levitt and Stephen J. Dubner (2014) remind us in *Think Like a Freak*:

> Human beings, for all our accomplishments, can be fragile animals. Most of us don't take criticism well at all. A spate of recent research shows that negative information "weighs more heavily on the brain," as one research team put it. A second team makes an even starker claim: in the human psyche, "bad is stronger than good." This means that negative events . . . make an outsized impression on our memories. (p. 180)

How many times has this happened to you? You meet a group of people at some social gathering, and your new acquaintances find out you're a teacher. The conversation turns to people's experiences in school, and someone tells a story about the way in which a teacher in elementary school, several decades ago, humiliated and embarrassed them in front of the class. Although this happened long ago, you can tell by the person's tone and expression that the hurt is still present, and the experience still affects them.

Or, perhaps you receive a performance evaluation from your administrator. It is very positive overall; in fact, it is glowing in some places. You get to the last section, which deals with recommendations for improvement, and your evaluator has made a couple of suggestions. Which do you focus on: the many positive and glowing comments or the two comments that you perceive as negative because the evaluator has indicated that you have room for improvement? If you answer like many teachers do (you just can't stop thinking about those areas for improvement), this is your negativity bias coming to center stage.

It is important to remember that students will respond in much the same way to the experiences they have in your classroom. The negative experiences they have with you will carry far more weight and have a much greater impact on them than will the positive ones. Your students will "remember traumatic experiences better than positive ones, recall insults better than praise, react more strongly to negative stimuli, think about negative things more frequently than positive ones, respond more strongly to negative events than to equally positive ones" (Cherry, 2019). That is why it is so important for you to be cognizant of any negative experiences your students may be having and work to shift the focus to make the experiences positive.

If your students are struggling with content, perhaps tell them the story of how Thomas Edison spent years trying to develop the light bulb. He is reputed to have said in regard to the myriad experiments that didn't work with no results, "Why, man, I have gotten a lot of results! I know several thousand things that won't work" (as cited in Dyer & Martin, 2006). Or tell them the WD-40 story we looked at in the Persist Until You Are Successful section (page 111 in chapter 8). And if you find that you have had a negative encounter with one of your students, know that the relationship will need some healing and that the onus is on you as the teacher to begin this healing process. You want your students to focus on the positive much more than the negative.

Adopting the Door in the Face Strategy

Another strategy you can use when implementing the contrast principle is sometimes called the *door in the face* strategy. Basically, the *door in the face* strategy begins when you make such an outrageous request of your students that you know in advance they will not accept it. You will metaphorically get the door slammed in your face. But you don't really want the outrageous request. What you really want comes next. Your second request appears very reasonable when contrasted with your initial request, and thus, the likelihood that the students will accept it is increased.

The strategy here is obvious—to those of you reading it in this book. In the moment of the actual conversation, however, your second request to the student will appear quite reasonable when compared to your initial request. You also appear to be flexible and willing to compromise. Students are much more likely to agree to your second request because it seems so much better for them than your first request.

The basketball coach who yells: "OK, fifty line sprints!" will hear many moans. This can be followed by, "All right, I'll settle for ten." It's the same with the mathematics teacher who says, "You are to do all twenty-five questions at the end of chapter 6 for homework," and,

after the whining stops, relents by saying, "OK, then, how about you just do the odd-numbered questions?"

TACTIC: USE THE BUTTERFLY EFFECT

We know that students are complex beings. We know that classrooms are complex places. It helps students and teachers alike to make sense of all that complexity by having an understanding of the *butterfly effect*. In "Understanding the Butterfly Effect," scientist and author Jamie Vernon (2017) writes:

> During the 139th meeting of the American Association for the Advancement of Science, Edward Lorenz posed a question: "Does the flap of a butterfly's wings in Brazil set off a tornado in Texas?" . . . The purpose of his provocative question, he said, was to illustrate the idea that some complex dynamical systems exhibit unpredictable behaviors such that small variances in the initial conditions could have profound and widely divergent effects on the system's outcomes. Because of the sensitivity of these systems, outcomes are unpredictable. This idea became the basis for a branch of mathematics known as *chaos theory*. . . . Small variances in the initial conditions could have profound and widely divergent effects on the system's outcomes. (p. 130)

What does that mean for you? How can you utilize the butterfly effect in your teaching practice?

I sometimes have guest speakers present to my preservice teacher classes. One such speaker is a former high school student of mine, Juanita, who always tells my preservice teachers a story about Ms. Perkis, one of her junior high school teachers. (As a reminder, I've changed all names for anonymity.) Juanita relates that she was an underachiever in those years, until one day, Ms. Perkis passed back a language arts assignment and then asked Juanita to step out into the hallway. The conversation was brief. All Ms. Perkis said to her was, "Juanita, I know you are so much smarter than this.

I know you can do so much better." She then walked back into the classroom. That was it.

Juanita tells these preservice teachers that brief conversation had a life-changing impact on her. She realized her teacher was right. She was smarter. She was capable of so much more. So that's what she did. She showed how smart she was (to herself and to her teacher). Several years later, Juanita graduated from university with a master's degree.

Please do not underestimate the power of a few well-chosen words or the power of a brief conversation that tries to show a student a different way forward. Remember our earlier discussion in this chapter about Rita Pierson's (2013) comments to the student who got two out of twenty correct on a spelling test? "You got two right; you didn't miss them all. And when we review this, won't you do better?" That's the kind of comment that has great butterfly effect potential for a student. You can never tell what the impact of those few words might mean to a student and the direction they take. They can, in fact, be life changing.

SUMMARY

In this chapter, you looked at the incredible power of rhythm and rhyme to help students remember key concepts, some ways to shift students' focus in the direction you want them to go, and how to overcome some of our inherent biases, such as negativity bias. There is great potential in you doing these little things well, as they have a lot of power to influence your students and nudge them in the right direction. As you reflect on this chapter, make sure to remember the following.

- Rhyming and repetition are powerful tools you can use to help students remember important content. If a concept is vital, teach it more than once or try and find a way to make a rhyme out of it and watch retention rates soar.

- The contrast principle is a very effective strategy for obtaining student cooperation. Show your students that what you want from them in the end is far better for them than what you asked for in the beginning.

- Be mindful of how the contrast principle can affect how you assess student work. If you mark two or three outstanding pieces of student work in a row, the next student's work may appear weaker than it really is—simply because it is not as good as the previous students' work.

- Images and metaphors that your students can see and relate to are effective ways to help them understand new content.

- Our tendency to focus much more on the negative than the positive—negativity bias—helped our ancestors survive, but you need to be mindful of how this can impact your students, both in terms of their achievements and in terms of their relationship with you.

- The butterfly effect tells us that we don't necessarily have to do something big to have a significant impact on a student. Small conversations can have dramatic results.

Reflective Practice

Use the following questions and activities to reflect on and make changes to your practice.

1. Choose a concept or some essential information that you want your students to memorize, and use the space provided to phrase it into some kind of rhyme. Using the combined strategies of rhyming and repetition, have your student sing this information at the beginning and the end of a few classes. After a period of time of your choosing, check to see how many students recall this critical information and how well.

2. Write down a request you want to make of your students. Simply write it in your usual language. Now, reword the request and insert positive words whenever possible. Assess the impact of this strategy on your success rate. Will you use this strategy again in the future?

   Original request: _____

   _____

   Revised request: _____

   _____

3. Think of an important concept you want your students to learn. Now, try to think of and write down ways in which you can make this into a visual representation of the idea. Remember the story from the chapter about having the two participants take steps to visually illustrate the impact of poor and good teachers. Try something similar, and see how this impacts student understanding.

4. Think about the one to three lowest-performing students in your class. Think about how you currently provide feedback to them on assessments. Now, with the Rita Pierson (2013) example in mind (minus eighteen becomes plus two), think of some ways in which you could turn the negative feedback into positive feedback. Write down your ideas, and implement this strategy over the course of the next several assessments and monitor the results.

5. Choose one of your most challenging students, a student who you feel could do much better in your class, either academically or behaviorally, or perhaps both. Now, write down what you see as being the primary problem with this student. Next, do some research in the form of one or two low-key conversations with this student. The key here is to explore, not criticize or challenge. Attempt to find out what is going on from the student's perspective, not from yours. Now reassess. What is the primary problem here, and how might you address it?

The student's primary problem: _____

_____

Notes from conversation 1:

Notes from conversation 2:

6. Write down a request that you want to make of your students. This could be with an entire class, a group of students, or of one student in particular. Now try the *door in the face* strategy. Make an outrageous request along the lines of what you want, but at the extreme end, knowing all the while the students will protest. Now make the actual request, what it is that you really want. Monitor the results.

Your outrageous request: _____

_____

Your more reasonable request: _____

_____

7. Think about your experiences with the butterfly effect. Has there been a time in your career when a few well-chosen words, spoken softly and sincerely to a student, have had a profound effect on that student's future performance in your class, be it academically or behaviorally? Be vigilant for opportunities to have these kinds of brief but potentially powerful conversations with your students, and watch the results.

Source: Pierson, R. (2013). Every kid needs a champion [Video file]. Accessed at www.ted.com/talks/rita_pierson_every_kid _needs_a_champion on June 14, 2021.

The Tactical Teacher © 2022 Solution Tree Press • SolutionTree.com
Visit **go.SolutionTree.com/behavior** to download this free reproducible.

CHAPTER 12

SOFT TACTICS FOR MOTIVATING STUDENTS THROUGH REWARDS

In *Punished by Rewards: The Trouble With Gold Stars, Incentive Plans, A's, Praise, and Other Bribes*, education and parenting expert and prolific author and speaker Alfie Kohn (1993) tells the story of an elderly man who, every day, endured verbal insults from a group of ten-year-olds who passed his house on their way to school:

> One afternoon, after listening to another round of jeers about how stupid and ugly and bald he was, the man came up with a plan. He met the children on his lawn the following Monday and announced that anyone who came back the next day and yelled rude comments about him would receive a dollar. Amazed and excited, they showed up even earlier on Tuesday, hollering epithets for all they were worth. True to his word, the old man ambled out and paid everyone. "Do the same tomorrow," he told them, "and you'll get twenty-five cents for your trouble." The kids thought that was still pretty good and turned out again on Wednesday to taunt him. At the first catcall, he walked over with a roll of quarters and again paid off his hecklers. "From now on," he announced, "I can give you only a penny for doing this." The kids looked at each other in disbelief. "A penny?" they repeated scornfully. "Forget it!" And they never came back again. (pp. 71–72)

What happened in this story? Psychologists have a name for this phenomenon, the *overjustification effect* (American Psychological Association, n.d.). Overjustification occurs when being rewarded for something lessens the intrinsic motivation that a person had for doing that thing in the first place. Put another way, if a person engages in an activity simply because they enjoy it, but now they get paid to do that same activity, the money they receive can effectively lessen the intrinsic motivation they initially had. The reward serves as an inhibitor, not an enhancer, of the activity. However, that doesn't mean you can't make tactical use of rewards to influence student behavior in positive ways.

In this chapter, we look at the use of rewards in your classroom, and explore when, how, and if you should use them. The tactics in this chapter are a bit different from previous chapters. The following are not individual approaches to guide your use of rewards with students but a process to support your understanding of the implications involved with using rewards. Use these tactics to determine whether to use rewards at all and, if you do, how to do so effectively.

- Understand your own thinking about rewards.
- Understand the connection between rewards and motivation.
- Know your methods for using rewards.

TACTIC: UNDERSTAND YOUR OWN THINKING ABOUT REWARDS

Before you use rewards as a tactic, it's critical that you fully understand your own approach and perspective about using them. To be sure, rewards can work to influence student behaviors. I once had three high school boys fail what I considered to be a fairly simple social studies vocabulary exam of fourteen new words and their meanings. This was new terminology that students needed to learn in order to work with several key concepts in the upcoming unit. So, I asked to speak to the boys for a few minutes at the end of class (it was lunchtime), and I told them that if they came back to class the next day and retook the test and *each* of them achieved at least 90 percent, I would give them $20 to split among themselves. I stressed that if any one of them achieved 89 percent or less, I would not give them anything. I wanted each of the boys to feel the pressure of not being the one to mess things up for the other two.

The boys retook the test the next day, and the lowest mark was 92 percent. They were very proud and waited with big smiles for their reward. As I passed a $20 bill to one of the boys, I asked them what they had learned from this experience. "Ripley's a baller!" replied one boy with a laugh. *Baller* was a slang term they used to describe someone who had a lot of money, as in a big ball of money in their pocket. Usually *ballers* refers to drug dealers, and this was a tough school with tough students, many of whom were involved with drugs.

I laughed at the imagery of myself as a baller and asked what else. One student answered, "We learned that when we study, we can pass, even get really high marks."

There it was! The lesson I wanted them to learn. Well worth my $20, I thought.

But were my actions *ethical*? Was I *bribing* them? Was I paying them to study? Was I rewarding bad behavior because they hadn't studied in the first place and, as a result of that, I was now giving them a chance to get money for doing what they should have done in the

first place? I could probably answer "Yes" to all of these questions. But I would do it all over again (and have on several occasions). And I sleep well at night. The real question is, How will *you* approach using rewards with your students?

There are many factors to take into consideration that are different and separate from the ethical issues you will confront in chapter 16 (page 193), so let's look at the unintended consequences of using rewards and the ethics of using them in general.

Beware of Unintended Consequences

Rewards almost always sound good. They imply you're going to get something for doing something well. But there is also the axiom, *Be careful what you wish for; you may get it.* In "What Data Can't Do," mathematician Hannah Fry (2021) tells the story of how former British Prime Minister Tony Blair tried to improve health services for the citizens of his country. Wait times for people to get an appointment to see their doctor were unacceptably long in his estimation, so Blair devised a reward program to incentivize doctors to shorten wait times. Doctors received a financial bonus if they saw patients within forty-eight hours. The result? Patients could not get doctor appointments unless they were willing to come in within forty-eight hours. People could no longer book an appointment for any time outside of that range (for example, next week) because there was no bonus in doing so for doctors. So much for long-term planning. It's also a good example of the potential for unintended consequences when using rewards.

There is clearly something innately attractive about using rewards to motivate students. After all, we see rewards used in a wide range of circumstances to motivate people. The business world gives financial bonuses and trips to the tropics to certain employees who achieve their targets. Parents "bribe" their children with promises of extra tablet or TV time if they behave in certain ways or perform extra household chores. Thus, it is easy to see how teachers would quite naturally carry assumptions regarding the effectiveness of rewards into their classrooms. Some of the tactics I've detailed in this book reflect a need to motivate positive behavior or learning outcomes through rewards.

If you ask most teachers to name the most significant behaviors that help determine whether a student will be successful in school, good attendance would very likely be somewhere near the top of that list. Thus, it makes sense that you want to encourage good attendance for your students by, for example, displaying a motivational attendance poster (page 80 in chapter 7), because the relationship between attendance and student success is clear (Birak & Cuttler, 2019). Behavior experts Carly D. Robinson, Jana Gallus, Monica G. Lee, and Todd Rogers (2021) tell us what every experienced teacher knows:

> In education, attendance is a particularly important input factor that affects both individual and organizational success. Because student absenteeism robustly predicts academic performance . . . and educational failure . . . local educational agencies have sought to make improving attendance a national priority. (p. 2)

Since good attendance is a critical factor in student success, shouldn't teachers find ways to motivate students to attend school as much as they possibly can? While the answer to this question is clearly yes, the question of *how* to motivate students to attend school as much as possible can be complex.

In their study, "The Demotivating Effect (and Unintended Message) of Awards," Robinson and colleagues (2021) describe an experiment they conducted to explore the impact of giving students rewards for attendance. They studied 15,329 students in grades 6–12. The students were divided into two random groups. One group received a *prospective award* in the form of a letter promising them they would receive a certificate if they had perfect attendance for the month of February. The other group received a *retrospective reward* in the form of a letter and a certificate for perfect attendance for one month in the fall semester.

Contrary to the researchers' expectations, neither the prospective award nor the retrospective award had any positive impact on attendance:

> The prospective awards did not on average improve behavior, and the retrospective awards *decreased* subsequent attendance. Moreover, we find a significant negative effect on attendance after prospective incentives were removed, which . . . suggests that awards may cause these unintended effects by inadvertently signaling that the target behavior (perfect attendance) is neither the social norm nor institutionally expected. In addition, receiving the retrospective award suggests to recipients that they have already outperformed the norm and what was expected of them, hence licensing them to miss school. (p. 1; emphasis added)

Giving students rewards for desired behaviors and accomplishments is complicated. Should you use rewards in your classroom? Is giving rewards ethical? When should you give rewards? What kinds of rewards work best, for what students, and in what circumstances? These are complex questions, and the answers will vary depending on the students, the context, the task, and the teacher.

Know the Ethics of Rewards

Many teachers give rewards of various kinds as motivation or reinforcement for positive student behaviors. Here, I want to explore the question: Are rewards ethical? Is it ethical to tell students *ahead of a task* (classical conditioning) that they will get a certain reward if they complete the task to a certain standard? Is it ethical to give students a reward *after* they have completed a task (operant conditioning) in recognition of a job well done?

Most students want to feel recognized when they do something commendable. Some students do not want public recognition, but a simple comment on an assignment or a quietly spoken "Nicely done!" means the world to them. Other students prefer recognition in a more public fashion, like the little boy who said to his father, "Let's play darts. I'll throw, and you say 'Wonderful!'" (Canfield & Hansen, 1996, p. 102).

If you choose to motivate through recognition of a student's accomplishments, it is critical that your praise be authentic. In his classic book *How to Win Friends and Influence People*, Dale Carnegie (1937) says that one of the fundamental ways to work with people is to give honest and sincere appreciation. Honest *and* sincere. Most students can tell when you're faking it, so don't bother. Psychologist, author, and expert on mindsets Carol S. Dweck (2016), in her approach to growth mindsets, would agree. She finds that empty praise of effort alone is unlikely to motivate students to believe in their own learning ability.

Further, Daniel Pink (2009) argues that goal setting and rewards can *induce unethical behavior*, an example of which we explore later in this chapter. If students are overly goal- or reward-driven, they may be tempted to cheat in order to achieve the goal and obtain the reward. Most teachers have had the experience of having a student attempt to cheat on heavily weighted assessments due to self-imposed pressure or pressure from caregivers. This pressure can be punitive in nature ("I'm taking your cell phone away if you don't get honors!") or seemingly more positive ("I'll buy you a new car if you graduate with distinction"). Both of these place significant pressure on the student to achieve to a certain level. And if a student cannot attain the prize or avoid the punishment via ethical means, cheating may become a very tempting option.

Two examples highlight my thinking about the risks involved in using rewards with students and where I most recommend teachers tread carefully: (1) what I think of as *jukin' the stats*, and (2) the way rewards can also inspire *unethical* behavior.

Jukin' the Stats

There is a scene from the television series *The Wire* (Simon, Colesberry, & Noble, 2002–2008) in which a detective (Roland "Prez" Pryzbylewski) leaves the police department to become a middle school teacher.

He joins a staff meeting where the school administration informs the entire teaching staff they now have to stop everything they are currently teaching and prepare their students for standardized state tests. The principal tells the teachers that the school board is looking for at least a ten-point increase on test results, which they plan to achieve by *teaching test questions directly*.

Prez teaches mathematics, but because the school's language arts marks are the lowest of all the subjects, he (like all of the teachers) is directed to teach language arts test sample questions during his mathematics classes, ignoring his own curriculum. Prez turns to a colleague after hearing the new directive (Simon et al., 2002–2008), and the following dialogue ensues:

> Prez: I don't get it. All this so we score higher on the state tests. If we're teaching the kids the test questions, what is it assessing in them?
>
> Colleague: Nothing, it assesses us. The test scores go up, they can say the schools are improving. The scores stay down, they can't.
>
> Prez: Jukin' the stats. Making robberies into larcenies.

Prez is thinking back to his days as a police officer, where officers in his department were rewarded with promotions for reducing robberies and rapes. Since they didn't have either the resources or the know-how to *actually* reduce robberies and rapes, senior police officers resorted to what they called "jukin' the stats." Robberies were *re-labeled* as larcenies; rapes were *re-labeled* as assaults. And thus, the number of robberies and rapes dropped significantly—at least on paper.

Some schools and school districts juke the stats on occasion, especially if there is enough pressure placed on them for failure or significant rewards given when the stats improve. I have witnessed firsthand high school administrators and teachers who encourage low-performing twelfth-grade students to drop out of university admission exam courses just so they can keep their class averages high.

Is that ethical?

Motivating Unethical Behavior

In the spring of 2019, one of the big news stories at the time was the college admissions scandal in the United States. Several dozen wealthy parents, including actresses Felicity Huffman and Lori Loughlin, were charged with arranging cheating on admission exams and applications in an effort to get their children into elite American colleges and universities (*Los Angeles Times*, n.d.). Netflix aired a documentary film about the scandal called *Operation Varsity Blues: The College Admissions Scandal* (Daly, Colson, & Smith, 2021), during which a Department of Justice spokesperson stated that the scandal was "the largest college admissions scam ever prosecuted by the Department of Justice. We've charged fifty people nationwide."

Huffman eventually served fourteen days in prison and was fined $30,000 (*Los Angeles Times*, n.d.). In 2020, Loughlin was sentenced to two months in prison and received one hundred hours of community service and a fine of $150,000 (*Los Angeles Times*, n.d.). Other parents were fined up to $50,000 and served between three weeks and five months in prison (Daly et al., 2021). Having their children accepted into schools like the University of Southern California, Duke, Yale, Harvard, and Stanford was enough to motivate these parents into committing unethical and illegal activities, a risk they were willing to take because they thought the reward was worth it. This story is a well-known example of rewards motivating unethical behavior.

TACTIC: UNDERSTAND THE CONNECTION BETWEEN REWARDS AND MOTIVATION

Kohn (1993) argues that the *equity principle*—which states that people should get what they deserve—has problems when applied to schools. What constitutes *deservedness*? Do teachers reward students on the basis of how much *effort* they have expended? Or should teachers only give rewards based on whether or not students' effort has produced the *desired results*, irrespective of effort and ability? Kohn (1993) concludes that, in a sense, rewards and punishments are essentially the same

things because removal of the reward *is* a punishment. The stick is the taking away of the carrot. And while rewarding a behavior may increase the likelihood that it repeats, it changes our attitudes toward the behavior.

For example, think of a person (let's call him George) who bakes really great cookies and gives them away to his friends and family on special occasions. George loves doing this for people he cares about. Some friends tell George he could make a killing selling his cookies at the local farmers' market every Saturday, and eventually, George decides to rent a booth for the summer and test this idea. His friends were right. George sells out every Saturday, and he makes an excellent profit. However, George now develops an intense dislike for baking cookies. Whereas he used to bake cookies for fun and to see the joy on his family's and friends' faces when they received a gift box full of his cookies, now he is doing it simply for profit. What used to be *play for the payoff of joy* has turned into *work for the payoff of money*. This is another example of the overjustification effect that we discussed at the beginning of the chapter.

Daniel Pink (2009a) warns us:

> Rewards can perform a weird sort of behavioral alchemy: They can transform an interesting task into a drudge. Than can turn play into work. And by diminishing intrinsic motivation, they can send performance, creativity, and even upstanding behavior toppling like dominoes. (p. 35)

Kohn (1993) makes a similar point:

> *Do this and you'll get that* automatically devalues the *this*. The recipient of the reward figures "If they have to bribe me to do this, it must be something I wouldn't want to do." . . . Promising a reward for an activity is tantamount to declaring that the activity is not worth doing for its own sake. (p. 76)

And of course, if you bribe a student to do something, you have to follow up to ensure they have fulfilled their part of the bargain. Remember, many students come from homes where they long ago learned that it is often possible to accept a bribe in advance and then not follow through on their end of the agreement. This can also happen in classrooms. The verbal commitment between you and a student is not enough. The student must live up to their end of the bargain, and you now have to make sure they have done so.

In *The Happy Teacher Habits,* Michael Linsin (2016), the founder of the Smart Classroom Management blog (www.smartclassroommanagement.com), says that the problem with extrinsic motivators (tokens, stars, prizes, and so on) is that they can take the intrinsic joy out of completing the work, and students may thus want greater and greater rewards for doing the work. Linsin (2016) argues that the secret to motivating your students is to shift the responsibility for learning and behaving to your students:

> It's doing your part by teaching compelling lessons through meaningful stories, connections, and context, and then letting your students loose to write the essay, perform the experiment, or solve for *x* with only reluctant additional support from you. It's giving your students increasing amounts of time to work, ponder, wrestle with, and overcome the challenges you place before them. It's planning projects, assignments, and presentations that take multiple steps and days, if not weeks, to complete. It's giving them the tools they need to do the work, and then letting them do it. This also changes the way students view their schoolwork—from busywork to get through to goals to be reached. (p. 89)

Look closely at what Linsin (2016) says. He advocates that teachers give students worthwhile and relevant goals to achieve, give them the tools they need to achieve these goals, and then get out of their way and let them do the work—offering additional support only in cases where they genuinely need it. Does this sound familiar to you? Because to me, it sounds a lot like the world of work when we become adults. Perhaps Linsin (2016) is on to something here.

TACTIC: KNOW YOUR METHODS FOR USING REWARDS

Should you ever reward your students? What kinds of rewards should you consider? Economics experts Steven D. Levitt and Stephen J. Dubner (2005) claim, "There are three basic flavors of incentive: economic, social, and moral. Very often a single-incentive scheme will include all three varieties" (p. 17). What reward "flavors" work best on which students? If so, how and when ought you give these rewards?

There are two perspectives I suggest you consider as you approach giving rewards: (1) what and (2) when. The *when* of influence is one of the most critical factors in our ability as teachers to lead, motivate, persuade, and inspire our students. *What* we do to motivate our students is important, but *when* we do it is vital in terms of our strategies actually being successful. The following sections explore these perspectives.

Knowing Your What

This perspective looks at the *kind of task* you are having your students perform. Kohn (1993) suggests that rewards do work well, but specifically for *simple kinds of tasks.* Pink (2009a) expands on this and shows that researchers find that rewards and punishments can work well for *algorithmic tasks,* but rewards and punishments do not work well for *heuristic tasks.* The following explains these task types.

- *Algorithmic tasks* are tasks where the process is defined and the outcome is predetermined. For example, when we teach students a particular way of multiplying two numbers by two numbers, we show them a series of steps that must be followed, and there is a single correct answer to the problem. This is an algorithmic task.

- *Heuristic tasks* have no defined process and no defined product. Students decide how to tackle a problem, and there may be many different—albeit equally good—answers to this problem. Examples abound, such as having primary students draw a picture and write a three-sentence story about the picture is an example of a heuristic task, or having high school language arts students write an essay in which they determine whether Hamlet is sane or insane, defending their conclusion. There are multiple ways in which students can accomplish these kinds of tasks. You get the idea. In giving students heuristic tasks, we give them a great deal of autonomy over both the process and the product. It is *their* work to figure out how to achieve the desired goals.

In the TED Talk "The Puzzle of Motivation," Pink (2009b) tells of an experiment by Sam Glucksberg of Princeton University. Glucksberg presented two groups with "the candle problem," in which participants were shown a table on which rests a candle, a box with thumbtacks, and a book of matches. There is also a corkboard attached to the wall. The task is to light the candle so the wax won't drip on the table.

Pink (2009b) describes how Glucksberg conducted this experiment:

> [He] gathered his participants and said, "I'm going to time how quickly you can solve this problem." To one group, he said, "I'm going to time you to establish norms, averages for how long it typically takes for someone to solve this sort of problem." To the second group, he offered rewards. He said, "If you're in the top 25 percent of the fastest times, you get five dollars. If you're the fastest of everyone we're testing here today, you get twenty dollars."

It took the incentivized group, the group getting money as a reward, *three and a half minutes longer* to perform the task. What is going on here? Why would the incentivized group perform so much more poorly than the group not getting any reward?

Pink (2009b), like Kohn (1993), believes this demonstrates that contingent motivators only work under the right circumstances and may, in fact, do harm if used in the wrong ones, stating, "If-then rewards work really well for those sorts of tasks where there's a simple set of rules and a clear destination to go."

This makes sense, because when we want to obtain the reward, we get focused on the problem. Thus, if the problem has a direct and simple conclusion, rewards can work quite well. However, if the problem is complex and requires creative thinking, focus is *not* what is required. A free flow of different ideas and an exploration of multiple ways to tackle the problem are required for this type of problem. Rewards appear to inhibit this kind of thinking. Thus, Pink (2009b) concludes that for tasks with a narrow focus (*algorithmic* tasks), incentives can work very well. However, for tasks that require more creative thinking (*heuristic* tasks), rewards can limit focus. Another way to describe this is that rewards seem to work better for tasks involving *convergent thinking*, where students are working toward a specific correct answer, but they do not work well (and can inhibit tasks) that require *divergent thinking*, where students are asked to be creative and to come up with a variety of creative solutions to a problem.

Knowing Your When

The second perspective to help you determine when to use rewards has to do with timing. The *when* aspect of giving rewards to students can be a critical variable in the effectiveness of the reward. Robinson and colleagues (2021) discuss what they call *prospective rewards*, rewards that are announced *in advance* and given based on performance achieved at a certain standard. (These are your *if-then rewards*.) They also describe *retrospective awards*, rewards given after a student completes a task such that it comes as a surprise to the student. (Think of these as *now-that rewards*.)

Levitt and Dubner (2015) describe a study they conducted called *Bribing Kids to Try Harder on Tests*. They told the students they would give them money if the students tried to improve their performance on tests. In order to see any improvement on exam results, the authors learned they had to pay the students *immediately after the tests*. Giving them the promised financial reward a month later resulted in no improvement in performance. Please pay special attention to this: promising your students financial rewards that only come years later if they stay in school and get a degree simply doesn't work. Their rewards, their payoff, have to be *much more immediate* if they have any chance of impacting performance in your classroom.

Levitt and Dubner (2015) got the best results in a very interesting way. They gave the students the financial reward *before* the exam and would then *take the money back* if the student did not meet the benchmark that had been set for improvement. This behavior on the part of the students is consistent with *loss-aversion theory*, the idea that *losing what we already have* has a much greater negative impact on us than would the positive impact of a similar gain. (See Use Loss Aversion, page 131 in chapter 10.)

Which of these strategies should you use: before or after? I suggest you try both and see what happens. After all, the question isn't which of these strategies works best—the real question is which of these strategies works best for *your* students, the ones you are teaching now? Timing isn't everything—but it is a very important thing.

SUMMARY

This chapter took a close look at the upsides and downsides of using rewards in classrooms. While giving rewards to students for desired performance intuitively seems to be a good strategy, you learned that there are times when rewards can actually hinder student performance. You also explored some ethical considerations detailing how rewards can actually encourage unanticipated and unethical behavior on the part of students when they want the reward so much they will cheat to attain it. As you reflect on this chapter, make sure to remember the following.

- You need to be careful about using rewards in the classroom to impact student behaviors and academic performance because, at times, rewards can have a negative impact rather than a positive one on student achievement or behavior.

- If a reward is extremely significant to students, they may be tempted to attain the reward through dishonest behavior. You need to ensure as much as possible that the reward is not so significant as to encourage dishonesty.

- Rewards work well for simple kinds of task performance. These are algorithmic tasks, tasks where the process is defined and the outcome is predetermined.

- Rewards actually decrease performance for creative and complex tasks. These are heuristic tasks, tasks that do not have a predetermined outcome nor a defined process.

- You can announce rewards *before* the task or desired behavior (classical conditioning) or *after* the task or desired behavior is accomplished (operant conditioning).

- Using classical conditioning, you can also give the reward *ahead* of the desired task, taking the reward away if the task is not performed to the agreed-on standard. This strategy utilizes loss aversion.

Reflective Practice

Use the five activities in this reproducible—(1) reflect on current practices, (2) use classical conditioning with students, (3) use operant conditioning with students, (4) combine classical conditioning with loss version, and (5) document your experiences—to plan and utilize rewards with your students.

Reflect on Current Practices

Think about your current views and practices in regard to using rewards in your classroom, and then complete the following chart. Why do you do what you do in regard to your use of rewards? Do you have strong beliefs about using rewards in your classroom? Do you have past experiences with rewards (either as a student or in your teaching practice) that have resulted in your beliefs and practices?

Three ways I currently utilize rewards in my teaching practice are:	I do or don't do this because of: (Describe your beliefs or past experiences with this reward strategy.)
1.	1.
2.	2.
3.	3.

Use Classical Conditioning With Students

Recall that *classical conditioning* involves promising the reward *before* the desired task or behavior. Implement the following steps for using this form of conditioning with your students.

1. Determine something you want from your class. This could be a change in certain behaviors, or it could be an improvement in a certain area of academic achievement.

   _____

2. Determine something that all or most of your students would want. It could be a movie afternoon, extended gym time, or a free class. You know your students best, so the reward is up to you.

   _____

3. Tell your students very specifically what it is you want from them, when you want it, and how you will know whether or not they have achieved this goal. Then tell them the reward they will get if they meet the mark. Please keep in mind what was discussed in regard to rewards being more effective for simple (algorithmic) tasks than for creative and complex (heuristic) tasks. *Optional: Try this strategy with both kinds of tasks or go with the research and only apply it to simpler tasks.*

4. Record your observations in the space provided. What impact, if any, does this have on future behaviors?

The Tactical Teacher © 2022 Solution Tree Press • SolutionTree.com
Visit **go.SolutionTree.com/behavior** to download this free reproducible.

Use Operant Conditioning With Students

Recall that *operant conditioning* involves promising the reward after the desired task or behavior. Implement the following steps for using this form of conditioning with your students.

1. Determine something you want from your class. This could be a change in certain behaviors, or it could be an improvement in a certain area of academic achievement. Do not tell your students about this.

   _____

2. Determine something that all or most of your students would want. As in the previous exercise, use your insider knowledge of students to decide what the reward should be.

   _____

3. On whatever occasion your students have met this expectation, whatever it may be, give them the reward you determined, and tell them what it is for. Again, please keep in mind this chapter's information with regard to rewards being more effective for simple (algorithmic) tasks than for creative and complex (heuristic) tasks. *Optional: Try this strategy with both kinds of tasks or go with the research and only apply it to simpler tasks.*

4. Record your observations in the space provided. What impact, if any, does this have on future behaviors?

Combine Classical Conditioning With Loss Aversion

Combining classical conditioning and loss aversion means giving the reward before the desired task or behavior but then committing to take the reward away if students don't achieve your expectations. Implement the following steps for using this form of conditioning with your students.

1. Determine something you want from your class. This could be a change in certain behaviors, or it could be an improvement in a certain area of academic achievement.

   _____

2. Determine something that all or most of your students would want. As in the previous exercise, use your insider knowledge of students to decide what the reward should be. However, in this case, the reward needs to be something tangible that you can take back.

   _____

3. Tell your students very specifically what it is you want from them, when you want it, and how you will know whether or not they have achieved this goal.

4. Give students their reward *before* they engage with the performance task you selected.

5. Let students know that if they do not achieve this task, let's say a 5 percent increase in the class average on the next unit test or a 10 percent improvement in attendance for the week, you will take the reward back from the entire class. Again, please keep in mind this chapter's information with regard to rewards being more effective for simple (algorithmic) tasks than for creative and complex (heuristic) tasks. *Optional: Try this strategy with both kinds of tasks or go with the research and only apply it to simpler tasks.*

6. Record your observations in the space provided. What impact, if any, does this have on future behaviors?

The Tactical Teacher © 2022 Solution Tree Press • SolutionTree.com
Visit **go.SolutionTree.com/behavior** to download this free reproducible.

Document Your Experiences

After experimenting with your class and the various kinds of reward structures and the different ways to apply them, determine what you have learned in regard to using rewards with your class. Describe your findings in the space provided. What would you do differently to improve your effectiveness with using rewards?

The Tactical Teacher © 2022 Solution Tree Press • SolutionTree.com
Visit go.SolutionTree.com/behavior to download this free reproducible.

CHAPTER 13

SOFT TACTICS FOR MAKING A GREAT FIRST IMPRESSION

The Successful Teacher's Survival Kit (Ripley, 2019) describes a shampoo company that made a commercial to sell an anti-dandruff shampoo in the 1980s. The tag line in the commercial was: "You never get a second chance—to make a first impression." This is both clever writing and a great lesson for teachers.

Why? Because first impressions lead to longer-term judgments that can enhance or inhibit effective relationship building with your students, and they happen quickly. Princeton University psychologists Janine Willis and Alexander Todorov (2006) conducted a study in which the participants made judgments about unfamiliar faces in approximately *one-tenth of a second*. The results show that, during that fraction of a second, people make judgments about numerous personality factors, such as "attractiveness, likability, trustworthiness, competence, and aggressiveness" (Willis & Alexander, 2006, p. 592).

Think about that for a moment. Your students will subconsciously begin making judgments about you in one-tenth of a second after they see you for the first time. And, by the way, you will be doing the same thing to them. As Gladwell (2009) puts it, "Apparently, human beings don't need to know someone in order to believe that they know someone" (p. 382).

Kahneman (2011b) makes a similar argument as he demonstrates that many of us make decisions based on the WYSIATI premise. (See The Impact of Grayscale, page 122 in chapter 9.) We often make quick judgments and snap decisions based on very partial and incomplete information, thinking that what we see is all there is to see. This is especially true when we meet new people: we judge their gender, their clothes, their overall appearance, and their looks, and this judging starts within a fraction of a second upon our seeing them for the first time.

While it is important to make a good first impression on colleagues, parents, and school administration as well, for our purposes, let's focus only on the first impressions you want to make on your students. Because first impressions are so powerful and their impact can be long-lasting, it is critical for you to be mindful of the kind of first impression you want to make on a new group of students. And just when can you make a first impression? Only once—on the first day of the school year or on the first day of the semester.

If your goal is to begin the process of building a *good* relationship, one that will nurture trust and respect, one that will increase your ability as the year progresses to have an impact on your students, it is crucial that the beginnings of this relationship start on a very solid foundation. The question is: How can you make a positive first impression on your students at the start of the school year, at the very beginning of your relationship with them? This chapter explores the following tactics to do this.

- Write a letter of introduction.
- Plan carefully.

TACTIC: WRITE A LETTER OF INTRODUCTION

One strategy you can implement even *before* the school year starts is to send your students a letter of introduction. This is something you can send via the school's email system or using whatever means is best for you, including regular paper mail. I have done this for years and have found it to have an extremely positive effect on my students. They begin to form an impression of me even before we meet, but it's an impression I get to influence instead of relying on that quick fraction of a second that they first see me in the classroom. It's a bit like watching the trailer before seeing the entire movie.

For this tactic to work, it's important to carefully construct your letter. While its content and style will naturally vary depending on the age level of the students and what you most want to communicate, I believe it's important for it to contain three parts.

1. Start off your letter by providing some *personal* information about you, your students' future teacher. I like to briefly go into my autobiography, telling them about my experiences with school as a student. I provide some information about my family, and so on. Generally, the older the students, the more I tell them about myself. The goal in this section is to have my upcoming students begin to see me as a *person*, not just as their teacher.

2. The second part of the letter gives students some information about you *professionally*. I do this—especially with older students—to start the process of establishing legitimacy. I want them to be confident that I know what

I'm talking about when it comes to teaching and the curriculum.

3. For the last section, give students some direction as to how you want them to *reply* to your letter. This emphasizes that you also want to start the process of getting to know your students prior to the first class. I provide my students with a series of questions that I ask them to answer before we meet on the first day of school. The nature of your questions will vary based on your students' ages and the school community, so use what you know about your students when determining what questions to ask.

While it's important to make your letter to students your own, here is an example of a letter I've used with high school students:

Allow me to introduce myself! My name is Dale Ripley, and I am old—very, very old (according to your standards). I was born, raised, and educated in Calgary, then moved to Edmonton in my early teens. Where did you grow up? Tell me about your parents or grandparents— whoever raised you!

I learned a great deal about myself and about other people in every school I had the good fortune of attending. What schools have you attended? I am grateful for all these experiences. What is one school experience that you will never forget (good or bad)? Tell me about it.

I graduated from Archbishop O'Leary High School in Edmonton (barely) with very poor marks (too much focus on cars, money, and girls—but I didn't think so at the time). After graduation, I worked at a number of jobs (janitor, railroad, mail delivery for Canada Post, a bakery, and a department store). What kind of jobs have you done thus far in your life?

After working for a year and discovering that I hated all the jobs I had, I decided to go back to school. I enrolled at the University of Alberta in education to become a teacher—something I had thought about for a very long time. I did this partly because school seemed much better than work, but there was also a woman I was dating who was going there, so it seemed like a good idea at the time. What are your educational goals? In other words, where do you want to go to work or school after you complete high school?

In addition to the letter, I also include a photograph of myself as an attachment with my letter. I put a great deal of thought into which photo I use. Most of us have great difficulty seeing ourselves in photos in the same way that others see us. We have all had the experience of looking at photos with friends or family, and while we may dislike the way we look in a particular photo, our friends say we look fine. That is why I recommend you consider a site like Photofeeler (www.photofeeler.com). Sites like this allow you to post a picture of yourself and get feedback in regard to your picture from people who don't know you. They only see your picture. You can get your photo rated in a number of different categories, but as a teacher, you will likely want to get ratings in areas such as leadership, professionalism, and trustworthiness.

Understand that your students (and their caregivers) who look at this photo and read your letter will *instantly* begin to make judgments about you, primarily at the subconscious level (Gladwell, 2007). In addition to the work I've previously cited in this chapter (such as Willis & Todorov, 2006), in "The Emotional Dog and Its Rational Tail," Haidt (2001) says, "Commentators on intuition have generally stressed the fact that a judgment, solution, or other conclusion appears suddenly and effortlessly in consciousness, without any awareness by the person of the mental processes that led to the outcome" (p. 808). Further, Todorov (2017) has conducted extensive research into the kinds of first impressions people make when seeing the faces of strangers. Todorov finds:

> We form this impression extremely rapidly. . . . We have done studies where (you) could see a face you've never seen before for as little as less than one-tenth of a second, and that gives enough time to most people to form complex impressions, like whether the person appears trustworthy, whether the person appears competent, whether the person appears aggressive, and so on. (as cited in The Brainwaves Video Anthology, 2019)

That is why it is so important that you write this letter carefully and that you choose an effective picture of yourself. Your future students and their caregivers will do this to you when they see your letter of introduction and your picture. They will immediately start to form impressions and opinions about you, and most of this will take place at the subconscious level. But the letter of introduction gives you a head start and an increased measure of control in the process of building effective relationships with your upcoming students. You are off and running before most teachers have even put on their sneakers.

TACTIC: PLAN CAREFULLY

In preparing both yourself and your classroom for the first day of school, you need to consciously ask yourself, "Exactly what kind of first impression do I want to make—and how am I going to go about making it?" This applies to how you will dress, how you will act, and how your classroom will look and feel.

First, it is extremely prudent for you to dress as the professional you are. Staff, parents, and students will judge you at first based on how you look. You need to act professionally, and this starts by dressing professionally. I always wanted my new students to know that while we (teachers) were here to work and learn, we could do this in ways that were fun. Therefore, on the first day of classes, I always wear a happy-face tie (see figure 14.1). It is really difficult to look at that tie and not smile.

Figure 14.1: Dale's happy-face tie sets a tone of professionalism and fun.

Along with your attire, consider how your students first see you. Are you present as they walk in the room? If you are, where are you, and what are you doing to acknowledge them as they enter? I like to stand at my classroom door, introducing myself, shaking hands, or doing fist bumps (yes, you can even do this with first-grade students), welcoming them to *our* classroom. This approach works alongside my attire to form that initial in-person connection as most students look at my tie . . . and smile.

You also need to think about the kind of first impressions that your *classroom* gives. How do you want your classroom to *feel* in regard to openness, friendliness, warmth, and learning? Give a great deal of thought to this, as it is of critical importance in getting your year off to a great start. Will you do all of the classroom decorating, or will you get some students to help? Will there be spaces on your walls for students to own, where they get to choose what gets displayed on these spaces? Or, will you exert sole control over wall and bulletin board decorations?

How will you arrange desks or tables and chairs? In groups? In rows? In a horseshoe or a circle? Will you have a preassigned seating plan where students find the desk or table with their name on it, or will you assign them places to sit once they are all in the room? Or can they sit wherever they want?

You will need to have answered all of these questions *before* your students show up on day one. Why? Because by doing so, you have already begun the process of creating impressions and building relationships with your students—milliseconds after they first see you. Thus, it is important for you to get these things right—whatever right is for you. Use the guidance in the Use Choice Architecture section (page 124 in chapter 9) to craft your plan.

Keep all of this in mind, and proceed accordingly, all the while remembering: *You never get a second chance—to make a first impression!*

SUMMARY

In this chapter, you learned about the importance of first impressions and how students will begin making judgments about their teachers in as little as one-tenth of a second after first seeing them. Because of this, it is critical that you purposefully stage the first impression you give to your students so that it sends the kinds of messages about you that you want students to begin learning. You can do this even prior to class, starting with a letter to each student. You can also influence students through your attire on the first day of school and how you set up your classroom. As you reflect on this chapter, make sure to remember the following.

- Your students will subconsciously begin to judge you based on how you look within one-tenth of a second after seeing you or your photograph. Remember: you never get a second chance to make a first impression.

- One way to make a good first impression is to send your students a letter that introduces you to them, telling them a bit about you personally and professionally. Include a photo you've carefully vetted with your letter.

- Have your students reply to your letter of introduction, telling you something about themselves that will give you a head start as you look for ways to establish similarity with challenging students once the school year or semester begins.

- Give a great deal of thought to what kinds of impressions you want to make on your students on the first day of classes—how you will dress, speak, act, and have your classroom arranged in order to give these impressions.

Reflective Practice

Use the following activities to set yourself up to make a great first impression with your students: (1) write your letter of introduction, and (2) plan for the first day.

Write Your Letter of Introduction

As you think about writing your students a letter prior to the start of the school year or semester to give them some sense of who their new teacher is and what you are like, use the following guided steps to craft your letter.

1. **Personal information:** The goal is to have your upcoming students see you as a person, not just as a teacher. Tell your future students something about the following.

   a. When and where you went to school

   b. What you were like as a student

   c. What your family is like (either your family while growing up or your adult family)

2. **Professional information:** The goal is to establish legitimacy that you have the skills and knowledge to teach the courses they are taking from you. While younger students will mostly give this to you automatically, this may help to establish legitimacy with older students who may be a bit more skeptical. List a number of things appropriate to your students' ages you think they should know about your expertise as a teacher.

3. **Student responses:** Give your future students some direction as to how you want them to reply to your letter. Provide them with a series of questions you want them to respond to prior to meeting them on the first day of school. Remember when we talked about establishing similarity in an earlier chapter? This is another way that you can find out about your students and get an initial look at potential areas of similarity with them, even before they walk into your classroom for the first time. Use the space provided to think of some questions to ask students.

4. **Photograph:** If you decide to include a photograph of yourself with your letter of introduction, give some consideration to what kind of image and feel you are attempting to convey with your choice of photo. Be sure to get some objective feedback on your choice of photograph before including it with your letter.

The Tactical Teacher © 2022 Solution Tree Press • SolutionTree.com
Visit **go.SolutionTree.com/behavior** to download this free reproducible.

Plan for the First Day

Think about what kinds of impressions you want to give to your students on the first day of class and how you will dress and set up your room in order to convey these impressions. Complete the following form.

1. **Dress:**

   a. What kinds of feelings and impressions am I trying to convey to my new students on day one of the school year based on how I dress?

   b. How will I dress in order to convey those kinds of feelings and impressions?

2. **Seating plan:**

   a. What kinds of feelings and impressions am I trying to convey to my new students on day one of the school year based on how I have set up the seating plan in my classroom?

   b. What kind of seating plan best conveys those kinds of feelings and impressions?

3. **Classroom decor:**

   a. What kinds of feelings and impressions am I trying to convey to my new students on day one of the school year based on how the classroom is decorated? Think about images, words, colors, and teacher—student spaces.

   b. How will I decorate my classroom in order to convey those kinds of feelings and impressions?

The Tactical Teacher © 2022 Solution Tree Press • SolutionTree.com
Visit **go.SolutionTree.com/behavior** to download this free reproducible.

CHAPTER 14

HARD TACTICS TO USE WITH EXTREME CAUTION

At the end of the first day of the semester at a high school where I was teaching, one of the new teachers (Garry) came into my classroom and asked if he could talk to me. He was clearly distraught, so I stopped what I was doing and listened. Garry told me that he had wanted to establish himself as the authority figure in the classroom on the very first day. This was important to him (remember, this was his first teaching position). He said that at the beginning of his first class that day, one eleventh-grade girl got up and was walking to the back of the room to sharpen her pencil. Garry immediately yelled at her to stop and then proceeded to berate her in front of the other students as she stood there, telling her she was "never to get up while he was teaching" and that she was "rude and inconsiderate and ought to know better at her age." He then commanded her to go back to her desk and sit down, which she did without a word. He noted that she was flushed in the face and was clearly embarrassed.

Mission accomplished, Garry thought. He was the boss, and now this young lady and all the other students knew it. The class proceeded, with Garry teaching without interruption. None of the other students said much of anything for the remainder of the lesson. Then came the backlash. Garry had proudly told this story to one of the other teachers over lunch. When his colleague

asked him the name of the student, Garry told him it was a girl named Joyce. His colleague then informed Garry that Joyce was one of the best students in the entire high school. She was bright and hardworking, and staff and students liked and respected her. In fact, she had a huge influence on the other students.

In his efforts to establish himself as the boss, Garry had chosen the worst possible student as a victim in his desire to prove that he was the one in charge of the classroom. He knew he had made a mistake and asked me how he might repair the damage so he had at least some chance of gaining trust and respect with this student.

I gave Garry some advice as to how he might go about trying to rectify this situation, which he wisely put into action the next day. He approached Joyce before class and asked to speak to her privately. He told her that he recognized he had made a mistake in his eagerness to establish his authority and that he realized that he had embarrassed her and that she didn't deserve any of the things he had said. His apology was genuine, and she accepted it. He then told her that since he had done this in front of the class, he would like her permission to apologize to her in front of the class, but he didn't want to embarrass her any further by doing this without her consent. In other words, he gave her control. She told him that an apology in front of the class would be fine, and that is how he started the class. By doing this, Garry was able to repair the damage he had caused with Joyce, and they quickly established an effective working relationship that served them both well for the rest of the year.

This story is a good example of what can happen if you choose to use hard tactics too soon, without sufficient knowledge of the context or students. There may be occasions where you need to depend on hard tactics, but use them sparingly, thoughtfully, and with extreme caution. With this premise in mind, this chapter explores the difference between soft and hard tactics and offers specific hard tactics on the following topics.

- Review your options.
- Build legitimacy with your students.
- Avoid the pitfalls of hard tactics.

KNOW THE DIFFERENCE BETWEEN SOFT AND HARD TACTICS

The fundamental difference between soft tactics and hard tactics lies in the *degree of freedom* you give your students in making choices in your classroom. Soft tactics allow for a much greater degree of freedom of choice for students than do hard tactics. However, this notion of freedom of choice needs some clarification, because it is not quite as simple as it appears at first glance.

In 1966, Louis E. Raths, Merrill Harmin, and Sidney B. Simon wrote a groundbreaking book entitled *Values and Teaching* that had an impact on social studies education in North America for decades. Raths and colleagues (1966) claim for a person to be considered *truly free* in making a choice, three things are necessary.

1. The person had to be free to choose *without any pressure or coercion*. The presence of coercion can be very challenging to discern. While the presence of the father with the shotgun in the old "shotgun wedding" cliché is obvious, sometimes coercion is internal. It can exist in the mind of the person doing the

choosing who is exerting significant pressure on themself.

The British comedian Eddie Izzard (2010) has a comedy routine he calls "Cake or death?" in which he asks his audience to choose between receiving a piece of cake or being executed. Not surprisingly, all choose cake. That is an extreme example—albeit humorous when you view Izzard's (2010) routine on YouTube—of the phrase *coloring the choices* in which a person may appear to have a choice but in reality does not.

2. The person has to be able to choose from among viable alternatives.

3. The person must have time to adequately *consider the positive and negative consequences* of their choice.

If your students really have a choice, then they should be able to: (1) choose freely; (2) have alternatives to choose from; and (3) carefully weigh the pros and cons of their choices. As a teacher, this is the standard you should hope to achieve when you use soft tactics to influence your students. You want to *maximize* the freedom your students have in making choices about their behaviors in your classrooms. Why? Because if it is the student who is making these choices, then the student is much more invested in making their choice work. After all, they are the ones who chose it.

Where soft tactics try to *maximize* student freedom, hard tactics seek to *minimize* the freedom that students have in making decisions. Hard tactics, by definition, leave students with much less freedom—if any freedom at all. Historically, that doesn't often work out so well.

In the introduction to this book, I cited Brown's (2013) description of hard tactics as an "attempt to get someone to think or do something specific by metaphorically pushing them in that direction. These tactics include making reference to formal authority, building a coalition, and applying pressure" (p. 76). Throughout history, governments have used some very hard tactics to ensure the "cooperation" of their citizenry. From Rome's public crucifixions (Geggel, 2019) to the over 2,600 people publicly guillotined during the French Revolution (Murat, 2014), one of the primary reasons nations and states use public execution is to send a message: "Look! This could happen to you if you do not fall into line."

Such brutal summary punishment obviously isn't part of the school experience, but schools do have their own long history of using corporal punishment as a means of motivating students to change their behaviors, and they often administered this punishment in public. *Corporal punishment* is any form of force designed to inflict physical pain on a student. This can and has included actions such as hitting the student with an object (such as a pointer or a strap); slapping, pinching, pulling, or twisting the student's skin; and so on (Gershoff & Font, 2016). Teachers and administrators administered these kinds of punishments in front of the class so as to send a message to the whole group: "Look! This could happen to you if you do not fall into line." Sounds familiar, doesn't it?

In the United States, corporal punishment remains legal in several states, and "over 160,000 children in these states are subject to corporal punishment in schools each year" (Gershoff & Font, 2016). In Canada, Section 43 of the Criminal Code (which came into force in 1892) allows teachers and parents to use physical violence against children if they deem such action as necessary to correct the child's behavior (Repeal 43 Committee, n.d.). However, in 2004, the Supreme Court of Canada narrowed the application of Section 43 such that teachers could no longer use it as justification for violence against students, and thus, such punishment is illegal throughout Canada (Canada Department of Justice, n.d.). Thus, the use of physical force as one of the hard tactics that teachers can use is either already completely gone (as in Canada) or on the way out (as is the current norm in the majority of U.S. states).

However, hard tactics in the classroom come in many other forms, and many teachers depend on such tactics to control their students. However, utilizing hard tactics comes with risks, so it's vital to understand the types of tactics at your disposal and whether you should use them at all.

TACTIC: REVIEW YOUR OPTIONS

There are numerous types of hard tactics you might use in your classroom. Researchers Anita Hall and Leverne Barrett (2007) from the University of Nebraska tell us, "Hard tactics include exchange, legitimating, pressure, assertiveness, upward appeal, and coalitions. These behaviors are perceived as more forceful and push the person to comply." Hall and Barrett (2007) describe four kinds of hard tactics, which I have modified in the following list to adapt them for a classroom context.

1. *Pressure* is a behavior that includes the teacher making demands, threatening, or intimidating students.

2. *Assertiveness* is a behavior where a teacher would repeatedly make requests or express anger toward students who do not meet or comply with their demands or expectations.

3. *Legitimating* happens when a teacher seeks to persuade students through their positional authority, saying things like, "I'm the teacher. I'm the one with the degree. Do what you're told!"

4. *Coalition* is where a teacher attempts to solicit the assistance of other teachers to force a student to comply. This could be a meeting where the student is confronted by several of his or her teachers, who then collectively address the student. Or, a teacher might say to a student, "All of the other teachers say you're lazy as well. Time for you to grow up and get your act together!"

Other hard tactics some teachers have used include threats and coercion. Threats in classrooms often take the form of either doling out punishments or taking away privileges. For example, we have all heard teachers say, "If you continue to do that, I am going to give you _____." This might be a detention after school, an essay or lines to write, dictionary pages to transcribe, laps around the gym, and so on. Or a teacher may withdraw a privilege, such as keeping a student in at recess or having lunch alone in an empty classroom.

Threatening a student poses several risks for a teacher.

- Teachers typically make threats when they're angry. As we've explored in this book, anger has a way of disconnecting the link between our brains and our tongues, and frequently the words that come rushing out of our mouths when we are angry are ill-chosen. Once voiced, you cannot take those words back, and you can do serious damage to your relationship with a student.

- If you threaten a student or group of students with a particular consequence for inappropriate behavior, you have little choice but to follow through with what you said you were going to do. Failure to do so sends a message that you don't really mean what you say. Doing this will confuse your students, who then have to guess whether or not you will follow through with what you threatened to do when you next utter a threat or if you will back down. Simply put, you can't do much bluffing in teaching. Why? Because if your students see that your threats are often simply a bluff, then you can forget about using threats effectively in the future.

- You need to be sure that you have the authority to actually enact the consequences that you have threatened. To tell a student that you—their classroom teacher—are going to expel them from school is not a threat that you can follow through on because teachers in the majority of school districts do not have that authority. Therefore, you need to be very sure that you have the authority and the ability to enact the consequences that you are describing when you threaten a student.

The lesson here is clear. If you tell a student that *action A* will result in *consequence B*, you are attempting to coerce the student, and you generally have to follow through. Thus, it is extremely important that you have the authority to do this and that you actually do what it is you said you were going to do. There are exceptions to the follow-through rule, however. For example, if you threaten a student with a consequence that you are not empowered to actually enforce, like expelling them from the school, then you need to backtrack on that. As well, if you say something in the heat of the moment, particularly threatening some kind of corporal punishment, you certainly should not follow through on that kind of threat. Again, the lesson here is clear: make sure you both know what you are and are not empowered to do in regard to student discipline under school policy, be cautious, and *never* utter threats in anger.

Coercion can take many shapes. However, in schools, it often takes the form of public shaming. A teacher who makes a student stand in class and then proceeds to berate the student at length over a transgression is using coercion. Think back to the story discussed earlier of Sedgewick Bell from the film *The Emperor's Club* (Hoffman, 2002), where his teacher embarrassed him in front of the class ("Stupid lasts forever"). That kind of behavior by a teacher—the humiliation and belittling of a student in the classroom—is analogous to a public execution in the town square. It is coercion, and it is bullying behavior on the teacher's part.

In *Why You Are Who You Are*, Mark Leary (2018) from Duke University argues that a person's preferred influence tactics relate closely to his or her personality. For example, people who tend to use reason as an influence tactic tend to score higher in conscientiousness and openness on personality tests, whereas people who use coercion and silent treatment tend to score low in agreeableness. Most elementary students feel quite helpless when teachers confront them with coercive behavior. They may cry and shut down as a result. High school students, however, have more options at their disposal. Some may cry or otherwise shut down, but others will choose to fight back. In either case, these kinds of hard tactics have almost no chance of changing the students' behaviors.

Hall and Barrett (2007) rate hard tactics like those described in this section as *low in effectiveness* and for good reason. While they can be very effective at encouraging students to dislike their teachers and to dislike school, they rarely have any positive effect on changing student behaviors over the long term. Why? Because any change in behavior is forced on the student, not freely chosen by the student. It is an attempt by the student to avoid embarrassment or punishment. The student is not choosing a course of action intrinsically. Therefore, the change in behavior is likely to be both superficial and temporary.

TACTIC: BUILD LEGITIMACY WITH YOUR STUDENTS

One of the keys to success when using hard tactics with students begins long before you should ever actually utilize a hard tactic—establishing legitimacy. In writing about the importance of legitimacy, Gladwell (2013) examines a different historical era and approach compared to the Romans and French Revolutionaries. In 1969, riots broke out in West Belfast between Irish Catholics and Ulster Protestant loyalists. This is seen as the beginning of a thirty-year conflict that is known in Ireland as *the Troubles* (Gladwell, 2013). The British sent in the army to try and keep the peace. However, Britain was predominantly Protestant, and to the Catholics of Northern Ireland, it seemed only natural that the sympathies of the British Army would fall toward their Protestant adversaries. This suspicion seemed to be confirmed when British soldiers took up positions between Protestant marchers and Catholic residents, but they faced the Catholics and had their backs to the Protestants—as if they were protecting the Protestant marchers from the neighborhood Catholics.

At this time, General Ian Freeland was in charge of the British forces in Northern Ireland. Gladwell (2013) writes:

General Freeland was trying to enforce the law in Belfast, but he needed to first ask himself if he had the legitimacy to enforce the law— and the truth is, he didn't. He was in charge of an institution that the Catholics of Northern Ireland believed, with good reason, was thoroughly sympathetic to the very people who had burned down the houses of their friends and relatives the previous summer. And when the law is applied in the absence of legitimacy, it does not produce obedience. It produces the opposite. It leads to backlash. (pp. 221–223)

A short time later, in response to a riot, General Freeland brought in reinforcements, soldiers from the Royal Scots, who were well-known to be one of the most stridently Protestant regiments in the entire British army. In the end, 337 people were arrested, 60 were injured, and several Irish Catholics had been killed, one having been crushed to death under the wheels of a British armored car. Gladwell (2013) sums up the abject failure of the British forces to establish any form of legitimacy in Northern Ireland because they "believed that all that counts are rules and rational principles. But what actually matters are the hundreds of small things that the powerful do—or don't do—to establish their legitimacy" (p. 228).

Think about that last sentence in relation to you and your students: "*What actually matters are the hundreds of small things that the powerful do—or don't do—to establish their legitimacy.*" Think about this in terms of "the laws" you have established in your classroom. Do your students view you as being the legitimate authority in your classroom?

Fortunately, there are many ways you can establish legitimacy in your classroom. While letting your students know about your academic credentials and knowledge of the subject matter is a start, most students will take this as a given. Legitimacy is primarily established with students, as Gladwell (2013) says, through the myriad ways that you interact with your students throughout the year, beginning on day one. Here are some examples.

- Tell your students at the beginning of the term that it is important to you that they see you as treating them fairly and that if they ever feel that you aren't doing this, they should come and talk to you about it.

- Have very few classroom rules but communicate those rules clearly to your students at the beginning of the term.

- Tell your students what consequences will occur if they choose to contravene your classroom rules, and always follow through with these consequences, no matter who the student is.

- Tell your students that you care about their success in your class, and you work very hard to help them be successful.

- Convey to students that you stick to your promises, much like the elephant in Dr. Seuss's (1968) *Horton Hatches the Egg*, who tells his friends he will not break a promise because "I meant what I said and I said what I meant" (p. 16). Live those words, and your students will know that your words matter, and they can count on what you say as being true.

- Lead by example by doing what you say. In other words, if you say that it is important for your students to show up on time, you should rarely, if ever, be late. If you say it is important for your students to keep up with their work, you come to class prepared. You walk your talk.

- Always come to class well prepared, and tailor-make your lessons when you can so that they include material that is interesting and relevant to your current students.

- Be empathetic and understanding with your students when things happen in their lives that may negatively impact their behavioral or academic performance in your classroom.

If you have established your legitimacy because your students see you as being fair and consistent, if your classroom rules are applied to all students equally all of the time, then it is highly unlikely that you will experience any significant backlash from your students when you put these rules into effect. However, if these principles are not in place, you can most certainly expect a backlash in a variety of forms from your students.

TACTIC: AVOID THE PITFALLS OF HARD TACTICS

There are reasons why hard tactics do not work over the long haul and why they rate low in terms of effectiveness in influencing students. While it may be necessary to use hard tactics in specific circumstances (like breaking up a fight between students), these kinds of tactics are not effective on a day-to-day basis in the classroom.

In describing their five effective strategies for gaining influence, Jeff Weiss, Aram Donigian, and Jonathan Hughes (2018), writing in the *Harvard Business Review*, claim that it is more effective to obtain genuine buy-in by using ". . . facts and the principles of fairness, rather than brute force, to persuade others." Greene (1998) puts it this way, "The main weakness of a show of force is that it stirs up resentment and eventually leads to a response that eats at your authority" (p. 256). No teacher wants to engage in strategies that will eventually eat at their authority.

There is an ancient parable from a 19th century Indian religious leader, Sri Ramakrishna (n.d.) called *Hiss You May, But Bite You Shall Not* that has a great deal of wisdom for you when you find yourself dealing with students who are behaving in unacceptable ways. I've retold it here with some adaptations designed to clarify the meaning of some of the original Hindi words:

Some cowherd boys used to tend their cows in a meadow where a terrible poisonous snake lived. All the boys were constantly on the alert for fear of the snake. One day a wise man was walking along the meadow. The boys ran to him and said, "Sir, please don't go that way. A poisonous snake lives over there."

"What of it, my good children?" said the wise man. "I am not afraid of the snake." So saying, he continued on his way.

A short time later, the snake saw the man and moved swiftly toward him, ready to strike.

As soon as the snake came near, the man asked kindly, "Look here. Why do you go about doing harm? Come, I will give you a holy word. By repeating it, you will learn to love God. Ultimately, you will realize Him and so get rid of your violent nature."

Saying this, he taught the snake a holy word. The snake bowed before the teacher and said, "Revered sir, how will I practice spiritual discipline?"

"Repeat that sacred word," said the teacher, "and do no harm to anybody." As he was about to depart, the old man said, "I shall see you again."

Some days passed, and the cowherd boys noticed that the snake would no longer bite. They threw stones at it. Still it showed no anger. One day one of the boys came close to it, caught it by the tail, and whirling it round and round, dashed it again and again on the ground and then threw it away. The snake vomited blood and became unconscious. It was stunned. It could not move. So, thinking it dead, the boys went their way.

Later that night, the snake regained consciousness. Slowly and with great difficulty, it dragged itself into its hole; its bones were broken, and it could scarcely move. The snake became a mere skeleton covered with a skin. It maintained its life on dirt, leaves, or the fruit that dropped from the trees.

About a year later, the wise man came that way again and asked about the snake. The cowherd boys told him that it was dead since they had not seen it for a very long time. But the old man didn't believe them. He went to the place where he first met the snake and called it by the name he had given it. Hearing the teacher's voice, the snake came out of its hole and bowed before him with great reverence.

"How are you?" asked the old man.

"I am well, sir," replied the snake.

"But why are you so thin?" the wise man asked.

The snake replied, "Sir, you ordered me not to harm anybody. So I have been living only on leaves and fruit. Perhaps that has made me thinner."

The old man said: "It can't be mere want of food that has reduced you to this state. There must be some other reason. Think a little."

Then the snake answered, "Now I remember. One day one of the boys dashed me violently against the ground. They are ignorant, after all. They didn't realize what a great change had come over my mind. How could they know I wouldn't bite or harm anyone?"

The old man exclaimed: "What a shame! You are such a fool! You don't know how to protect yourself. I asked you not to bite, but I didn't forbid you to hiss. Why didn't you scare them by hissing?"

The circumstances in which you will need to utilize hard tactics are usually rare; however, there will likely be occasions when you are dealing with students who have stepped over the line, and you will have to hiss! However, be very selective in how you hiss.

Note that hissing, in this context, is *not* arguing. Greene (1998) reminds us that "Any momentary triumph you think you have gained through argument is really a Pyrrhic victory. The resentment and ill will you stir up is stronger and lasts longer than any momentary change of opinion" (p. 69). At a surface level, you may very well win most—if not all—of the arguments you have with your students. You may *win the argument*, but the real goal is to *win the student*.

Some teachers lose control of their emotions and get very angry at students who misbehave and break the rules. They may then direct some insulting and disparaging comments toward the students in an attempt to wield their power and make the student comply. Teachers need to remember that these students will be back in class soon, and they will have to teach them for the remainder of the school year. Be careful what you say and be careful what you do, because after the discipline incident is dealt with, you will have to work with these students to rebuild the relationship. Simply put, if you truly want to positively influence student learning and classroom behavior, you will need to have more than just a hammer in your toolbox.

SUMMARY

Over 2,500 years ago, the Greek fabulist Aesop (2010) wrote a story called "The North Wind and the Sun." The wind and the sun were arguing which of them was stronger. They saw a traveler wearing a cloak and agreed that whoever could make the traveler discard his cloak was the stronger. The wind blew a cold gust at the traveler, but the harder the wind blew, the more tightly the traveler clung to his cloak. Now it was the sun's turn. The sun beamed warmly and brightly on the traveler, and soon, the man became hot and removed his cloak.

Although hard tactics are sometimes necessary, this story is an excellent reminder that gentle persuasion is often far more effective than brute force. As you reflect on this chapter, make sure to remember the following.

- One set of strategies that teachers sometimes use to influence student behaviors can be labeled *hard tactics*.

- Hard tactics include strategies such as pressure (demands, threats, and intimidation), assertiveness (repetitive requests and anger to comply), legitimating (persuasion through authority), and coalition (using group pressure to force compliance).

- Teachers tend to use influence tactics that are in accord with their personalities. You can find out a great deal about yourself by the kinds of influence and discipline strategies you use with students.

- It is virtually impossible to utilize hard tactics effectively with students unless you have first established legitimacy.

- Hard tactics are, at their very core, problematic in that they can cause serious and long-term damage to student-teacher relationships. Students may be resentful and angry for months, years, or even decades at a teacher who used hard tactics on them in an attempt to change their behavior.

Reflective Practice

Use this reproducible to assess how often you use soft and hard tactics, reflect on your classroom rules and enforcement methods, and review your use of tactics to build legitimacy with your students.

Assess Your Use of Soft and Hard Tactics

Think about how you currently attempt to influence behaviors in your classroom at this point in your career. On the following spectrum, place an X where you currently see yourself.

I use soft tactics 100 percent of the time.   **I use hard tactics 100 percent of the time.**

Reflect on the following questions and respond.

1. Am I happy with where I see myself in terms of my use of hard and soft tactics?

2. Do I utilize hard and soft tactics in an appropriate fashion, using hard tactics rarely and only when the circumstance calls for their use?

3. If I am not happy with where I see myself in terms of these questions, what three steps will I take to change my current practice?

    a. _____

    _____

    b. _____

    _____

    c. _____

    _____

The Tactical Teacher © 2022 Solution Tree Press • SolutionTree.com
Visit **go.SolutionTree.com/behavior** to download this free reproducible.

Reflect on Your Classroom Rules and Enforcement Methods

Think about the rules you have established in your classroom for this school year and the consequences that you have outlined for your students if they choose to violate these rules. Answer the following questions.

1. Have I been consistent in my application of consequences for my students, for all of my students, all of the time?

2. In what ways do I show favoritism, allowing some students to occasionally get away with transgressions?

3. What message do I send students in my use and enforcement of classroom policies?

Review How You Build Legitimacy

The following are a number of strategies that you can enact in your classroom to establish legitimacy with your students. Put a checkmark beside the ones that you have already done, and think about the ones that you may not have yet put into practice. What's stopping you?

☐ I told my students at the beginning of the term that it is important to me that they see me as treating them fairly and that if they ever feel that I am not doing this, they should come and talk to me about it. When that happens, I listen carefully and do not become defensive.

☐ I have very few classroom rules, but the ones that I do have I communicate clearly to my class at the beginning of the term.

☐ I told my students what consequences would occur if they chose to violate our classroom rules, and I always enact these consequences, no matter who the student is.

☐ I told my students that I care about their success in my class, and I work very hard to help them be successful.

☐ I ensure students know that I mean what I say and say what I mean. I am acutely aware that most students know hypocrisy when they see it. Therefore, I always model the behaviors I ask of them.

☐ I come to class with my lessons always well prepared, and I tailor my lessons when I can to include material that is interesting and relevant to my current students.

☐ I am empathetic and understanding with my students when things happen in their lives that may negatively impact their behavioral or academic performance in my classroom.

☐ When I make promises and commitments to my students, I always follow through.

☐ I reflect on things I can do or change to establish legitimacy with my students. These things include the following.

a. _____

b. _____

c. _____

d. _____

e. _____

The Tactical Teacher © 2022 Solution Tree Press • SolutionTree.com
Visit **go.SolutionTree.com/behavior** to download this free reproducible.

CHAPTER 15

SOFT TACTICS FOR KNOWING WHEN TO INFLUENCE YOUR STUDENTS

How old were you when you first became aware of when it was not a good time to ask mom or dad or a caregiver for something you wanted? Three years old? Maybe four? Even as young children, most of us were aware enough to "take a read" of adults before asking for something. If they were busy, in a bad mood, or tired, we were often discerning enough to know that it would be better to wait for a more opportune time to make our request. We knew instinctively that this was not a good time to ask. It just didn't feel right. It always makes me think of this quote from *The Newsroom* (Sorkin, Rudin, Poul, Liberstein, & Biggs, 2012) as a character explains to a colleague why her timing was wrong: "Ask a boxer who's just been knocked unconscious when he'd like to schedule his next bout."

When is it the right time or the right circumstances to ask for something from another person? How do we know? What do we look for? How does it feel? For you, as a teacher, the questions become: When are your students ready to learn the next set of concepts? When is the right time to ask for more effort or improvement in work or classroom behavior? When should you try to influence or persuade your students to do something you want them to do?

When it comes to our attempts to influence and persuade our students, *timing is key*. Timing often means

the difference between success and failure—and its importance should never be underestimated. This chapter details the following tactics for honing your timing with students.

- Discern when students are ready for new learning.

- Reduce student anxiety when they struggle.

- Move students from a fixed mindset to a growth mindset.

- Know when to push and when to nudge.

- Get the real picture first.

- Understand your relationship to students.

TACTIC: DISCERN WHEN STUDENTS ARE READY FOR NEW LEARNING

Teaching, by its very nature, requires you to attempt to change your students. You are expected to intervene in students' lives, convince them to let go of immature beliefs, develop their literacy skills, help them grow in character and understanding of the world, and so on. To accomplish this, you must have some kind of impact on your students. You must encourage and motivate them to let go of past behaviors and beliefs and adopt new and more mature views of the world and ways of being in it. We want our students—at the appropriate time—to "put away childish things" and grow. However, to figure out whether or not your students are ready for the new knowledge you want to teach them, there are a number of things you need to consider.

First, you must determine whether your students are *intellectually* capable of understanding this new knowledge. For example, we don't teach calculus to sixth-grade students. We know that a typical sixth-grader's brain is not sufficiently developed or mathematically experienced enough to handle the abstract concepts necessary to do symbolic mathematics. This is the same reason we don't teach *Hamlet* in third grade, with students who don't have the necessary literacy skills to tackle literary works of such complexity in structure, vocabulary, and themes. Instead, we move students forward gradually, building steadily over time based on what they already know.

In education, we call this *scaffolding*—the building of more advanced knowledge on the foundations of previous knowledge (Grafwallner, 2021). Scaffolding is one of the factors you must take into consideration when attempting to gauge whether or not your students are intellectually ready for any kind of new learning. Do they possess the requisite knowledge and skills that new learning requires? About scaffolding, education consultant and author Barbara Blackburn (2018) writes, "Student success occurs when you create an instructional environment that sets high expectations for each student and provide scaffolding without offering excessive help." She says the key is engaging students in *productive struggle*, which she describes as the "sweet spot between scaffolding and support" (Blackburn, 2018).

Second, you need to determine if your students are *emotionally* ready for new learning. For example, imagine teaching elementary students about nutrition and food sources. While it is true that the drumsticks, bacon, and roasts their caregivers purchase for supper come from chickens, pigs, and cows, many students don't know much about slaughterhouses and how animals are killed to provide them with these kinds of food. Imagine the horror of a first-grade class in a large city if they see a YouTube video of a chicken or pig slaughterhouse in operation (which are out there). Most young students are not emotionally ready for the cold, hard fact that animals get killed so they can eat bacon and burgers. If they are aware of this at an intellectual level, most certainly aren't ready to see a video of this actually taking place.

Another factor associated with emotional readiness has to do with teachers making an informed determination as to whether or not it is their place or a caregiver's place to teach certain things. I once read a newspaper article in which a sixth-grade parent complained to the local media about her son's teacher. She was incensed because the student's teacher mentioned in class there was no Santa Claus. She claimed her son came home in tears and was upset because his teacher had shattered his belief in Santa, and his classmates had made fun of him because he still believed in Santa Claus. While it would certainly be unusual for most sixth-grade students to believe in Santa, it's not unheard of. However, it would be far less unusual for most kindergarten or first-grade students to believe that Santa, the Easter Bunny, and the Tooth Fairy are real. Yet, a first-grade substitute teacher also got caught in this trap in November 2018, upsetting numerous parents (News 12 Staff, 2018). Whether first-grade students are emotionally ready to learn that none of these mythical creatures actually exist is one question. However, other considerations are whether or not it is the teacher's place to tell them these creations are fictitious or when such knowledge is best left for caregivers to teach.

When is it our place as educators to teach certain things, and when is it more appropriate that we leave these particular lessons to caregivers? That is a question most teachers have to answer at multiple points throughout their career. I consider factors such as my students' ages, my relationship with them, the subject under discussion (questions about the Tooth Fairy are in an entirely different category from questions about gender fluidity), and so on. In the end, I rely on an a saying that has served me well throughout my teaching career: *When in doubt, don't!*

TACTIC: REDUCE STUDENTS' ANXIETY WHEN THEY STRUGGLE

Anxiety and other emotional and environmental factors can impact how a student responds to an assignment or assessment in ways that don't reflect their proficiency with learning goals. For example, in a sixth-grade mathematics class I taught, the content we explored included how percentages, fractions, and decimals were different ways of expressing the same mathematical concept. I was attempting to teach my students that 25 percent as a percentage, 1/4 as a fraction, and 0.25 as a decimal all express the same relative value, just in different forms.

One student in the class simply couldn't grasp this idea. She was a very bright and hardworking student, but on this particular day, she was in an intellectual slump, and the concept eluded her. She asked me if I would try and teach her this over the lunch break, which I did. Still no progress. She then asked to stay after school to try again, which we did. She still couldn't understand this idea and was, by this time, visibly frustrated and on the verge of tears. When would she understand this? I didn't know. But I did know that it wasn't going to be that day.

"I don't understand this! I'm *never* going to learn this!" she exclaimed, eyes watering, cheeks red. I responded, "It's true that you can't do this—*today*. We will try again tomorrow, and maybe then you will understand it. And if you don't, we will try the day after that. You *will* eventually understand this, just not today, and that's OK. You're smart and hardworking, and you will learn this, but not today. I think it best if you go home now, forget about this, and we will try again tomorrow."

This student's *when* (as in, *when* she learned this mathematical concept) came the next day—*when* she was ready, *when* she had taken a break.

As teachers, we need to understand that time is variable in learning, but the eventual accomplishment of learning must be a constant (DuFour, DuFour, Eaker, Many, & Mattos, 2016). Be discerning about *when* students are ready to learn what you want them to learn and if their *when* is not today. You can always provide more work and more scaffolding to help them be more prepared. The image I use with students is waves washing up on the shore. The knowledge I am teaching is like the waves, and they are the shore. It may stick after the first wave, or the second, or it may take three or four waves. But eventually, they will get it.

TACTIC: MOVE STUDENTS FROM A FIXED MINDSET TO A GROWTH MINDSET

In *Mindset: The New Psychology of Success,* Dweck (2016) argues that people (including students) essentially have one of two mindsets, a *fixed mindset* or a *growth mindset.* Students with a fixed mindset believe that their level of intelligence is fixed and cannot be changed, that having to work hard at school simply shows they are not naturally smart, and that being "naturally stupid" is an excuse for them not to try. On the other hand, students with a growth mindset believe they can develop their abilities through effort, that setbacks and failures simply mean they have to try harder or try in different ways to achieve their goals, that their focus should be on improving as opposed to getting it right the first time, and that persistent effort is valuable and will most often lead to success.

Let's look through the lens of Dweck's (2016) theory at the previous section's story about the sixth-grade student who was frustrated with her inability to understand how percentages, fractions, and decimals were different ways of expressing the same mathematical notion—this student initially exhibited a fixed mindset. She believed that she needed to learn the concept immediately, that very day, and if she couldn't learn it then, she was a failure. I had to shift her fixed mindset thinking toward a growth mindset, to convince her that she was smart enough to master the concept, perhaps just not that day.

The construct of fixed and growth mindsets can be helpful to you, with some caveats. First, very few students are of either one mindset or the other. These are binary, either-or notions, and most students fall somewhere along the continuum, not at polar opposite places. Second, you will often find that students vacillate between having a fixed mindset and then a growth mindset. Some students may be of a growth mindset in physical education but a very fixed mindset in mathematics. Here, it is the subject being taught that is the variable. Other students may be of a fixed mindset on one particular day and of a growth mindset another day, all due to circumstances, mood, and so on.

If you want to influence students to change behaviors, to learn, to improve, it is imperative that you move them in a direction toward a consistent growth mindset. This is fairly easy to do, but it requires that *you* have a growth mindset about your students. If you don't believe a student can grow and improve, and if you convey that thinking to that student, you will utterly fail to influence their behavior. I simply ask students to tell me something they learned within the last week or describe something they can do now that they couldn't do when they were three years old. Examples abound. I then point out to them the obvious fact that, at some time between then and now, they learned this information or developed this skill. And in just the same way, they will ultimately learn what they cannot figure out today or master the skill that eludes them at that moment.

I end our conversation with this little rhyme about when they will learn what we are working on: *Just not today, and that's OK.*

TACTIC: KNOW WHEN TO PUSH AND WHEN TO NUDGE

Robert Wright is a journalist and author who writes on a range of topics from science and history to politics and religion. In his book, *The Moral Animal: Why We Are the Way We Are*, he writes:

> The anthropologist notes recurring themes in culture after culture; a thirst for social approval, a capacity for guilt. You might call these, and many other such universals, "the knobs of human nature." Then the psychologist notes that the exact tunings of the knobs seem to differ from person to person. One person's "thirst for approval" knob is set in the comfort zone, down around (relatively) "self-assured," and another person's is up in the excruciating "massively insecure" zone; one person's guilt knob is set low and another person's is painfully high. So the psychologist asks: How do these knobs get set? . . . Human nature consists of knobs and of mechanisms for tuning the knobs, and both are invisible in their own way. (Wright, 1995, p. 9)

The image that Wright (1995) describes is accurate and powerful. While you may not use the image of tuning the knobs like Wright did, you learned long before you became a teacher that people were different—that if you wanted to get along with one person or obtain a favor from another person, you needed to know how to tune the knobs properly.

This proper tuning is of critical importance if you are to be successful in your work with students. However, the act of dialing in properly to each student *in the right way* and *at the right time* is challenging. It is complicated by several factors, especially the following.

- Your students change from day to day (their moods, friendships, what is happening in their lives, and so on) as well as all of this changing significantly over the course of the year. The shy eighth-grade girl and the nervous eighth-grade boy who sat behind her in the fall may well grow into a much more confident young lady and a composed and "cool" young man come spring.

- It is very difficult to *read* another person accurately all of the time, to gauge with precision what motivational strategies will work best at any given moment. Accurately tuning in to your students and dialing the knobs correctly all of the time simply aren't possible. However, the better you know a student, the more likely you will get it right.

Getting to know your students may seem a challenge, but it's not as complicated as it might seem. *The Americans* (Fields & Weisberg, 2014) is a story of two Soviet Union KGB spies, Philip and Elizabeth Jennings, who are posing as an American couple living in the suburbs of Washington, D.C. In one episode, Philip and Elizabeth are discussing various ways to co-opt an American naval officer named Brad Mullin to help them. Philip had done the necessary background research and learned a great deal about Mullin's life. He tells Elizabeth, "Mullin's a computer nerd, camera buff, classical music lover. There's a million ways in on this" (Fields & Weisberg, 2014).

In much the same way, if you take the time to really learn about the students you are trying to influence, you will find the same thing. There are a million ways in, but you have to look for them deliberately and continuously. Never doubt that these ways in exist for every student you teach, but you have to spend the time looking. As teachers, our inherent biases and assumptions sometimes trick us into thinking we already know what these ways in with our students actually are. And sometimes we look in the wrong places. But if you want to influence your students, you have to know where the doors are because they are the only way inside.

Any teacher who has taught for a while has had the experience of finding the doors and getting to know a student well enough to determine which strategies for motivation or persuasion they think will work well with that particular student. For example, with Taylor, dialing the knob is usually a gentle reminder that she wants to pass with honors. For Riley, it's letting him know that the basketball coach checks in regularly to make sure his grades are up and his behavior in class is appropriate, because Riley badly wants to stay on the team. For Brendan, a reminder that school attendance is a condition of his parole, and if he skips, he could end up back in jail—this usually dials him in quite effectively. For Hannah, humor works best, such as telling her (with a big smile on your face and a twinkle in your eye) that if she fails the upcoming test, she may get discouraged, drop out, turn to a life of crime, and spend the rest of her life behind bars, and you are just too busy to have to visit her in jail on the weekends.

However accurately you read your students, there will be times when you get it wrong. For example, I use my life behind bars routine with Hannah, and where she normally laughs in response and gets to work, today she snaps back at me. I tell Riley about the coach stopping by, and he replies abruptly, "Basketball sucks!" and he doesn't care what the coach thinks. *When* do you push hard, *when* do you nudge, and *when* do you back off? There is no answer key at the back of any *How to Be a Great Teacher* book to address these questions. You know that students are emotionally complex, that they change from day to day, and some days you will simply dial the knobs incorrectly.

There are, however, several things you *can* do to determine *when* to attempt to persuade a student or group of students and what strategies might work best. We explore this in the next section.

TACTIC: GET THE REAL PICTURE FIRST

In "Extreme Negotiations," Weiss and colleagues (2018) recommend the first step to successfully influencing others is to *get the big picture first*. For teachers, this means letting go of the assumptions and preconceptions that we have about students and actively soliciting their perspectives.

If you truly want to know when and how to best motivate your students, you need to learn about the students in front of you *now*—both as a group and as individual students—and dismiss the assumptions and expectations that you may have about them based on past experience. Even if one or more individual students have been in your classroom before, this term's students are still *not* the class you had last year. They are who they are now, which may not be the same as yesterday—and at the beginning of a school year, teachers typically don't know the students in their classes very well. If you don't take the time to genuinely learn about them, you will make mistakes in both the *how* and the *when* of your influence strategies (Weiss et al., 2018).

Unfortunately, sometimes teachers tend not to test or revisit their assumptions, especially if they have taught the same age level of students for an extended period of time. They tend to think that after teaching a specific grade or class for several years, they already know the students at that age level. There is some truth to this belief. We *do* know students at these grade levels—*in a general sense*. We *do not*, however, know the *particular* student or group of students in front of us *now*.

Earlier, I noted that Voss (2016) contends if we want to have influence over other people (students in your case), we need to embrace a mindset of discovery:

> Your goal at the outset is to extract and observe as much information as possible. Which, by the way, is one of the reasons that really smart people often have trouble being negotiators—they're so smart they think they don't have anything to discover. Too often people find it easier to simply stick with what they already believe. (p. 25)

Avoid being the teacher who considers yourself so smart and experienced with your students' age group that you think you have little or nothing new to learn. This is wrong. It is *always* wrong. You do not know the *new* group of students as individuals and as a group at all, or as Voss (2016) sums it up, "Until you know what you're dealing with, you don't know what you're dealing with" (p. 26).

When are you ready to attempt to have a significant impact on your students? Part of that answer is when you know them well enough to have some degree of understanding as to what might work well. And that takes an open mind, a willingness to discover and learn, and an ability to really see the students in front of you, not the students that exist only in your mind.

TACTIC: UNDERSTAND YOUR RELATIONSHIP TO STUDENTS

Never forget that at its essence, teaching is about relationships. However, building great student-teacher relationships takes time, energy, and thoughtfulness. You cannot effectively influence students you barely know. Thus, the influence you have early in the school year is likely insignificant compared to the influence you can have later in the year, provided that you have done the necessary work.

Remember, when it comes to having a profound impact on your students, first you crawl, then you walk, and only then can you run. There is a scene in the movie *Jurassic World* (Trevorrow, 2015) where Claire, the Jurassic World park manager, visits Owen, the man who trained the velociraptors. Claire wants Owen to come back to work for the park and train some new dinosaurs, and the following exchange takes place (FRESH Movie Trailers, 2015):

> Claire: . . . since you're able to control the raptors . . .
>
> Owen: See, it's all about control with you. I don't control the raptors. It's a relationship. It's based on mutual respect.

That conversation is a wonderful metaphor for effective student-teacher relationships. Teachers who genuinely want to have a profound and positive impact on their students know this is a great truth about teaching. You don't control your students, but if you establish mutual respect with them, you can influence them. Effective teaching can only happen over the long haul when your students like *and* respect you, when you have established a good working relationship with them based on mutual trust and respect. Remember Pierson (2013): "Kids don't learn from people they don't like!"

This basic fact about teaching manifests itself more and more as students get older. A first-grade student may give you a great deal of trust and respect on day one simply because you're the teacher. However, most high school students need convincing that you genuinely care about them and their success, that you are trustworthy and respect them, and that you have something worthwhile to teach. Early in the school year, at some level, most of them are thinking, "Show me! Prove to me that this class matters and that you care about me." That takes deliberate, thoughtful action over an extended period of time.

Ideally, you want your students to move from dependence to independence, to move from being extrinsically motivated to being more intrinsically motivated as they get older. You want your students to learn to set goals that are productive and meaningful to them and to be self-motivated to achieve these goals. However, until your students reach that level of autonomy, you have a significant role to play in motivating them.

When can you really have a significant impact on your students' motivation to succeed at their schoolwork? When you matter to them. When you've established a relationship with them that is strong enough that your opinion of their behavior and work matters to them, and it matters a lot. When can you ask for big changes in a student's quality of work or kinds of behavior? When you have asked for small changes, and they gave you what you asked for.

It's a journey, and it takes time. Remember, first you crawl, then you walk, then you run.

SUMMARY

In this chapter, you explored questions around *when* it is best to attempt to influence your students. The *when* of influence depends on a number of factors, such as whether your students are intellectually and emotionally ready for the new material and whether it's your place to deal with a topic. You also looked at how important it is for you to genuinely see the students in front of you without reacting to any internal, implicit prejudices and biases you may have. Understanding who your students are is foundational to your ability to influence them. As you reflect on this chapter, make sure to remember the following.

- The concept of scaffolding requires teachers to know when students are ready for new learning. Students need sufficient background knowledge to enable them to comprehend more complex information at the next levels of understanding.

- Emotional readiness can be as important as intellectual readiness when introducing new information to students.

- Every student will have their own particular "knobs of human nature" tuned to different levels. All students are unique, and they are always changing. This makes it difficult to accurately assess which influence strategies will work best with an individual student from day to day.

- Let go of the assumptions and stereotypes you may hold about students. Frequently, these are the result of past experiences and are often based on age, gender, grade, and so on. These stereotypes and biases can blind you from seeing the students who are actually in your classroom right now.

- You need to enter your classroom with a mindset of discovery and extract as much information as you can about each student and your class as a whole. Once you achieve a deeper level of understanding of your students, you can choose appropriate influence strategies that have the potential to be highly effective.

Reflective Practice

Use the following questions and activities to reflect on and make changes to your practice.

1. This chapter talked about student readiness for new learning, specifically in the form of scaffolding. What do you do in your classroom to determine if your students are ready for new learnings?

   a. Intellectually:

   _____

   _____

   _____

   b. Emotionally:

   _____

   _____

   _____

2. This chapter also described two stories in which elementary teachers told their students that Santa Claus was fictitious, both of which upset parents. In your teaching practice, do you ever face the question of whether or not it is appropriate for you to teach certain content to your students, or whether this type of knowledge is better taught to your students by their caregivers? If so, list the factors that you consider in making your determination as to whether or not you or the caregivers should teach this to your students.

   a. _____

   b. _____

   c. _____

   d. _____

   e. _____

3. Think about the strategies discussed in this chapter to reassure students when they are working hard to grasp new content, but they just can't get it. What do you do when this happens in your class? What approaches, such as using the imagery of waves washing over a shoreline, do you think might help some of your students?

4. Choose one of your most challenging students, one whom you feel you can reach but haven't been able to thus far. Now, think about the quote from *The Americans*, "There's a million ways in" (Fields & Weisberg, 2014). Begin a journey of exploration with this student to find out as much as you can about their interests, likes, dislikes, and activities outside of your class in school, outside of school, and so on. What ways do you see in, and what might you be able to accomplish with this student given your new knowledge?

The Tactical Teacher © 2022 Solution Tree Press • SolutionTree.com
Visit **go.SolutionTree.com/behavior** to download this free reproducible.

5. Answer this question honestly: On a scale of 1 to 10, with 10 being high, how important do you think it is that your students like you in order for you to be effective as their teacher? Circle your response.

   1   2   3   4   5   6   7   8   9   10

6. The information we explored in this chapter argues that students don't learn from people they don't like. If you circled any number below a 7, think about why you feel that way and the arguments in this chapter. What changes might you make in your teaching practice as a result of your reflections?

Source: Fields, J., & Weisberg, J. (Executive Producers). (2014). The Americans [Television series]. Los Angeles: Twentieth Century Fox Home Entertainment.

The Tactical Teacher © 2022 Solution Tree Press • SolutionTree.com
Visit **go.SolutionTree.com/behavior** to download this free reproducible.

Part 3

ETHICS AND UNSEEN MOTIVATORS

CHAPTER 16

THE ETHICS OF INFLUENCE

In *Split-Second Persuasion: The Ancient Art and New Science of Changing Minds*, research psychologist and author Kevin Dutton (2011) describes an interaction with a fellow passenger on an airline flight with a twenty-something man who didn't have an address to put on his (required) immigration form:

> "No problem," he said. "Just watch." I wasn't so sure. Standing behind him in the queue at JFK, I was all ears. Was he really going to pull it off? If so, how? There was the usual exchange with the officer on the desk as she took his prints and photograph. But then, when she eventually got around to processing his form, he suddenly remarked on her name.
>
> "Wow—Verronica with two r's! That's amazing! The only other person I've ever known spell their name like that was my mum. That's great!"
>
> The officer beamed. She agreed it was quite a coincidence. Know what? First time she, too, had come across another Verronica. She stamped his passport. Handed it back to him. And that, pretty much, was that.
>
> Bit of distraction. Bit of empathy. And he was in. (p. 189)

The passenger described in this story is certainly an effective influencer. Using tactics such as *likability* and

you and me—we're alike, he effectively accomplished his goal of getting past airport security with an incomplete immigration form. However, given the fact that his mother's name wasn't Verronica with two *R*s, what do you think about his masterful use of influence to achieve his goal, albeit that it involved being dishonest? This situation gives rise to one of ethics' classic questions: Do the means justify the ends?

To help you answer this question for yourself, this chapter explores the following aspects of ethics you should consider as you determine your approach to being a tactical teacher.

- Ethics and great teaching
- The right and the responsibility to influence students
- The gentle art of nudging
- The right to be wrong
- A final ethics check

ETHICS AND GREAT TEACHING

Teachers are faced with ethical decisions daily. In recognition of this reality of teaching, educational institutions and organizations routinely develop and publicize various codes of ethics to both guide their members and to hold them accountable to the high standards the public expects from teachers. For example, in 1975, the U.S. National Education Association (2020) first adopted its code of ethics, which now states in part, "The educator accepts the responsibility to adhere to the highest ethical standards," and further on, "The educator strives to help each student realize his or her potential as a worthy and effective member of society."

In Canada, where education is a provincial responsibility, each of the provinces has its own code of ethics or code of conduct for teachers. All of these codes address the teacher's ethical responsibilities toward students, colleagues, and the various teachers' associations. However, these ethical codes speak in the language of generalities, and thus it is often difficult for teachers to find guidance in these codes to determine an ethical course of action for a specific situation.

One example of such a dilemma has to do with student achievement. In "What Makes a Teacher Great?" (in press), I argue that one of the qualities of a great teacher is "they consistently give honest, prompt and accurate feedback to students with regards to their learning." In examining effective teaching practices, *The Economist* (2016) states that giving students prompt feedback is the single most significant factor in helping students learn. But the type of feedback given matters, with some types of feedback more powerful than others (Hattie & Timperley, 2007). Renowned education research specialist John Hattie states:

> There are two things I have learned about feedback that are important—first, think of feedback that is received, not given. And while teachers see feedback as corrections, criticism, comments, and clarifications, for students, unless it includes "where to next" information, they tend to not use it. Students want feedback just for them, just in time, and just helping nudge forward. So worry about how students are receiving your feedback much more than increasing how much you give. (as cited in Visible Learning, n.d.)

John Hattie and Helen Timperley (2007) further state that feedback where a teacher praises student efforts with phrases like "Great job" or "Nice work" does little to impact learning because it provides little to no information about task performance and, therefore, doesn't result in student engagement or commitment to learning or understanding.

Finally, in "The Power of Feedback Revisited," Benedikt Wisniewski, Klaus Zierer, and John Hattie (2020) examine the power of three types of feedback in regard to their impact on student learning: (1) reinforcement and punishment, (2) corrective feedback, and (3) high-information feedback. They find:

> Feedback is more effective the more information it contains. Simple forms of reinforcement and punishment have low effects, while high-information feedback is most effective. . . . High-information feedback contains information on task, process, and (sometimes) self-regulation level. . . . Students highly benefit from feedback when it helps them not only to understand what mistakes they made but also why they made these mistakes and what they can do to avoid them next time. (Wisniewski et al., 2020)

The takeaway of all this is that it's incumbent on teachers to provide students with quality assessments derived from the curriculum standards they are studying and then provide feedback that is prompt, honest, and informative. Yet, one of the most difficult ethical dilemmas teachers face has to do with providing your students with honest feedback.

What is the right thing to do if you want to encourage a student to keep trying, but the student achieves a failing grade of, say, 45 percent on a written assessment? You know the student well and believe he or she will be crushed and discouraged with the failing grade. Do you give the 45 percent the student achieved? That's the honest thing to do. Or do you award some additional marks (my students called these *pity marks*) in order to get the student into the 50 percent or higher range—a passing grade so the student doesn't become discouraged? In situations like these, I found some ethical guidance in the film *Star Trek II: The Wrath of Khan* (Bennett, 1982). Spock, a Vulcan who is "incapable" of lying, is caught in a lie (one told in the form of coded communication to protect the crew and ship). A crew member confronts him and says in disbelief, "You lied." Spock replies, "I exaggerated" (Bennett, 1982).

I like to believe that I never lied to my students about their marks—but in certain circumstances, I did exaggerate. Ethically, was what I did right? Was it right to give them pity marks because I believed that doing so would keep them engaged, while not doing so ran the risk of discouragement, possibly to the point of them giving up? What if you knew, particularly in the case of high school students, that a failing grade might even be the last straw before dropping out of school? What do you do in these kinds of situations, and how can you determine that your choices are ultimately ethical? To help untangle these questions, the following exceptions explore ends and means from the perspective of Machiavellian thinking and the degree to which you might be a kindred spirit with Machiavelli.

Ends and Means

In the early 16th century, an Italian diplomat and politician named Niccolò Machiavelli (2016) published a book that came to be titled *The Prince*. Machiavelli argued that the objectives of princes—goals such as glory, expansion of wealth, territory and power, and ultimately the goal of survival—can justify the use of virtually any means in order to achieve them. In the book, Machiavelli (2016) posits:

> In the question whether it is better to be loved rather than feared, or feared rather than loved, it might perhaps be answered that we should wish to be both; but since love and fear can hardly exist together, if we must choose between them, it is far safer to be feared than loved. (p. 42)

I have seen many teachers debate this question, although teachers usually frame the issue along these lines, "Is it better for your students to *like you* or to *respect you*?" And the debate begins—assuming that liking and respecting are mutually exclusive and completely binary concepts in their classrooms.

There are teachers who are quite Machiavellian in their teaching strategies. They are convinced that the ends do justify the means. While most draw the line at physical punishment, they do believe that threatening, bribing, lying, intimidating, and deceiving their students are all actions that are ethically justified if these actions lead to better performance on the part of their students.

There are also teachers who cover for students' inappropriate behaviors ("I'm not going to call your parents *this time*"), but they make it clear that the student now owes them by bringing up this favor whenever they want the student to do something—the quid-pro-quo strategy of classroom management. Do you remember the reciprocation tactics from chapter 4 (page 39)?

At the end of each reporting period, I have always looked closely at every student's grade prior to finalizing it. What I look for is to see how close they are to achieving the next higher letter grade. For example, if a student has a mark of 72.3 percent (which equates to a C+ on the scale where I teach) and they would have received a B if they had achieved 73 percent (only 0.7 percent more), I will usually bump them up. After all, a B feels so much higher than a C+. I do this in recognition of the fact that I simply don't believe my assessment practices are accurate to within less than 1 percent, and I do it to motivate my students.

It's entirely fair to ask if it's ethical to give select students additional marks that are unearned or change a student's final grade from a failing grade to a passing grade if you believe it will avert a decision to drop out. After all, you want this student to succeed; you want to influence him or her to stay in school. Do the ends justify the means in a situation such as this?

A principal colleague of mine (let's call him Mr. Williams) was transferred to a junior high school in the middle of the school year. He had been warned that the school had a bad reputation in the community and that the students were undisciplined. After his first week there, Williams's worst fears were confirmed. The school was highly dysfunctional. The quality of teaching in many of the classes he observed was poor, discipline was lax, and grade 9 students (U.S. eighth grade) thought, with some justification, that they were running the school.

Williams reasoned that he needed to work hard to establish good working relations with the seventh- and eighth-grade students, as he saw these students as the future leaders in the school. As for the grade 9s, however, he believed with only a few months left in the school year before they graduated and moved on, there was little to be gained from putting a lot of time and effort into winning them over. In light of this, Williams chose to use a different approach with the ninth-grade students.

There was one particularly influential student, Jason, who was a leader among his peers. He continually gave teachers a difficult time in class, but he also knew where the boundaries were. He would disrupt the class and challenge the teachers, oozing bad attitude but never behaving quite badly enough to get suspended. He was a master manipulator, and most teachers were at a loss as to how to deal with him.

Mr. Williams decided on a strategy to persuade this boy to change his ways. He called Jason into his office one day, and the conversation, as he related it to me, went something like the following.

Mr. Williams: Jason, do you know that I have final approval over what goes into the school yearbook?

Jason: So?

Mr. Williams: Well, you recall how all the grade 9 students filled out a form describing what they wanted to say beside their yearbook pictures. The grade 7 and 8 kids only get their photos and names, but the grade 9s get to tell things about themselves—like their favorite memories, future ambitions, who their heroes are—and so on. Do you remember filling out that form for the yearbook?

Jason: Yeah. So what?

Mr. Williams: Well, if you don't start to behave properly in your classes and around the school, I will take your yearbook entry and change it when I get the final copy for approval in the first week of summer holidays. Your favorite memory will read, "The day I met Mr. Williams." Your future ambition will read, "To grow up to be just like Mr. Williams." Your hero will read, "Who else? Mr. Williams!"

Jason (turning red and obviously upset): You can't do that!

Mr. Williams: It will be summer holidays. Who's going to stop me? And when the kids all come back to pick up their yearbooks in the fall, you will become a legend. They will laugh at you and harass you about this for years. You will never live it down, and your classmates will never forget it.

Jason (his tone much softer now): But you can't do that.

Mr. Williams: However, you don't need to worry about any of that actually happening, if you start to behave around here. It's up to you. You can go back to class now.

In telling me this story, Mr. Williams let me know that he never had a single problem with this boy for the rest of that school year. Jason stopped challenging teachers and disrupting classes, graduated, and moved on to high school—his yearbook entry unaltered.

I asked Williams if he would have actually changed Jason's yearbook entry if the boy had not changed his ways. He replied, "I was confident I would never have to face that decision. I figured that the fear of me changing his yearbook entry in the way I described was more than enough to get the kid to change his ways. He didn't know me very well and thus couldn't be sure whether or not I was bluffing. And I was right; it worked."

This story gives rise to a number of ethical questions. While this principal's influence strategy was clearly effective, did the ends justify the means? I wrote in detail in chapter 14 (page 171) about how important it is for teachers to be willing to back up any consequence they articulate to students aimed at influencing student behavior in a beneficial direction. Consider that Mr. Williams would have found himself in quite the predicament had Jason not changed his ways. So before proceeding, I ask you to spend some time with this question: Was the principal's behavior *ethical?* That is a very different question than were his actions *effective* and a much more difficult one to answer. If you think Williams's behavior was unethical, reflect on your justification for this conclusion. If you think Williams's behavior was ethical, spend some time discerning why you believe this. What is your reasoning? What do your reflections tell you about how much of Machiavelli is in you?

How Machiavellian You Are

How Machiavellian are you in your teaching? Richard Christie and Florence Geis (1970) from Columbia University reviewed Machiavelli's work and developed twenty statements they thought were vital to his arguments. They devised a test, known as the MACH-IV test, which asks the respondents the degree to which they agree or disagree on a five-point scale with the twenty statements. The results suggest the extent to which a respondent is or is not Machiavellian. Visit https://openpsychometrics.org/tests/MACH-IV if you want to take this test online.

In "The Dirty Dozen: A Concise Measure of the Dark Triad," Peter K. Jonason and Gregory D. Webster (2010) from the University of Florida similarly use twelve questions that attempt to determine the extent to which an individual possesses three socially undesirable traits: (1) narcissism, (2) psychopathy, and (3) Machiavellianism. They call these traits *the dark triad.* By having participants respond to questions such as "I tend to manipulate others to get my way," "I tend to lack remorse," and "I want others to admire me," the authors then score respondents in terms of the degree to which they possess the dark triad of these three characteristics. Visit

https://openpsychometrics.org/tests/SD3 if you want to take this test online.

If you do have some Machiavellian beliefs and behaviors that are part of your teaching practice, that gives rise to the question, where did they come from? Mark Leary (2018), a professor of psychology and neuroscience at Duke University, says that children as young as ten or eleven years old have shown Machiavellian personality traits. He concludes that children of parents who score high in Machiavellianism are better liars because they model from their parents.

If you take these online tests to discover where you score in regard to your Machiavellian personality traits, what can you then do with this information? There is no ideal teacher score that you should strive to achieve on the Machiavellian scale. The point of the exercise is for you to glean a greater degree of self-insight in this regard, asking yourself how your score reflects in your interactions and relationships with your students. If you find your current practice works for you, you might conclude you are quite content to leave things as they are. However, if you discover something about yourself and your Machiavellian traits that give you pause, perhaps this could be the beginning of some work on your part to change this. It really is up to you.

THE RIGHT AND THE RESPONSIBILITY TO INFLUENCE OUR STUDENTS

Do teachers have the right to affect their students' lives? It seems obvious that this is inherent in the very nature of teaching. It's hard to imagine a parent or a principal who would be pleased to hear a teacher say at the end of the school year, "Well, here they are: my class. I had no impact on them whatsoever because I felt uncomfortable exerting any influence on them and their lives. They have to make their own choices."

You are supposed to influence, persuade, coax, motivate, and inspire your students. You are supposed to give your students certain kinds of experiences and challenge their thinking so that your students develop and grow toward their potential as persons through their experiences in your classroom. That is every teacher's responsibility.

Having said that, however, this does not automatically give teachers the right to achieve these goals—however laudable they may be—through any means possible. The following sections explore these questions by reflecting on your use of influence through positional authority and determining what to do with your approach to students if it runs in conflict with a caregiver's wishes or beliefs.

Influence Through Positional Authority

Some teachers believe the very title of *teacher* gives them the power to impact students simply by the nature of the position. They view themselves as the *de facto* authority in the classroom, and their primary influence strategy is to simply tell the students what to do. We looked at this in our exploration of hard tactics in chapter 14 (page 171).

Being the teacher does give you a certain kind of power, but exactly what kind of power should you exercise? What kind of power is most ethical? Ronald Rolheiser (2018) claims:

> Our world understands power precisely as a force that can lord it over others and compel them to obey. In our world, power is understood to be real only when it can forcibly assert itself to make others obey it. . . . But such a notion of power is adolescent and superficial. Power that can make you buckle under is only one kind of power and ultimately not the most transformative kind. Real power is moral. Real power is the power of truth, beauty, and patience. (pp. 138–139)

What might this vision of ethical, transformative power look like in a classroom? I would propose the following examples of what a transformative teacher might ethically do with the power he or she has. A transformative teacher:

- Takes in foolishness and gives back wisdom
- Takes in childishness and gives back maturity
- Takes in laziness and gives back ambition
- Takes in lethargy and gives back energy
- Takes in confusion and gives back clarity
- Takes in anger and gives back peace

These are not easy things to do. There is no book or manual guaranteed to help you achieve these aims, but there are numerous resources that can inform and support your efforts, such as *Reclaiming Youth at Risk* (Brendtro et al., 2019) and *Poor Students, Rich Teaching* (Jensen, 2019).

In many ways, the traits of a transformative teacher I listed fly in the face of our natural instincts to give back what we're getting. "Hey kid, you're angry and yelling at me! I'll show you yelling!" Or "You're lazy and don't care how well you do in school. Well, watch how little I care." These kinds of responses are very human but not very helpful—and not very ethical either.

Ethics in Conflict With Caregivers

I once taught in an inner-city junior high school that had numerous students whose parents were first-generation Canadians. One of the classes I taught was ninth-grade guidance, which was designed to help students figure out what stream (academic, general, or technical-vocational) they should go into when they started high school the following year. I had the students write a number of aptitude tests and begin to explore their areas of interest to see what jobs and careers might be a good fit for them.

Most of the boys in the class took to this task with enthusiasm, but most of the girls (who were normally quite engaged in the course) were relatively indifferent to the notion of high school as preparation for a job or career. I took a couple of the girls aside privately, shared my observations about their lack of interest in regard to career exploration, and asked them in a very low-key and non-threatening way, what was going on. Their answer both shocked and informed me, as it may you, but don't be too quick to judge how this group came to adopt such a mindset:

Girls: Sorry, Mr. Ripley, but we don't really need to learn any of this stuff. It doesn't apply to us.

Me: I don't understand. How can this not apply to you? You need to go to high school, and you need to get some sort of job to support yourself. Why not get trained and educated for something you like, something you're good at?

Girls: You don't understand. We're going to go to high school, take the easiest courses we can, graduate, and then get whatever kind of job we can get. But we're not going to be working for long because then we're going to get married and have kids, and our husbands will take care of us. [Their response seemed very sincere.]

Me: OK, that might work out for some of you. But what happens if your marriage falls apart? What happens if your husband dies or cheats or becomes an alcoholic who can't hold down a job? Don't you want to be able to take care of yourself and your kids?

Girls: Oh, that will never happen to us! [Said with absolute certainty]

As I delved further into where these ideas had come from—and why most of the boys were interested in preparing for specific jobs, but the majority of the girls was not—I discovered that these notions were primarily cultural in origin. The girls had been raised to believe that their roles in life were to be wives and mothers, just as their mothers and grandmothers had been. Their mothers had been telling them this for years, as had their fathers. The boys, on the other hand, had been raised with the idea that they were supposed to provide for their families. Thus, it was important that these boys had a trade or a career of some kind.

What was the ethical thing for me to do in this situation? Was it right for me to tell these girls that their parents were wrong and had old-fashioned views and inappropriate sex-role stereotypes about the "proper" place of men and women in the home? Should I have barraged them with statistics about divorce rates and abused women, and husbands who cheated on their wives? Or should I have kept my nose out of this whole

situation and respected their parents and their parents' traditions?

What would you have done in this situation? What do you do when this kind of situation presents itself to you today, when what you are trying to teach clashes with cultural or family norms? What is the ethical thing to do? Near the end of this chapter, I will give you a few questions to ask in situations such as this. Your answers to these questions will help you determine how ethical your actions might be.

THE GENTLE ART OF NUDGING

In *Nudge*, Thaler and Sunstein (2008) explore the ethical aspects of having an impact on another person's decisions through the gentle art of nudging. Nudging is when small (sometimes subconscious) stimuli are applied to influence people's decisions and behavior. Thaler won the Nobel Prize in 2017 for his work on how people make decisions in the area of finance, and one of his key ideas is that a great deal of the time, *human beings do not act rationally* (The Royal Swedish Academy of Sciences, 2017). Rather, they often make decisions on the basis of feelings and faulty reasoning. Remember the rider and the elephant from chapter 5 (page 49)?

I believe that nudging a student toward the choice you want him or her to take is usually very ethical. Why? First, because a nudge is *not* a mandate. The student still has a choice and still has control over what course of action he or she decides to take. Second, you are a teacher, and as such, you should have more knowledge than the student about the student's true potential, the way life works, the importance of a good education, what kinds of knowledge have value for your students, what is true and what is not, and so on. Is that an ethical mindset for teachers? Thaler and Sunstein (2008) argue that this aspect of nudging:

> Lies in the claim that it is legitimate for choice architects to try to influence people's behavior in order to make their lives longer, healthier, and better. In other words, we argue for

self-conscious efforts . . . to steer people's choices in directions that will improve their lives. (p. 5)

Take another look at that last phrase, "to steer people's choices in directions that will *improve their lives.*" While you must be careful in presuming you know what is in a specific student's best interests, particularly with regard to your own invisible biases, this is still an excellent description of great teaching. With this in mind, let's explore some additional tactics for nudging: a default strategy and coloring the choices.

Nudging by Using the Default Strategy

Companies often nudge us to purchase their products through what is known as the *default strategy* (Samson & Ramani, 2018). A default strategy is when the targeted person has to . . . *do nothing.* That's right, they don't have to do a single thing, and thus the default position kicks in automatically.

For example, we see this a great deal in the selling of software online or the selling of video streaming services. "Get this service or item free for thirty days, and if you no longer want it, simply email us and cancel. We won't start billing you until after your thirty-day free trial is up." In order to stop the monthly payments from starting, subscribers have to *do something*: they have to go online and cancel their subscription within thirty days. If most people *do nothing* after that time, the default position kicks in, and the billing begins.

Governments also use the default strategy to nudge their citizens toward behaviors they deem as desirable. For example, in the 2000s, several European nations (Austria, Belgium, France, Hungary, Poland, and Portugal) all convinced over 90 percent of their citizens to participate in their country's organ donation programs (Ariely, 2008a). This compares to other European countries such as Denmark, the Netherlands, the United Kingdom, and Germany—which all have a participation rate below 30 percent (Ariely, 2008a). How did the first group of nations manage to get such a high participation rate? They used the default strategy.

When people applied for licenses at the Department of Motor Vehicles, the form had a section that read: *Check the box below if you* don't *want to participate in the organ donor program.* Doing nothing meant that you were automatically a participant in the program. The other countries? Their form at the Department of Motor Vehicles read: *Check the box below if you* want *to participate in the organ donor program.* You had to *do something* in order to participate, and most people simply didn't bother.

In 2019, the government of Nova Scotia, Canada, became the first provincial or state government in North America to make organ donation the default position of all its citizens (Brean, 2019). Citizens can opt out of organ donation by signing opt-out documents. But that's the catch—people have to *do something* to opt out, whereas if they *do nothing*, they automatically become organ donors.

Nudging via the default strategy doesn't have to be something you use as a form of manipulation. One example of the default strategy in a classroom setting has to do with students who are dissatisfied with their marks. Most teachers have had the experience of passing back assignments or exams, only to be inundated with students asking, "How come you only gave me a _____ percent? I deserve more!" and so on. You can avoid these situations using the default strategy.

Simply inform your students *prior* to them doing the first assessment of the year that you would be very happy to hear any appeals in regard to their marks when they get their assessments handed back. If they feel they have been shortchanged, they are welcome—even encouraged—to seek a higher grade. In order to do so, they must write an appeal paper to you in which they clearly describe how you have inappropriately interpreted the standards as outlined on the scoring rubric of the assignment to their work. Tell them you will then read their appeal and then set up a meeting with them to review the assessment.

Notice the default nudge—*if they do nothing*, their original mark automatically stands. For their mark to increase, they have to do a fair bit of thinking in regard to their work and the rubric and then follow that up with a written appeal. The default position is the status quo—their mark stays the same. As you can probably guess, it will be a rare occurrence for you to receive an appeal in regard to a student's mark if you implement this default strategy. And if it does happen, you can be assured that particular student is serious and perhaps even correct in their arguments.

Another example of a default nudge is giving your students a range of choices, but some students want to go outside of that range. For example, if you conduct a novel study in language arts, you might say to your students that they can "Choose any of the following five novels to read," then provide your predetermined list of five novels selected to appeal to a variety of students in your class. However, you may then tell your students that if none of the five chosen novels appeals to them, they can choose another novel that they would like to read . . . *if* they: (1) bring the novel to show you so that you can assess its appropriateness in terms of content and reading level and (2) write a one-page persuasive essay attempting to convince you that they should be allowed to read the novel of their choosing.

Notice the default position. Inaction means the students must automatically choose one of the five novels you selected for the class. In order to step outside of your five selections and choose for themselves, they must *do something*. It has been my experience that on those rare occasions when a student decides they want to read a novel of their choosing, and they write the persuasive essay to defend their choice, I always let them have their way. This does not happen often, but if a student is that serious about wanting to work with a novel that they chose, and they are willing to do that kind of work, I say good for them.

Notice that neither of these scenarios involves anything that could be construed as unethical behavior. In fact, both of these approaches to the default strategy involve engaging students in high-level cognitive thinking about learning they've done or that they want

to do. Think about the kinds of default positions that you can set up in your classroom with your students—situations where *doing nothing* and accepting what you have established are the choices you prefer them to make.

Knowing How to Color the Choices in Your Classroom

Thaler and Sunstein (2008) discuss the idea of using choice architecture in attempting to influence another person, which you will remember from chapter 9 (page 124) occurs when the person endeavoring to influence (you, the *teacher*) attempts to give the person being influenced (your *students*) some degree of choice. However, you've specifically designed how you present these choices to lead students to the choice you want them to make. I refer to this in Use the Contrast Principle to Nudge Students in a Direction (page 140 in chapter 11) as *coloring the choices*—making the option you want the student to choose stand out as the most preferable. Greene (1998) writes:

> [Coloring the choices] was a favored technique of Henry Kissinger. As President Richard Nixon's Secretary of State, Kissinger considered himself better informed than his boss, and believed that in most situations he could make the best decisions on his own. But if he tried to determine policy, he would offend or perhaps enrage a notoriously insecure man. So Kissinger would propose three of four choices of action for each situation, and *would present them in such a way that the one he preferred always seemed the best solution compared to the others.* (p. 259; emphasis added)

Note that the difference in this tactic from the chapter 11 tactics is that the focus previously was on directly influencing behavior, whereas this tactic relies on a more subconscious form of nudging. Many caregivers use choice architecture in this way and with great skill. Imagine a teenager who has just recently obtained his or her driver's license having a parent give him or her the following two choices.

1. "Would you like to be home by midnight, in which case you can take my car?"

2. "Or, would you like to stay out until 2:00 a.m., in which case you can't take the car?"

In a classroom, teachers do not typically use terminology like *nudge*, *choice architecture*, or *color the choices*. Nonetheless, most experienced teachers have practiced these kinds of influence strategies for years. Consider the following.

- An elementary teacher asks a student in his or her fourth-grade class, "Do you want to write one hundred lines that say, *I will stop swearing in class*, or do you want to look me in the eye, shake my hand, and promise me you will work really hard to stop swearing?"

- A junior high or middle school teacher asks the class, "Do you want to write a three-hundred-word essay or a five-hundred-word essay on this topic?"

- A high school teacher asks an eleventh-grade student who is misbehaving in class, "Do you want to follow me into the hallway where we can discuss this quietly and privately now, or do you want me to kick you out and then set up a meeting with you and your parents?"

Most educators would look at these three examples and say they are examples of effective class management techniques and would not categorize them as being unethical in any way, even though the choices for the student have been carefully constructed to make one more desirable than the other.

THE RIGHT TO BE WRONG

Earlier in this chapter, I wrote about the importance of teachers acting on behalf of students' best interests. In teaching relative to this issue, one of the questions I ask future teachers in my undergraduate classes is this: "Do students have the right to fail?" The question usually disturbs them, mostly because they have never thought about it before. I then ask them to consider, before determining their response to this question,

factors such as the age and grade level of the students, the nature of the course the student is in, and the consequences of not passing a particular course.

Do students have the right to be wrong? Most teachers would reply with a resounding "Yes!" because students can be wrong frequently throughout each school day. However, the impact of giving the incorrect response to a question in class and the impact of choosing to drop out of school or drive while seriously impaired are not the same. The consequences of some choices are minor, while the consequences of other choices can be life-altering.

Although we generally want to give students as much freedom as possible to make choices, even if they choose foolishly or poorly at times, it is also incumbent upon us to do whatever we can to help students make the best choices when it comes to decisions that can have a significant impact on their lives, both now and in a future they cannot yet see. While you certainly have this ethical responsibility to your students, where is the line between not influencing a student enough and interfering in their lives beyond what is reasonably your purview as their teacher? There are some guidelines that may prove helpful in considering this question.

First, consider the age and maturity of the students. Are they socially, emotionally, and intellectually capable of truly understanding the choices they are making? Have they explored and do they understand all or most of the options available to them in this particular circumstance?

Second, what are the consequences if the student chooses poorly? You do not let a second-grade student go outside for recess without their coat when it is below freezing, but you may have no problem with them coloring the giraffe purple in art class.

On the other hand, you may encourage a high school student to drop out of school and get a job for the present time if this student sees no value whatsoever in the long-term benefits of a high school education and shows it by missing most of his or her classes and doing nothing constructive even when present. After all, that student can always come back if the world of work isn't as peachy as the student thinks it is going to be. Life can be a very effective teacher.

However, a good student whose heart is broken because their girlfriend or boyfriend broke up with them and they want to drop out of twelfth grade is a completely different story. While we can empathize with the very real pain of such a circumstance, we can also see a future where this student's heart has healed, and life is good once again. *We* can see this, but *the student* might not. In this kind of circumstance—where the short-term consequences of dropping out are simply too negative, while the long-term rewards of graduating can be significant—do we not have an ethical responsibility to try and persuade the student to stay in school?

A FINAL ETHICS CHECK

If you are still unsure whether or not the approaches you are using with your students are ethical, I suggest you put them to this test—*make them public.* Discuss your persuasion strategies with other teachers, your administrators, some trusted parents, and friends. Listen closely to their reactions. If you cannot defend the strategies you use (to influence, to motivate, to persuade your students) to respected colleagues, parents, and friends—or if you find yourself even hesitant to have such a discussion—this is likely a sign that you have stepped across an ethical threshold.

Another powerful way to scrutinize the ethical dimension of your actions or planned actions is to ask yourself this question, *Who is going to benefit from my choosing this course of action?* There are three possible responses to this question.

1. If it is a *student* or *group of students* who will ultimately benefit from what you are planning to do, you are probably pursuing an ethical course of action.

2. If you *and* your students are *both* going to benefit from your implementing a persuasion strategy, you are still likely on solid ethical ground.

3. However, if *you* are the *only one* benefiting from a particular course of action—or worse, your students may suffer some degree of harm—then it is time to take a look at what's motivating you. Look closely, and you will likely see an ethical line—the one you are planning to step over (or already have). At this point, it's time to consider alternatives.

SUMMARY

In *Duped: Truth-Default Theory and the Social Science of Lying and Deception,* Timothy Levine (2020) from the University of Alabama reminds us, "The motives behind truthful and deceptive communication are the same" (p. 155). In other words, *people who tell the truth and people who lie both have the same goals.* Levine (2020) continues: "They want to be seen as good people, they don't want others to think they did a bad thing, and they want to avoid punishment" (p. 155). The same can be said about the use of influence strategies with students. Teachers who want what they believe to be best for their students, and teachers who want what they believe to be best for themselves, utilize the same influence strategies, and they both have the same goals—to get the students to agree to what they want. As Cialdini (2016) puts it:

> Just because we can use psychological tactics to gain consent doesn't mean we are entitled to them. The tactics are available for good or ill. They can be structured to fool and thereby exploit others. But they can also be structured to inform and thereby enhance others. (p. 11)

This book has provided you will a multitude of ways to influence your students. Now that you have the tools, you also have the responsibility to use these tools ethically. As you reflect on this chapter, make sure to remember the following.

- Several ethical problems can arise around the strategies you use to influence your students. You need to examine what kinds of *means* are acceptable for you to use in attempting to motivate your students toward the *ends* that you want them to achieve.

- One common dilemma you face is in the area of student assessment. Is it ethical for you to give a student extra marks in order to keep the student engaged and motivated, perhaps even to keep them from dropping out of school?

- At times, you may find that what you are teaching your students is in direct conflict with what caregivers teach these students at home. This results in a particularly challenging ethical dilemma for teachers.

- Many times, it is better to nudge students subtly in the direction you want them to go or toward making the choices you want them to make, rather than acting in a very overt or coercive manner. One such nudge is the *default strategy*, whereby your students do nothing, and in doing nothing, they end up making the choice you wanted them to make.

- Choice architecture is an effective method of nudging students toward making the choices you want them to make. You can accomplish this by coloring the choices to make the one you want students to choose the easiest and most attractive of the alternatives available.

- When you master the influence techniques described in this book, you need to be mindful that you can use these techniques for good or ill; consider the ethical issues involved before utilizing these influence strategies with your students.

Reflective Practice

Use the following questions and activities to reflect on and make changes to your practice.

1. Have you ever given a student extra marks (pity marks) in order to bump up their grade? Write down your insights about who benefited (you, the student, or both of you) from this and why. What was your goal? Did you achieve what you wanted by awarding these extra marks?

2. Think about the story of the principal, Mr. Williams, who threatened a student with changing his yearbook entry unless the student improved his behavior. Do you think the principal's actions were ethical? Why or why not?

   What about you? Have you ever threatened a student by telling them you would embarrass them unless they complied with something you wanted, such as a change in classroom behavior? If so, how did that work out for you and the student? Do you feel your behavior in this instance (while it may have been effective) was ethical?

3. This chapter described two online tests you can take to find out how Machiavellian you might be: (1) the MACH-IV test (Open-Source Psychometrics Project, n.d.b) and (2) the dark triad personality test (Open-Source Psychometrics Project, n.d.a). Take these tests using the links at the end of this reproducible, and reflect on what you discovered about yourself. How might this knowledge impact your current teaching practices?

4. Think about the *default strategy* described in this chapter and the idea of nudging your students to choose what you want them to by simply doing nothing. What is one way that you could implement a default strategy in your classroom? Describe it, and then take it for a test drive. How did it work?

The Tactical Teacher © 2022 Solution Tree Press • SolutionTree.com
Visit **go.SolutionTree.com/behavior** to download this free reproducible.

5. Describe two ways in which you currently color the choices in your classroom. (Use the examples in this chapter as models.)

a. _____

_____

b. _____

_____

What is an additional way you could nudge your students to choose what it is you want them to choose?

6. Think about something you have done with a student or students in order to have them choose what it is you wanted them to do, but you were somewhat uncomfortable with your actions. Now, apply the following three criteria to what you did:

a. Did the student benefit from your actions? _____

b. Did you and the student benefit from your actions? _____

c. Were you the only one who benefited from your actions, and was the student harmed in some way?

_____   _____

How comfortable would you be telling a person you hold in high regard about what you did and why?

In light of your answers to the preceding questions, would you do the same thing again in a similar circumstance, or would you choose a different path? If so, why?

Sources: Open-Source Pyschometrics Project. (n.d.a). Dark triad personality test. *Accessed at https://openpsychometrics.org/tests /SD3 on June 8, 2021; Open-Source Pyschometrics Project. (n.d.b).* MACH-IV: Machiavellianism test. *Accessed at https:// openpsychometrics.org/tests/MACH-IV/1.php on June 8, 2021.*

The Tactical Teacher © 2022 Solution Tree Press • SolutionTree.com
Visit **go.SolutionTree.com/behavior** to download this free reproducible.

CHAPTER 17

HOW YOUR STUDENTS MIGHT SUBCONSCIOUSLY MOTIVATE YOU

This book has explored how essential it is for you to establish effective relationships with your students if you are going to have any chance of successfully having a positive influence on them. However, a relationship, by definition, is a two-way street. Make no mistake, while you are doing the work of deliberately—albeit subtly—influencing them, your students are also influencing you, sometimes in ways of which you are completely unaware. Let's take a look at how the road of influence looks when it runs in the opposite direction.

John Malouff of the University of New England, Australia, devoted much of his life to studying teacher bias in student grading after he found it particularly difficult to mark a specific student's essay without considering her background:

> The friendly and hardworking young woman had previously confided in him that she had suffered a lot, and had been abused. "It was very hard for me to put all that aside—that she was such a pleasant hardworking person bringing herself up," he said. "It was hard to mark her." (as cited in Cook, 2016, p. 1)

Motivated by this experience, John M. Malouff and Einar B. Thorsteinsson (2016) conducted a meta-analysis of bias in grading and found that teacher bias—whether it be a positive bias or a negative bias—can have a significant impact on the grade a student achieves. Malouff and Thorsteinsson (2016) find: "The focus of the bias could be prior experience with a student (e.g. a halo effect), some physical characteristic such as sex, race, or physical attractiveness or some assigned status, such as being classified as gifted or learning disabled" (p. 245). They also found that bias was reduced when teachers used a rubric to score students' work.

This final chapter explores the following ways students influence teachers (often without students themselves knowing it) and why all teachers must tread carefully.

- The halo effect
- Inherent charisma
- Thinking you *know* students

THE HALO EFFECT

The *halo effect* occurs when teachers have positive opinions and ideas about students based on a student's performance in *one area* but then allow this positive impression to influence their views of the student in *other areas* of the student's performance.

An example of the halo effect (used to great advantage by many clever high school and university students) is when a student—let's call this student

Dakotah—performs extremely well on the first few assessments at the beginning of the school year. Dakotah achieves honors marks on the first major assignment and the first two exams in social studies. As a result, the social studies teacher now views Dakotah as a bright, hardworking honors student. Subsequently, if Dakotah's performance diminishes slightly on subsequent assessments, the teacher is still likely to assess Dakotah at the honors level. Why? Because in the mind of the social studies teacher, Dakotah is an honors student, and unless the quality of Dakotah's work drops noticeably and in a sustained way, she will still receive honors marks.

This application of positive opinions in one area (the first few assessments) onto other areas (subsequent assessments) is a classic example of the halo effect all teachers must be self-aware of. While it is relatively simple to get around the halo effect on written assessments by having students put their names on the *back* of their assessments and not look at who wrote the assessment until after it has been marked, few teachers actually do this, and thus the halo effect lives on in many classrooms.

INHERENT CHARISMA

Another way students impact their teachers has to do with the effect that their inherent charisma (appearance and bearing) has on the way they are treated and assessed in schools—but perhaps not in the way you might first assume. Cialdini (2007) tells us, "Research has shown that we automatically assign to good-looking individuals such favorable traits as talent, kindness, honesty, and intelligence. Furthermore, we make these judgments without being aware that physical attractiveness plays a role in the process" (p. 171). In *A Natural History of the Senses*, Ackerman (1990) further says:

> We pretend that beauty is only skin deep, but Aristotle was right when he observed that "beauty is a far greater recommendation than any letter of introduction." The sad truth is that attractive people do better in school, where they receive more help, better grades, and less punishment. (p. 271)

Cialdini (2007) and Ackerman (1990) are claiming not only that teachers favor students who are inherently charismatic in some way but that they do this without even being aware of it. It is difficult to imagine any well-adjusted teacher knowingly doing this, let alone admitting it. "Oh yes, I give all the pretty girls and all the good-looking guys in my classes extra marks" said no teacher ever in the staff room. But does this happen subconsciously, as Cialdini claims? Subsequent research suggests the answer is yes.

A 2017 study from researchers Rey Hernández-Julián and Christina Peters, titled "Student Appearance and Academic Performance," focused on a post-secondary institution in Denver. They had twenty-eight "raters" score an average of four hundred student identification photographs for levels of attractiveness. They then separated the images into three categories of appearance: (1) below average, (2) average, and (3) above average. Next, they looked at student grades relative to their placement in these three categories. Their conclusion— *appearance matters*. Students who were rated as being above average received higher grades (Hernández-Julián & Peters, 2017).

However, there is a chicken-and-egg pedagogical puzzle here:

> It is also possible that throughout the course of a semester, professors pay less attention and offer less support to less attractive students. As a result, these students learn less, accumulate less human capital, and perform worse in the evaluation of the course. The more attractive students do earn higher grades, but these higher grades are actually a result of higher learning. However, the reason they are learning more is because of their appearance. In this case, appearance does produce more learning. (Hernández-Julián & Peters, 2017, p. 261)

Think about that. While the research clearly suggests students who are inherently charismatic tend to achieve higher grades, the question of *why* they achieve higher grades remains unanswered. Is it because teachers unconsciously award inherently charismatic students higher grades, or is it because teachers tend to spend more instructional time with more charismatic students, which then results in these students achieving higher grades because they have learned more?

Perceived levels of charisma affect other areas of students' experiences in school as well. Cialdini (2007) tells us, "Research on elementary-school children shows that adults view aggressive acts as less naughty when performed by an attractive child and that teachers presume good-looking children to be more intelligent than their less-attractive classmates" (p. 172). Clearly, being viewed as charismatic by teachers has advantages in school, from elementary to post-secondary. It has positive effects on achievement, and it can lessen the consequences of misbehavior. Are there differences in outcomes for the students whose appearance you find charismatic versus those you don't?

THINKING YOU *KNOW* STUDENTS

We have all seen TV shows and movies where both we—the viewers—and the detectives doing the questioning, figure out who the bad guy is really quickly. We can just tell. The villain seems dishonest, is jittery, won't look questioners in the eye, or has defensive body language. You, the viewer, much like the detectives on the screen, know for certain you have figured out who the perp is due to the physical and verbal cues they are giving us. Simply put, they act guilty.

Teachers often use the same strategies as TV law enforcement when trying to "read" students' behaviors and body language. We do this especially when we are investigating some form of wrongdoing in our classroom. When questioning students about cheating on a test or who did what to whom, we rely on cues such as eye contact, body language, and pace and tone of voice to help us determine which of our students

is telling the truth and who is lying. A lot of teachers think they're pretty good at this. How about you?

Many police departments in Canada and the United States interview suspects using the Reid technique (Reid, 2014), which notes the following about the significance of eye contact.

- It's important to observe a suspect answer generic questions to establish the subject's normal verbal and nonverbal behavior, including their default disposition related to eye contact.

- Truthful suspects tend to maintain direct eye contact when answering questions.

- Questioners must themselves maintain eye contact while in close proximity to a suspect.

Think about these items, and then ask yourself if you share similar beliefs about the behaviors of your students. As Gladwell (2019) writes, this is a common way to interpret the significance of eye contact in Western culture:

> Mutual gaze (maintained eye contact) represents openness, candor, and trust. Deceptive suspects generally do not look directly at the investigator; they look down at the floor, over to the side, or up at the ceiling as if to beseech some divine guidance when answering questions. . . . Truthful suspects, on the other hand, are not defensive in their looks or actions and can easily maintain eye contact with the investigator. (p. 328)

As you will see in a moment, Gladwell (2019) does not hold this view; rather, he highlights how these beliefs have seeped into our culture and into our classrooms. Many teachers assume they can differentiate between honest students and dishonest students based on their observations of how students act while being questioned. Perhaps these assumptions hold true in some instances, but certainly not all, as former lawyer, judge, and U.S. Supreme Court clerk Alex Kozinski (2017) states: "There is growing evidence that the Reid technique results in a significant number of false confessions, especially among the young, the mentally impaired and those of low intelligence" (p. 1). *Especially among the young.* These are the very people we work with in schools.

Gladwell (2019) makes a compelling argument that, in actuality, we are *not* good at reading other people. We do *not* (as often as we like to think) arrive at valid conclusions about other people based on our observations of their facial expressions and body language, and there is something flawed with the tools we use to do this and our belief in their precision. Gladwell (2019) describes some people as "mismatched: when they do not behave the way we expect them to behave" (p. 330).

While Gladwell's (2019) research focuses primarily on how humans misinterpret the intentions and meanings of *strangers* due to flaws and assumptions in our perceptive abilities, ask yourself this question, "How well do you *really* know your students?" Teachers may argue that their students certainly are not strangers and thus, Gladwell's (2019) conclusions simply don't apply, but let's take a closer look at this.

At the beginning of the school year, teachers generally don't know their students very well at all. In elementary schools, however, where teachers usually spend much more time with their classes than occurs in secondary school, the opportunity to get to know their students well is clearly present. Getting to know your students well is, however, more difficult in secondary grades because students typically only spend one or two classes with the same teacher and then move on to the next subject-area specialist.

Given this reality, if you assume that you know most of your students reasonably well, and if you also assume that you can "read them" because of this knowledge and your well-honed perceptive skills, you are in serious danger of misreading and misunderstanding your students. And this misread can cause unnecessary conflict, seriously damage your relationships with students, and can even result in profound harm to them. And it will most certainly impact your ability to influence them in any significant way.

I encourage you to take a close look at the assumptions you have about your students. If Teacher A believes that students are fundamentally good ("Oh, they can mess up on occasion for sure, but as a general rule they are kind, honest, and work hard")—then Teacher A will read students through that lens. The teacher's default, thinking-fast, automatic go-to position will naturally lean toward believing what students tell him or her. Contrast this with Teacher B, who believes most students are fundamentally untrustworthy, lazy, and duplicitous. Teacher B's default, thinking-fast position is to read deception in the actions and words of students who are under investigation for some classroom incident.

In the section Use the Positive-Word Strategy With Students You Dislike (page 55 in chapter 5), I mentioned a proverb that states, *Two-thirds of what we see is behind our eyes.* A wise teacher is aware of this when attempting to read how a student is feeling or whether or not a student is telling the truth. If you are going to effectively convince your students to buy what you are selling in your classroom—whether that be knowledge, skills, values, life lessons, good behavior, and so forth—then you need to get to know them and know them well.

Voss (2016) tells us that to truly get to know someone, we must really listen and observe. Gladwell (2019) reminds us that really understanding another person is exceedingly difficult and that we often misread the strangers in our lives. The lesson for teachers here is clear: If you want to influence your students in profound and meaningful ways, then you must do the work of getting to know your students beyond a superficial level. Only then can you effectively choose the influence strategies that will resonate best with a particular student or a particular group of students. Then, and only then, will you maximize the chance that they will choose to follow where you want them to go.

SUMMARY

As you reflect on this chapter, make sure to remember the following.

- It is very difficult for a teacher who knows (or thinks he or she knows) about a student to avoid letting this knowledge influence their assessment of that student's work.

- Bias can be positive (the halo effect), or it can be negative. In either case, this bias takes away from an objective assessment of the quality of a student's work.

- Teachers seem to be less biased when they use a rubric in assessing students' work. Another tactic you can use to reduce or eliminate bias is to use numbers on an assessment in place of student names or have students put their name on the back of the assessment. This way, you don't know which student has submitted the assessment until after you have graded it.

- Students who are deemed to be physically attractive generally achieve higher grades in school and are disciplined less severely in elementary schools.

- Many teachers read body language cues when working with students. However, there is a very real danger that you may be misreading these cues, thus resulting in an inappropriate course of action based on this misreading of the student.

Reflective Practice

Use this reproducible to change your approach to assessment, assess your own biases, and analyze your thinking about students' body language.

Change Your Assessment Approach

If this is not your current practice, conduct an experiment for the next three assessments in your class. Have your students put their names on the back of the assessment, and then conduct your assessment before looking at which student submitted it. Answer the following questions.

1. How did you feel while doing your grading when you didn't know which student had submitted the work?

2. What impact has this change had on students' overall mark?

3. Do you believe that assessing your students this way makes your assessment more objective and accurate? If so, why? If not, why not?

Assess Your Biases

We all have biases. The problem that arises in your teaching practice is when these biases remain at the subconscious level, where they affect your relationships with students and your assessments without your conscious knowledge. Use the following chart to list a minimum of five biases you have, why you have them, and at least one course of action that you are going to commit to that will help you either remove or reduce this bias in your relationships and assessments with your students.

Five biases that I have are . . .	Why I have these biases; where they came from	In order to remove or reduce the effect of this bias, I will . . .
1.		
2		
3.		
4.		
5.		

The Tactical Teacher © 2022 Solution Tree Press • SolutionTree.com
Visit **go.SolutionTree.com/behavior** to download this free reproducible.

Analyze Your Thinking About Body Language

Think about the assumptions you currently have about what messages body language tells you. Do you believe that:

1. Students who don't look at you when you are talking to them are more likely to be lying?

   ☐ Yes

   ☐ No

2. Students who fold their arms across their chest or who turn away from you while talking are most likely hiding something?

   ☐ Yes

   ☐ No

3. Students who take long pauses before answering your questions, especially when you are investigating a "classroom crime," are most likely trying to concoct a cover story?

   ☐ Yes

   ☐ No

After answering, ask yourself the following questions, writing down your answers in the space provided.

1. How many of these student behaviors might be culturally based? In other words, are you making assumptions about how students ought to behave based on your cultural biases?

2. Where did your assumptions come from (culture, media, and so on), and how accurate are they really?

The Tactical Teacher © 2022 Solution Tree Press • SolutionTree.com
Visit **go.SolutionTree.com/behavior** to download this free reproducible.

EPILOGUE

Anyone who picked up this book looking for a quick fix for the problem students in their class will, by this point, be somewhat disappointed. There are no silver bullets or magic wands when it comes to changing the way challenging students behave. On the other hand, if you approach this book's tactics and knowledge with an open mind, you will find a multitude of powerful and effective ideas you can use with your students to change the way they conduct themselves in your classes.

In the introduction to this book, I promised that teachers who read this book and utilized even a fraction of the strategies described herein would see a significant improvement in their ability to positively impact student behaviors and achievement in their classrooms. That was a promise that I did not make lightly, and I am confident that if you chose to read this book, and if you implemented some of these strategies, you have experienced how well they can work. I know things are (or will be) better in your classroom, for you and for your students.

I would like to close by complimenting you on your work. Any teacher who reads a book like this and then works hard to put these strategies into practice is a teacher who genuinely cares about students' success. I know, as well, that your relationships with some of your more challenging students are more peaceful and less confrontational than they were in the past, all due to the effort you put into making your classroom a better place for all of your students.

I wish you and your students continued success on your educational journeys. Enjoy the ride.

APPENDIX

In this book, you encountered references to an exercise and a youth-support program you may want to use in your practice. The first is a reproducible for the Newspaper of the Self activity, which you can conduct with students as part of a start-of-year or start-of-semester exercise to get to know them better. Use the information you gather to inform your tactical approach to supporting positive behavioral and academic growth. The second reproducible offers a series of frequently asked questions about implementing an Adopt-a-Kid program in your school. Use this in conjunction with school leadership and other specialists in your school or community to design and launch this program.

The Newspaper of the Self

This assignment asks you to create an unusual newspaper. Most daily newspapers (whether they are in print or digital) contain a number of different sections, such as current events, sports, entertainment, business, and so on. Like these typical newspapers, you will create a newspaper with similar kinds of sections included, but the entire newspaper is all about you!

This assignment has three purposes:

1. Provide the reader (that would be me, your teacher) with some information about you and your life

2. Give me some idea, as we begin our work together at the start of the school year, of your writing abilities

3. Give you the opportunity to take a more in-depth look at your life as it is at this time and where you see yourself heading in the future

Assignment Requirements

- Your newspaper must have a title at the top of the front page and an index at the bottom left corner of the front page showing the page numbers where each section can be found in your newspaper.

- Your newspaper is to include all fourteen sections described after this list.

- You may add original (meaning YOU drew them) cartoons or drawings where you feel this is appropriate to enhance any particular sections.

- You may add photographs to illustrate the content of any of the sections.

Make sure you include the following fourteen sections in your newspaper. These are in no particular order of importance. You are free to arrange your Newspaper of the Self in any way that you feel is best.

1. **Current Events:** In this section, describe something that is going on in your life right now that you feel is either really interesting, very important to you, or perhaps both.

2. **Family Section:** Here, you are to describe your family. Tell me about your parents or caregivers and any other people who live with you, such as siblings. Explain how you get along with them, and any particular things that you have in common or like to do together. The more detail, the better!

3. **Dear Abby:** Write a letter to the paper outlining a problem you are actually experiencing at this time. Then think of a possible solution to your problem and write a reply to yourself. This is an opportunity for you to show what a great problem solver you are.

4. **Births, Deaths, and Marriages:** Here, you are to tell about any births, deaths, or marriages that have taken place during your life thus far that are important to you.

5. **Book Review:** Describe a book you read recently (one that you *chose* to read, not one that you *had* to read for school). Why did you choose to read this book? What did you like and dislike about it? If you have not read a book on your own for a very long time, use this section to describe the last book you read and why you gave up reading.

6. **Business:** Describe what you do to earn or obtain money and what you do with the money once you get it.

7. **Letter to the Editor:** Here you are to write a letter to the editor of your newspaper giving your opinion about something that is important to you. It could be local (something going on in the school or the town or city you live in) or some issue that is of national or even international importance. The most important thing here is that you chose to write about something that really matters to you. Describe what you see as the issue and how you think it ought to be addressed.

8. **Leisure:** Describe what you do in your free time. When you have no responsibilities (school, homework, job, chores, and the like), what do you like to do, and why these kinds of activities?

9. **Music:** Describe what kinds of music you like and why. Describe what kinds of music you don't like and why. Who are your favorite recording artists? Why these?

10. **Sports:** What is your favorite sport to play? What is your favorite sport to watch? Why do you like these sports? If you hate sports, describe how you came to dislike sports so much. (Remember, you weren't born hating sports, something happened.)

11. **Movies:** Describe a movie you recently saw (either in the theater, on TV, or streaming). Why did you choose this particular movie to watch? What happened in the movie? Did you like it or not, and why? Would you recommend it to a friend? Why or why not?

The Tactical Teacher © 2022 Solution Tree Press • SolutionTree.com
Visit **go.SolutionTree.com/behavior** to download this free reproducible.

12. **Travel:** Describe the most interesting trip you have ever taken in your life. If you haven't taken any trips that you found interesting, describe your ideal fantasy trip—the place you could go if you could go anywhere in the world. Where would you go, what would you do, and why this particular destination?

13. **TV:** Describe your three favorite TV shows in some detail. Why are these three shows your favorites?

14. **Me in the Future:** Here, you are to imagine that whatever you want to be and whatever you want to do actually come to be. Describe what your life will be like in the future (you get to choose how old you want to be for your writing of this section of the newspaper). Explain where you will be living, what you will be doing for work, and whether or not you will have a family. This is a chance for you to describe your dreams coming true.

Remember, you are creating a newspaper that is all about you. Be specific and detailed—provide a wealth of information about you and your life. Remember, this is your first major assignment for this class, so show me the best writing you can.

Scoring Rubric

Student's Name: _____

Part 1: Requirements Completed

Note: For this section, you will automatically receive 50 out of the 50 available marks simply by (1) completing all fourteen of the required sections and (2) providing answers to all of the information for each of the sections of your newspaper as described in the following assignment requirements, which also include a front page with a title and an index.

Current Events: _____   Business: _____   Movies: _____

Family Section: _____   Letter to the Editor: _____   Travel: _____

Dear Abby: _____   Leisure: _____   TV: _____

Births, Deaths, and Marriages: _____   Music: _____   Me in the Future: _____

Book review: _____   Sports: _____   Front page has a title and an index: _____

Total Marks for Completion: _____ / 50

Part 2: Marking Standards and Weightings

The following explains how I will assess your writing for this assignment.

A. **Thought and detail:** This refers to the degree of thought and insight you have demonstrated throughout the various sections of the assignment, as well as to the degree of detail demonstrated in your written responses to each section.

 10 = Exceptional   8 = Proficient   6 = Satisfactory   5 = Basic   3 = Limited   1 = Poor

B. **Organization:** This refers to how well you have organized each section; how interesting your opening sentence is, and how well you keep your writing focused on the specific topic of each section.

 10 = Exceptional   8 = Proficient   6 = Satisfactory   5 = Basic   3 = Limited   1 = Poor

C. **Writing mechanics:** This refers to the degree to which your writing is free from errors in spelling, grammar, punctuation, and capitalization.

 10 = Exceptional   8 = Proficient   6 = Satisfactory   5 = Basic   3 = Limited   1 = Poor

D. **Grammar and word usage:** This refers to the degree to which your writing is free from errors in word usage, sentence fragments, awkward phrasing, unclear meaning, and the like.

 10 = Exceptional   8 = Proficient   6 = Satisfactory   5 = Basic   3 = Limited   1 = Poor

E. **Matters of choice:** This refers to the appropriateness of the choices you have made in your writing, the examples you have chosen to illustrate your points, and the words you have chosen to get your message across to the reader.

 10 = Exceptional   8 = Proficient   6 = Satisfactory   5 = Basic   3 = Limited   1 = Poor

The Tactical Teacher © 2022 Solution Tree Press • SolutionTree.com
Visit **go.SolutionTree.com/behavior** to download this free reproducible.

Total marks: _____ / 50

General Comments

Part 1 marks: _____ / 50

Part 2 marks: _____ / 50

Final mark: _____ / 100 = _____%

The Tactical Teacher © 2022 Solution Tree Press • SolutionTree.com
Visit **go.SolutionTree.com/behavior** to download this free reproducible.

Adopt-a-Kid Program FAQs

The following sections highlight the purpose of an Adopt-a-Kid program and answer frequently asked questions (FAQs) about such programs.

What Are an Adopt-a-Kid Program's Goals?

- Create a positive and meaningful relationship between a caring, capable adult and a student who is at risk of eventually dropping out of school.
- Learn about the issues and problems that are affecting the student's academic performance causing negative behaviors.
- Empower students to realistically face their problems and deal with these problems successfully on their own.
- Interrupt the downward spiral in which a student may be caught.

Who Are the Staff Mentors?

- Any staff member who volunteers to participate in the program, including non-teaching staff

Who Needs a Mentor?

- Students identified as at risk by their teachers, according to the indicators found at the end of this program description

What Does a Mentor Do?

- Provides a positive role model for their students
- Provides a supportive relationship—someone who is genuinely interested in the student
- Builds self-esteem—"I must matter because this person cares about me."
- Acts as a resource person—a link to other helpers, agencies, and organizations
- Advocates for the student when and where appropriate
- Challenges the student's negative patterns of thinking—shows the student that there are more positive alternatives in terms of the way the student sees the world and how he or she deals with problems
- Coaches the student in the development of social skills
- Encourages the student to establish positive goals and work toward achieving them

What Are Useful Guidelines for an Adopt-a-Kid Program?

- Contact between the mentor and the student should occur daily at the beginning of the program to help build the relationship. Set a time and place that are mutually agreeable and that will not embarrass the student in front of his or her peers. If you want to meet your student in the hallways, get his or her permission first.
- If you cannot meet with your student on a particular day, make sure you explain this to your student and establish a time when you can connect again. It is essential that you be an adult that the student can count on. You show up when you say you will, and you follow through on your commitments.
- The length of the contact will vary, perhaps a moment in the morning ("How are you?" "Did you have a nice evening?" "Did you get your homework done?" "Do you have all your books, pens, and a calculator?" "See you later!" and so on). The contact may take longer later in the day if the student has specific needs that have to be addressed.
- If you have time during the day to meet with your student and deem doing so as necessary or appropriate, consider taking him or her out of class with the teacher's consent.
- You may increase or decrease the frequency and duration of contacts as suits your student's needs and your availability.

The Tactical Teacher © 2022 Solution Tree Press • SolutionTree.com
Visit **go.SolutionTree.com/behavior** to download this free reproducible.

What About Discipline?

- Mentors are not expected nor encouraged to discipline their student.

- Mentors should not become directly involved in the discipline process between their student and a teacher or administrator.

- Mentors can explain discipline policies and reasons for particular behavioral expectations to their students. They can also listen to complaints from their students and respond appropriately.

- Mentors can help their students examine actions that led to problems when these arise and help the students devise ways to avoid or appropriately deal with similar situations in the future.

- If an administrator is a mentor, a different administrator should handle the discipline of that administrator's Adopt-a-Kid students.

When Does the Mentorship End?

- The relationship can be terminated by mutual agreement. In this case, it is the mentor's option to take another student or not.

- The relationship may carry on into the next school year if both parties want this.

What If Problems Develop?

- The relationship should be given at least one month to form. If, after that time, your student continues to be hostile or uncooperative, contact the Adopt-a-Kid coordinator to have a dialogue about whether the student may be safely transferred to another mentor.

What Else Should I Be Aware of?

- It is essential that staff freely volunteer to participate in this program. It is not possible to create or force a positive relationship between a staff member and a student unless the staff member is freely committed to working on this.

- Staff who volunteer to participate in this program must sincerely want to share their time and wisdom and learn about their students' lives, helping to make their students' lives better.

- If your student reveals that they are the victim of a neglect or abuse situation, in many countries, you are legally bound to report this to the appropriate authorities. Regardless of legal considerations, it is your professional responsibility to do so even if the student gave you this information in confidence. You may reassure your student that you will be there to support him or her throughout the investigation should one occur.

- If you are ever in doubt about what is an appropriate course of action in regard to an issue brought to you by your Adopt-a-Kid student or what you may be legally required to do in a specific situation, you are to discuss this with an administrator at the earliest opportunity.

- Mentors should not attempt psychological therapy. If your student needs professional help, please facilitate this through the appropriate school personnel.

What Logistics Are Involved?

- Ascertain who wants to become a mentor.

- Have the teaching staff generate a list of potential students at risk using the indicators in the next section.

- Match the students to their mentors at a meeting with all mentors present. Mentors will choose the students with whom they want to work based on the best chances of success according to the mentor's current relationship with particular students.

- There will be a maximum of two students per mentor. No exceptions.

- A mentor may opt to take only one student.

- If there are more students identified as at risk than there are mentors available, then the students chosen to participate in this program will be the ones deemed by staff to be the highest priority cases.

The Tactical Teacher © 2022 Solution Tree Press • SolutionTree.com
Visit **go.SolutionTree.com/behavior** to download this free reproducible.

How Do I Identify Students Who Might Be at Risk?

Students at risk often exhibit some or all of the following characteristics. These descriptors should serve only as general guidelines in selecting students for inclusion in this program. Students at risk tend to:

- Have established patterns of poor school attendance

- Display a variety of problem behaviors in multiple settings—home, school, and community

- Are currently or are likely to become involved with law enforcement

- Have difficulty coping in a regular classroom learning environment, often despite the addition of various remedial measures

- Experience academic failure as evidenced by low grades, despite average or above-average aptitude for learning goals (underachievers)

- Come from a family that offers little in terms of emotional support or school support with limited or no monitoring of school progress from the home

- Have caregivers who have infrequent positive contact with the school; most contacts with caregivers are school initiated and are negative and unproductive in nature

- Frequently demonstrate an inability to establish or maintain satisfactory relationships with peers and significant adults

- Demonstrate a poor self-concept (low level of personal motivation, tendency to give up easily, low self-esteem, pessimistic about their future, and so on)

- Have poor physical health habits, as evidenced by poor nutrition, inadequate exercise, poor dental care, inadequate sleep, and substance abuse

The Tactical Teacher © 2022 Solution Tree Press • SolutionTree.com
Visit **go.SolutionTree.com/behavior** to download this free reproducible.

REFERENCES AND RESOURCES

Ackerman, D. (1990). *A natural history of the senses*. New York: Vintage Books.

Adnot, M., Dee, T., Katz, V., & Wyckoff, J. (2017). Teacher turnover, teacher quality, and student achievement in DCPS. *Educational Evaluation and Policy Analysis, 39*(1), 54–76.

Aesop. (2010). *Aesop's fables: 240 short stories for children*. New York: Frank F. Lovell & Company.

Alberta Government. (2015). *Every student counts: Make the attendance connection*. Accessed at https://education.alberta.ca/media/373 9680/school-reference-guide_final.pdf on August 4, 2021.

Amdur, E. (2020). *The power of the positive word*. Accessed at www.forbes.com/sites/eliamdur/2020/11/22/the-power-of-the-positive -word/?sh=194013f87a71 on June 2, 2021.

American Psychological Association. (n.d.). Overjustification effect. In *APA dictionary of psychology*. Accessed at https://dictionary.apa .org/overjustification-effect on August 26, 2021.

Ariely, D. (2008a). *Are we in control of our own decisions?* [Video file]. Accessed at www.ted.com/talks/dan_ariely_are_we_in_control _of_our_own_decisions#t-433637 on June 2, 2021.

Ariely, D. (2008b). *Predictably irrational: The hidden forces that shape our decisions*. New York: Harper.

Ariely, D. (2016). *Payoff: The hidden logic that shapes our motivations*. New York: Simon & Schuster.

Aslan, R. (2017). *God: A human history*. New York: Random House.

Balfanz, R., & Byrnes, V. (2012). *Chronic absenteeism: Summarizing what we know from nationally available data*. Baltimore: Johns Hopkins University Center for Social Organization of Schools. Accessed at https://ies.ed.gov/ncee/edlabs/regions/west/rel westFiles/pdf/508_ChronicAbsenteeism_NatlSummary_Balfanz_Byrnes_2012.pdf on August 4, 2021.

Barkley, R. (2021). *What is executive function? Seven deficits tied to ADHD*. Accessed at www.additudemag.com/7-executive-function -deficits-linked-to-adhd on August 19, 2021.

Barsade, S. G. (2000). *The ripple effect: Emotional contagion in groups (Yale SOM Working Paper No. OB-01)*. Accessed at https://ssrn .com/abstract=250894 on June 2, 2021.

Bennett, H. (Executive Producer). (1982). *Star trek II: The wrath of Khan* [Motion picture]. United States: Paramount Pictures.

Birak, C., & Cuttler, M. (2019). *School absenteeism can set off troubling chain of events, pediatricians say*. Accessed at www.cbc.ca/news /health/school-absenteeism-pediatrics-1.5005670 on June 2, 2021.

Blackburn, B. (2018). Productive struggle is a learner's sweet spot. *Productive Struggle for All, 14*(11). Accessed at www.ascd.org/ascd -express/vol14/num11/productive-struggle-is-a-learners-sweet-spot.aspx on February 3, 2021.

Bower, G. H., & Bolton, L. S. (1969). Why are rhymes easy to learn? *Journal of Experimental Psychology, 82*(3), 453–461. Accessed at https://psycnet.apa.org/record/1970–03124–001 on June 2, 2021.

The Brainwaves Video Anthology. (2019). *Alexander Todorov—Face Value: The irresistible influence of first impressions* [Video file]. Accessed at www.youtube.com/watch?v=c_vbCzWnpEk on August 26, 2021.

Brean, J. (2019). *Nudging the dead: How behavioural psychology inspired Nova Scotia's organ donation scheme*. Accessed at https://nationalpost.com/news/canada/nudging-the-dead-how-behavioural-psychology-inspired-nova-scotias-organ-donation -scheme on August 12, 2021.

Brendtro, L. K., Brokenleg, M., & Van Bockern, S. (2019). *Reclaiming youth at risk: Futures of promise* (3rd ed.). Bloomington, IN: Solution Tree Press.

Brown, K. G. (2013). *Influence: Mastering life's most powerful skill*. Chantilly, VA: The Great Courses.

Bruner, J. S. (1960). *The process of education*. Cambridge, MA: Harvard University Press.

Buehner, C. (1971). *Richard Evans' quote book*. Accessed at http://listserv.linguistlist.org/pipermail/ads-l/2014-April/131770.html on June 8, 2021.

Burger, J. M., Messian, N., Patel, S., del Prado, A., & Anderson, C. (2004). What a coincidence! The effects of incidental similarity on compliance. *Personality and Social Psychology Bulletin, 30*(1), 35–43.

Burkett, R. (2013). An alternative framework for agent recruitment: From MICE to RASCLS. *Studies in Intelligence, 57*(1), 7–17. Accessed at www.cia.gov/static/3e909813c3f24ffea6481524038bcace/Alt-Framework-Agent-Recruitment.pdf on July 20, 2021.

Canada Department of Justice. (n.d.). *Criminal law and managing children's behavior*. Accessed at www.justice.gc.ca/eng/rp-pr/cj-jp /fv-vf/mcb-cce/index.html on August 11, 2021.

Canfield, J., & Hansen, M. V. (1993). *Chicken soup for the soul: 101 stories to open the heart & rekindle the spirit*. Deerfield Beach, FL: Health Communications.

Canfield, J., & Hansen, M. V. (1996). *A 3rd serving of chicken soup for the soul: 101 more stories to open the heart and rekindle the spirit*. Deerfield Beach, FL: Health Communications.

Carnegie, D. (1937). *How to win friends and influence people*. New York: Simon & Schuster.

Chellappa, S. L., Steiner, R., Blattner, P., Oelhafen, P., Götz, T., & Cajochen, C. (2011). Non-visual effects of light on melatonin, alertness and cognitive performance: Can blue-enriched light keep us alert? *PLoS ONE, 6*(1). Accessed at https://pdfs.semantic scholar.org/bb2b/79cbc25edd5ee64263a692d8aaee34c815dc.pdf?_ga=2.149702706.560335669.1548903917–536850301 .1548903917 on June 8, 2021.

Cherry, K. (2019). *What is the negativity bias*? Accessed at www.verywellmind.com/negative-bias-4589618 on June 8, 2021.

Christian, D. (2018). *Origin story: A big history of everything*. New York: Little, Brown.

Christie, R., & Geis, F. L. (1970). *Studies in Machiavellianism*. New York: Academic Press.

Cialdini, R. B. (2007). *Influence: The psychology of persuasion* [Rev. ed.]. New York: HarperCollins.

Cialdini, R. B. (2016). *Pre-suasion: A revolutionary way to influence and persuade*. New York: Simon & Schuster.

Clear, J. (2018). *Atomic habits: An easy and proven way to build good habits and break bad ones*. New York: Avery.

Cohen, E. (2015). "All day, all week, Occupy Wall Street!": Space, biopower, and resistance. In S. Stapleton & A. Byers (Eds.), *Biopolitics and utopia: An interdisciplinary reader* (pp. 141–166). New York: Palgrave Macmillan.

Colburn, L., & Beggs, L. (2021). *The wraparound guide: How to gather student voice, build community partnerships, and cultivate hope*. Bloomington, IN: Solution Tree Press.

Conzemius, A. E., & O'Neill, J. (2014). *The handbook for SMART school teams: Revitalizing best practices for collaboration* (2nd ed.). Bloomington, IN: Solution Tree Press.

Cook, H. (2016). *The 'halo effect' that helps beautiful students get better marks*. Accessed at www.theage.com.au/national/victoria /the-halo-effect-that-helps-beautiful-students-get-better-marks-20160901-gr6l30.html on June 8, 2021.

Covey, S. R. (1989). *The seven habits of highly effective people: Restoring the character ethic*. New York: Simon & Schuster.

Covey, S. R. (2005). *The seven habits of highly effective people: Powerful lessons in personal change*. New York: Simon & Schuster.

Covey, S. R. (2020). *The seven habits of highly effective people: Powerful lessons in personal change* [30th anniversary ed.]. New York: Simon & Schuster.

Dadich, S. (Executive Producer). (2019). *Abstract: The art of design* [Television series]. Los Angeles: RadicalMedia/Tremolo Productions.

Daly, K., & Colson, L. (Producers), & Smith, C. (Director). (2021). *Operation varsity blues: The college admissions scandal [Documentary]*. Los Gatos, CA: Netflix. Accessed at www.netflix.com/watch/81130691?trackId=14277281&tctx=-97%2C -97%2C%2C%2C%2C on June 8, 2021.

Damasio, A. R. (1994). *Descartes' error: Emotion, reason, and the human brain*. New York: Putnam.

Damasio, A. R. (2005). *Descartes' error: Emotion, reason, and the human brain*. New York: Penguin.

Darwin, C. (1958). *On the origin of species by means of natural selection, or the preservation of favored races in the struggle for life*. New York: New American Library. (Original work published 1859)

de Mello, A. (1982). *The song of the bird*. New York: Doubleday.

Descartes, R. (1637). *Discourse on the method of rightly conducting the reason, and seeking truth in the sciences*. Accessed at www.gutenberg .org/files/59/59-h/59-h.htm on June 8, 2021.

Desmond, A. J. (n.d.). Charles Darwin: British naturalist. *Britannica*. Accessed at www.britannica.com/biography/Charles-Darwin on July 13, 2021.

Dobelli, R. (2013). *The art of thinking clearly*. New York: HarperCollins.

Dobbs, D. (2011). Teenage brains. *National Geographic, 20*(4), 37–59.

Donne, J. (1624). *No man is an island*. Accessed at www.commonlit.org/en/texts/no-man-is-an-island on July 13, 2021.

Dr. Seuss. (1968). *Horton hatches the egg*. New York: Random House Children's Basics.

DuFour, R., DuFour, R., Eaker, R., Many, T. W., & Mattos, M. (2016). *Learning by doing: A handbook for Professional Learning Communities at Work* (3rd ed.). Bloomington, IN: Solution Tree Press.

Duane, D. (2018). *How the startup mentality failed kids in San Francisco*. Accessed at www.wired.com/story/willie-brown-middle -school-startup-mentality-failed on June 8, 2021.

Duhigg, C. (2012). *The power of habit: Why we do what we do in life and business*. New York: Random House.

Duhigg, C. (2016, September 8). *The power of habit: Why we do what we do in life and business* [Video file]. Accessed at www.youtube .com/watch?v=szgoDIkimNU on June 8, 2021.

Dukes, R. L., & Albanesi, H. (2013). Seeing red: Quality of an essay, color of the grading pen, and student reactions to the grading process. *Social Science Journal, 50*(1), 96–100.

Dutton, K. (2011). *Split-second persuasion: The ancient art and new science of changing minds*. Boston: Houghton Mifflin Harcourt.

Dweck, C. S. (2016). *Mindset: The new psychology of success* (Updated ed.). New York: Ballantine Books.

Dyer, F. L., & Martin, T. C. (2006). *Edison: His life and inventions* [ebook]. New York: Harper & Brothers. (Original work published 1910) Accessed at www.gutenberg.org/files/820/820-h/820-h.htm on August 26, 2021.

The Economist. (2016, June 11). *Teaching the teachers*. Accessed at www.economist.com/news/briefing/21700385-great-teaching-has -long-been-seen-innate-skill-reformers-are-showing-best on June 15, 2021.

Eiseley, L. (1969). *The unexpected universe*. New York: Harcourt Brace Jovanovich.

Elliot, A. J. (2015). Color and psychological functioning: A review of theoretical and empirical work. *Frontiers in Psychology, 6*(368). Accessed at www.researchgate.net/publication/275049913_Color_and_psychological_functioning_A_reviewof_theoretical_and _empirical_work on June 8, 2021.

Elliot, A. J., Maier, M. A., Moller, A. C., Friedman, R., & Meinhardt, J. (2007). Color and psychological functioning: The effect of red on performance attainment. *Journal of Experimental Psychology, 136*(1), 154–168. Accessed at https://pubmed.ncbi.nlm.nih.gov /17324089 on June 8, 2021.

Emerson, R. W. (1903). *The complete works of Ralph Waldo Emerson: Essays* [2nd series, vol. 3]. Boston: Houghton Mifflin. (Original work published 1844) Accessed at https://quod.lib.umich.edu/e/emerson/4957107.0003.001/1:8?rgn=div1;view=fulltext on June 8, 2021.

Feinberg, W., & Soltis, J. F. (1992). *School and society* (2nd ed.). New York: Teachers College Press.

Ferreri, L., Bigand, E., & Bugaiska, A. (2015). The positive effect of music on source memory. *Musicae Scientiae, 19*(4), 402–411. Accessed at https://doi.org/10.1177/1029864915604684 on June 8, 2021.

Fields, J., & Weisberg, J. (Executive Producers). (2014). *The Americans* [Television series]. Los Angeles: Twentieth Century Fox Home Entertainment.

Fordham, D. R., & Hayes, D. C. (2009). Worth repeating: Paper color may have an effect on student performance. *Issues in Accounting Education, 24*(2), 187–194.

French, M. T., Robins, P. K., Homer, J. F., & Tapsell, L. M. (2009). Effects of physical attractiveness, personality, and grooming on academic performance in high school. *Labour Economics, 16*(4), 373–382. Accessed at DOI: 10.1016/j.labeco.2009.01.001 on June 8, 2021.

FRESH Movie Trailers. (2015, April 9). *Jurassic World "I don't control the raptors" movie clip # 1* [Video file]. Accessed at www.youtube.com/watch?v=jzA1FSIG1ZQ on June 8, 2021.

Friedman, H. S., Prince, L. M., Riggio, R. E., & DiMatteo, M. R. (1980). Understanding and assessing nonverbal expressiveness: The affective communication test. *Journal of Personality and Social Psychology, 39*(2), 333–351.

Frimer, J. A., Skitka, L., & Motyl, M. (2017). Liberals and conservatives are similarly motivated to avoid exposure to one another's opinions. *Journal of Experimental Social Psychology, 72*, 1–12. Accessed at https://pdfs.semanticscholar.org/14a8/0ae14fdfb8c7ea115 373bfee39812d0f03e9.pdf?_ga=2.81267475.504010076.1544109833–1122966822.1544109833 on June 8, 2021.

Fry, H. (2021, March 29). What data can't do. *The New Yorker.* Accessed at www.newyorker.com/magazine/2021/03/29/what-data -cant-do on August 10, 2021.

Galef, J. (2016, April 4). *Why "scout mindset" is crucial to good judgment* [Video file]. Accessed at www.youtube.com/watch?v=3MYEt Q5Zdn8 on June 8, 2021.

Gardner, B., Lally, P., & Wardle, J. (2012). Making health habitual: The psychology of 'habit-formation' and general practice. *British Journal of General Practice, 62*, 664–666.

Gardner, B., & Rebar, A. (2019). *Habit formation and behavior change.* Accessed at https://oxfordre.com/psychology/view/10.1093 /acrefore/9780190236557.001.0001/acrefore-9780190236557-e-129 on August 28, 2021.

Geggel, L. (2019). *Jesus wasn't the only man to be crucified. Here's the history behind this brutal practice.* Accessed at www.livescience.com /65283-crucifixion-history.html on August 11, 2021.

Gershoff, E., & Font, S. A. (2016). Corporal punishment in U. S. public schools: Prevalence, disparities in use, and status in state and federal policy. *Society for Research in Child Development, 30*(1). Accessed at www.researchgate.net/publication /322568694_Corporal_Punishment_in_US_Public_Schools_Prevalence_Disparities_in_Use_and_Status_in_State_and_Federal _Policy on June 8, 2021.

Gladwell, M. (2002). *The tipping point: How little things can make a big difference.* Boston: Back Bay Books.

Gladwell, M. (2007). *Blink: The power of thinking without thinking.* New York: Back Bay Books.

Gladwell, M. (2009). *What the dog saw and other adventures.* New York: Little, Brown.

Gladwell, M. (2013). *David and Goliath: Underdogs, misfits, and the art of battling giants.* New York: Little, Brown.

Gladwell, M. (2018). *The future of humanity* [Video file]. Accessed at www.youtube.com/watch?v=leRRAvnDc6s on June 8, 2021.

Gladwell, M. (2019). *Talking to strangers: What we should know about the people we don't know.* New York: Little, Brown.

Goldstein, N. J., Martin, S. J., & Cialdini, R. B. (2008). *Yes! 50 scientifically proven ways to be persuasive.* New York: Free Press.

Grafwallner, P. (2021). *Not yet . . . and that's OK: How productive struggle fosters student learning.* Bloomington, IN: Solution Tree Press.

Greene, R. (1998). *The 48 laws of power.* New York: Viking.

Groopman, J. (2019, October 28). Can brain science help us break bad habits? *The New Yorker.* Accessed at www.newyorker.com /magazine/2019/10/28/can-brain-science-help-us-break-bad-habits on June 8, 2021.

Haidt, J. (2001). The emotional dog and its rational tail: A social intuitionist approach to moral judgment. *Psychological Review, 108*(4), 814–834.

Haidt, J. (2006). *The happiness hypothesis: Finding modern truth in ancient wisdom.* New York: Basic Books.

Haidt, J. (2012). *The righteous mind: Why good people are divided by politics and religion.* New York: Pantheon Books.

Haley, K. J., & Fessler, D. M. T. (2005). Nobody's watching? Subtle cues affect generosity in an anonymous economic game. *Evolution and Human Behavior, 26*(3), 245–256.

Hall, A., & Barrett, L. (2007). *Influence: The essence of leadership.* Accessed at http://extensionpublications.unl.edu/assets/pdf/g1695 .pdf on June 8, 2021.

Hamachek, D. (1995). Self-concept and school achievement: Interaction dynamics and a tool for assessing the self-concept component. *Journal of Counseling & Development, 73*(4), 419–425.

Hamblin, J. (2019, September 29). The most dangerous way to lose yourself. *The Atlantic.* Accessed at www.theatlantic.com/health /archive/2019/09/identity-fusion-trump-allegiance/598699 on June 8, 2021.

Hanushek, E. (2010). The difference is great teachers. In K. Weber (Ed.), *Waiting for "Superman": How we can save America's failing public schools* (pp. 81–103). New York: Participant Media. Accessed at https://hanushek.stanford.edu/sites/default/files/publications /Hanushek%202010%20Superman.pdf on June 8, 2021.

Hanushek, E. (2018). Education reform. In S. W. Atlas et al. (Eds.), *Economic policy challenges facing California's next governor* (pp. 19–23). California: Hoover Institution. Accessed at www.hoover.org/sites/default/files/research/docs/ economicpolicychallengescalifornia_ohanian_hooverinstitution_10-2018_updated .pdf on September 30, 2021.

Harari, Y. N. (2017). *Homo deus: A brief history of tomorrow.* New York: Harper.

Harari, Y. N. (2018). *21 lessons for the 21st century.* New York: Spiegel & Grau.

Harvard Health Publishing. (2020). *Understanding the stress response.* Accessed at www.health.harvard.edu/staying-healthy /understanding-the-stress-response on June 16, 2021.

Hatfield, E., Cacioppo, J. T., & Rapson, R. L. (1994). *Emotional contagion.* New York: Cambridge University Press.

Hattie, J., & Timperley, H. (2007). The power of feedback. *Review of Educational Research, 77*(1), 81–112.

Hawking, S. (2018). *Brief answers to the big questions.* New York: Bantam Books.

Heid, M. (2018). The blueprint for changing your habits. In *The power of habits: Start good ones, break bad ones, change your life* (pp. 68–71). New York: TIME Books.

Hernández-Julián, R., & Peters, C. (2017). Student appearance and academic performance. *Journal of Human Capital, 11*(2), 247–262.

Hoffman, M. (Director). (2002). *The emperor's club* [Motion picture]. United States: Universal Pictures.

Holiday, R., & Hanselman, S. (2016). *The daily stoic: 366 meditations on wisdom, perseverance, and the art of living.* New York: Portfolio.

Iminvestorsworld. (2015, April 23). *We all abide by "Henry's rule"* [Blog post]. Accessed at https://lminvestorsworldwide.wordpress .com/2015/04/23/we-all-abide-by-henrys-rule on June 14, 2021.

Inglis-Arkell, E. (2013). *The experiment that led to the concept of "thinking outside the box."* Accessed at https://io9.gizmodo.com /the-experiment-that-led-to-the-concept-of-thinking-out-1463883774 on June 8, 2021.

Ito, T., & Cacioppo, J. T. (2005). Variations on a human universal: Individual differences in positivity offset and negativity bias. *Cognition and Emotion, 19*(1), 1–26. Accessed at www.researchgate.net/publication/237934035_Variations_on_a_Human _Universal_Individual_Differences_in_Positivity_Offset_and_Negativity_bias on June 8, 2021.

Iyengar, S. (2010). *The art of choosing.* New York: Twelve.

Izzard, E. (2010). *Eddie Izzard "cake or death" sketch from Dress to Kill* [Video file]. Accessed at www.youtube.com/watch?v=PVH0g ZO5lq0 on June 8, 2021.

Jensen, E. (2019). *Poor students, rich teaching: Seven high-impact mindsets for students from poverty* (Rev. ed.). Bloomington, IN: Solution Tree Press.

Jonason, P. K., & Webster, G. D. (2010). The dirty dozen: A concise measure of the dark triad. *Psychological Assessment, 22*(2), 420–432.

Kahneman, D. (2011a). *"Focusing illusions" and the myth of California happiness* [Video file]. Accessed at www.youtube.com/watch?v =DMi9g4mkY04 on June 8, 2021.

Kahneman, D. (2011b). *Thinking, fast and slow* (7th ed.). Toronto, Ontario, Canada: Doubleday Canada.

Kahneman, D., Krueger, A. B., Schkade, D., Schwarz, N., & Stone, A. A. (2006). *Would you be happier if you were richer? A focusing illusion.* Accessed at www.morgenkommichspaeterrein.de/ressources/download/125krueger.pdf on June 8, 2021.

Kang, H. J., & Williamson, V. J. (2014). Background music can aid second language learning. *Psychology of Music*, *42*(5), 728–747.

Kaplan, J. T., Gimbel, S. I., & Harris, S. (2016). Neural correlates of maintaining one's political beliefs in the face of counterevidence. *Scientific Reports*, *6*(39589). Accessed at www.nature.com/articles/srep39589 on June 8, 2021.

Kaptchuk, T. J., Friedlander, E., Kelley, J. M., Sanchez, M. N., Kokkotou, E., Singer, J. P., et al. (2010). Placebos without deception: A randomized controlled trial in irritable bowel syndrome. *PLoS One*, *5*(12). Accessed at https://journals.plos.org/plosone/article?id=10.1371/journal.pone.0015591 on June 8, 2021.

Keckeisen, G. (2002). The Korean War 'brainwashing' myth led to U.S. countertechniques against communist indoctrination. *Military History*, *19*(3), 70–72.

Kluger, J. (2018). How to tame the wild inside you. In *The power of habits: Start good ones, break bad ones, change your life* (pp. 11–21). New York: TIME Books.

Koerner, B. (2019). How cities reshape the evolutionary path of urban wildlife. *Wired*, *26*(11), 72–85.

Kohn, A. (1993). *Punished by rewards: The trouble with gold stars, incentive plans, A's, praise, and other bribes*. Boston: Houghton Mifflin.

Kolbert, E. (2017, February 27). Why facts don't change our minds. *The New Yorker*. Accessed at www.newyorker.com/magazine/2017/02/27/why-facts-dont-change-our-minds on June 9, 2021.

Kotler, S. (2021). *The art of impossible: A peak performance primer*. New York: HarperCollins.

Kozinski, W. (2017). *The Reid interrogation technique and false confessions: A time for change*. Accessed at https://papers.ssrn.com/sol3/papers.cfm?abstract_id=3002338 on June 9, 2021.

Kraft, T. L., & Pressman, S. D. (2012). Grin and bear it: The influence of manipulated facial expression on the stress response. *Psychological Science*, *23*(11). Accessed at www.researchgate.net/publication/231211974_Grin_and_Bear_It_The_Influence_of_Manipulated_Facial_Expression_on_the_Stress_Response on August 28, 2021.

Kurke, L. B. (2004). *The wisdom of Alexander the Great: Enduring leadership lessons from the man who created an empire*. New York: American Management Association.

Lambert, B. (2018, November 19). *Chris Voss's tactical empathy: 6 reflective listening skills combined* [Video file]. Accessed at www.youtube.com/watch?v=wQwP4j0AqmU on June 9, 2021.

Leary, M. (2018). *Why you are who you are: Investigations into human personality*. Chantilly, VA: The Great Courses.

Lebowitz, S., Akhtar, A., & Ward, M. (2020). *61 cognitive biases that screw up everything we do*. Accessed at www.businessinsider.com/cognitive-biases-2015–10 on June 9, 2021.

Lecky, P., & Thorne, F. (Ed.). (1945). *Self-consistency: A theory of personality*. New York: Island Press.

Levine, T. (2020). *Duped: Truth-default theory and the social science of lying and deception*. Tuscaloosa, AL: University of Alabama Press.

Levitt, S. D., & Dubner, S. J. (2005). *Freakonomics: A rogue economist explores the hidden side of everything*. New York: William Morrow.

Levitt, S. D., & Dubner, S. J. (2014). *Think like a freak: The authors of* Freakonomics *offer to retrain your brain*. New York: William Morrow.

Levitt, S. D., & Dubner, S. J. (2015). *When to rob a bank: . . . And 131 more warped suggestions and well-intended rants*. New York: William Morrow.

Lewis, M. (2017). *The undoing project: A friendship that changed our minds*. New York: W. W. Norton.

Linsin, M. (2016). *The happy teacher habits: 11 habits of the happiest, most effective teachers on earth*. San Diego, CA: JME Publishing.

Lombardi, L., & Joshua, E. (Eds.). (2020). *The science of emotions* (TIME special ed.). New York: Meredith Corporation.

Los Angeles Times. (n.d.). *Full coverage: The college admissions scheme*. Accessed at www.latimes.com/california/story/la-me-college-admissions-storygallery on August 10, 2021.

Lukianoff, G., & Haidt, J. (2018). *The coddling of the American mind: How good intentions and bad ideas are setting up a generation for failure*. New York: Penguin Press.

Lynn, M. (2003). *Mega tips: Scientifically tested techniques to increase your tips*. Accessed at https://ecommons.cornell.edu/bitstream/handle/1813/71300/Mega_Tips.pdf?sequence=1&isAllowed=y on July 27, 2021.

Machiavelli, N. (2016). *The prince* (N. H. Thomson, Trans.; original work published 1532). Accessed at Digireads.com on November 30, 2021.

MacLellan, L. (2018). *You can be a better negotiator just by listening for verbal tells.* Accessed at https://qz.com/work/1283784/how-to -negotiate-anything-the-common-verbal-tells-worth-listening-for on June 9, 2021.

Maddux, W. W., Mullen, E., & Galinsky, A. D. (2008). Chameleons bake bigger pies and take bigger pieces: Strategic behavioral mimicry facilitates negotiation outcomes. *Journal of Experimental Social Psychology, 44*(2), 461–468.

Malouff, J. M., & Thorsteinsson, E. B. (2016). Bias in grading: A meta-analysis of experimental research findings. *Australian Journal of Education, 60*(3), 245–256.

Maron, D. F. (2018). *Under poaching pressure, elephants are evolving to lose their tusks.* Accessed at www.nationalgeographic.com /animals/2018/11/wildlife-watch-news-tuskless-elephants-behavior-change on June 14, 2021.

Marshall, M. (2016, July 7). *A placebo can work even when you know it's a placebo* [Blog post]. Accessed at www.health.harvard.edu/ blog/placebo-can-work-even-know-placebo-201607079926 on June 14, 2021.

Martin, J. (2015). Working the crowd: Behavior management through strategic classroom arrangement. *Journal of Instructional Research, 4,* 52–56.

Maslow, A. H. (1943). A theory of human motivation. *Psychological Review, 50*(4), 370–396. Accessed at http://citeseerx.ist.psu.edu /viewdoc/download?doi=10.1.1.318.2317&rep=rep1&type=pdf on June 14, 2021.

MathRaps. (n.d.). *The Rappin' Mathematician decimals* [Video file]. Accessed at www.youtube.com/watch?v=V6pZyY6mM3g on August 26, 2021.

McGlone, M. S., & Tofighbakhsh, J. (2000). Birds of a feather flock conjointly: Rhyme as reason in aphorisms. *Psychological Science, 11*(5), 424–428.

McIntyre, G., & Blanchard, A. (Executive Producers). (2012). *Born to be good?* [Documentary]. Toronto, Ontario, Canada: Stormy Nights Productions.

Meacham, J. (2018). *The soul of America: The battle for our better angels.* New York: Random House.

Merriam-Webster. (n.d.). Placebo. In *Merriam-Webster.com dictionary.* Accessed at www.merriam-webster.com/words-at-play/placebo -word-origin on August 22, 2021.

Miller, R. (2017). *Arthur Miller: Writer* [Documentary]. United States: HBO Documentary Films.

Mitchell, S. (1988). *Tao te ching: A new English version.* New York: HarperCollins.

Munro, A. (1968). *Boys and girls.* Accessed at www.giuliotortello.it/shortstories/boys_and_girls.pdf on June 14, 2021.

Murat, L. (2014). *The man who thought he was Napoleon: Toward a political history of madness.* Chicago: University of Chicago Press.

MyFootage.com. (2018). *1968 Vietnam protests* [Video file]. Accessed at www.youtube.com/watch?v=16Z670bdH9k on August 26, 2021.

National Education Association. (2020). *Code of ethics for educators.* Accessed at www.nea.org/home/30442.htm on June 14, 2021.

News 12 Staff. (2018, November 30). *Christmas ruined? Teacher upsets students by saying Santa isn't real.* Accessed at https://newjersey .news12.com/christmas-ruined-teacher-upsets-students-by-saying-santa-isnt-real-39569563 on August 11, 2021.

Nietzsche, F. (1974). *The gay science: With a prelude in rhymes and an appendix of songs* (W. Kaufmann, Trans.). New York: Vintage Books. (Original work published 1878) Accessed at https://philoslugs.files.wordpress.com/2016/12/the-gay-science-friedrich -nietzsche.pdf on June 14, 2021.

Nossiter, B. D. (1978, June 11). Ring of clumsy forgers finally ends two-year run. *The Washington Post.* Accessed at www.washingtonpost.com/archive/business/1978/06/11/ring-of-clumsy-forgers-finally-ends-2-year-run/bbd7f20b-d13d-4cd6 -901b-5d68eb6e62a7/ on June 16, 2021.

Open-Source Pyschometrics Project. (n.d.a). *Dark triad personality test.* Accessed at https://openpsychometrics.org/tests/SD3 on November 8, 2021.

Open-Source Pyschometrics Project. (n.d.b). *MACH-IV: Machiavellianism test.* Accessed at https://openpsychometrics.org/tests /MACH-IV on November 8, 2021.

Ortberg, J. (2017). *I'd like you more if you were more like me: Getting real about getting close.* Carol Stream, IL: Tyndale House Publishers.

Papaeti, A. (2020). *On music, torture and detention: Reflections on issues of research and discipline. Transposition, 2.* Accessed at https://journals.openedition.org/transposition/pdf/5289 on August 6, 2021.

Paris, O. (2021). *From the archives: A brief history of film music.* Accessed at www.filmindependent.org/blog/know-score-brief-history-film-music on August 6, 2021.

Pattillo, A. (2020). *Emotional contagion: How humans catch and spread feelings without ever knowing.* Accessed at www.inverse.com/mind-body/emotional-contagion-catch-feelings on June 14, 2021.

Peterson, J. B. (2018). *Twelve rules for life: An antidote to chaos.* Toronto, Ontario, Canada: Random House Canada.

Peterson, J. B. (2021). *Beyond order: Twelve more rules for life.* New York: Penguin.

Pierson, R. (2013). *Every kid needs a champion* [Video file]. Accessed at www.ted.com/talks/rita_pierson_every_kid_needs_a_champion on June 14, 2021.

Pink, D. H. (2009a). *Drive: The surprising truth about what motivates us.* New York: Riverhead Books.

Pink, D. H. (2009b). *The puzzle of motivation* [Video file]. Accessed at www.youtube.com/watch?v=rrkrvAUbU9Y on June 14, 2021.

Pink, D. H. (2012). *To sell is human: The surprising truth about moving others.* New York: Riverhead Books.

Pink, D. H. (2018). *When: The scientific secrets of perfect timing.* New York: Riverhead Books.

Przybylski, A. K., Murayama, K., DeHaan, C. R., & Gladwell, V. (2013). Motivational, emotional, and behavioral correlates of fear of missing out. *Computers in Human Behavior, 29*(4), 1841–1848.

Ramakrishna, S. (n.d.). *Hiss you may, but bite you shall not.* Accessed at www.ramakrishnavivekananda.info/parables/1_files/1-189.html on August 11, 2021.

Raths, L. E., Harmin, M., & Simon, S. B. (1966). *Values and teaching: Working with values in the classroom.* Columbus, OH: C. E. Merrill Books.

Read, K., Macauley, M., & Furay, E. (2014). The Seuss boost: Rhyme helps children retain words from shared storybook reading. *First Language, 34*(4), 354–371.

Reid, J. (2014). The Reid Technique. In B. C. Jayne & J. P. Buckley (Eds.), *The investigator anthology: A compilation of articles and essays about the Reid Technique of interviewing and interrogation* (2nd ed.). Chicago: John E. Reid & Associates. Accessed https://reid.com/resources/critics-corner/ch-1-the-reid-technique on August 12, 2021.

Reiss, M. B. (2010). *Negotiating with evil: When to talk to terrorists.* New York: Open Road Integrated Media.

Repeal 43 Committee. (n.d.). *Why we advocate repeal.* Accessed at www.repeal43.org/why-we-advocate-repeal on August 11, 2021.

Ripley, D. (in press). What makes a teacher great? *Canadian Teacher Magazine.*

Ripley, D. (2019). *The successful teacher's survival kit: 83 simple things that successful teachers do to thrive in the classroom.* Lanham, MD: Rowman & Littlefield.

Robinson, C. D., Gallus, J., Lee, M. G., & Rogers, T. (2021). The demotivating effect (and unintended message) of awards. *Organizational Behavior and Human Decision Processes, 163*, 51–64. Accessed at doi: 10.1016/j.obhdp.2019.03.006 on June 15, 2021.

Rolheiser, R. (2018). *Wrestling with God: Finding hope and meaning in our daily struggles to be human.* New York: Image.

Ronfeldt, M., Loeb, S., & Wyckoff, J. (2013). How teacher turnover harms student achievement. *American Educational Research Journal, 50*(1), 4–36.

Rosling, H. (2018). *Factfulness: Ten reasons we're wrong about the world—and why things are better than you think.* New York: Flatiron Books.

Rowe, M. B. (1972). Wait-time and rewards as instructional variables, their influence on language, logic, and fate control: Part one—wait-time. *Journal of Research in Science Teaching, 11*(2), 81–94. Accessed at http://eric.ed.gov/?id=ED061103 on June 15, 2021.

The Royal Swedish Academy of Sciences. (2017). *The prize in economic sciences 2017* [Press release]. Accessed at www.nobelprize.org/uploads/2018/06/press-43.pdf on August 12, 2021.

Samson, A., & Ramani, P. (2018, August 27). *Finding the right nudge for your clients.* Accessed at www.investmentnews.com/article/20180827/BLOG09/180829939/finding-the-right-nudge-for-your-clients on August 12, 2021.

Schenk, T. (2012). *Negotiation and neuroscience: Possible lessons for negotiation instruction.* Accessed at www.pon.harvard.edu/research _projects/negotiation-pedagogy-program-on-negotiation/negotiation-and-neuroscience-possible-lessons-for-negotiation-instruction on June 15, 2021.

Scott, R. (Director). (2007). *Blade runner: The final cut* [Motion picture]. United States: Warner Brothers.

Scott, R. (Director). (2017). *All the money in the world* [Motion picture]. United States: Imperative Entertainment & Scott Free Productions.

Seinfeld, J. (2017). *Night guy, morning guy, day guy* [Video file]. Accessed at www.youtube.com/watch?v=UEe2pN8oksc on June 15, 2021.

Seuss, D. (1968). *Horton hatches the egg.* New York: Random House.

Shakespeare, W. (2005). *Macbeth.* New Haven, CT: Yale University Press. (Original work published 1606)

Shatner Method. (2016, November 19). *Peanuts' teacher calls out Charlie Brown & Linus - "Wah wa wa wah wa wa" - 1969* [Video file]. Accessed at www.youtube.com/watch?v=CxC_AjFxS68 on June 14, 2021.

Shi, J., Zhang, C., & Jiang, F. (2014). Does red undermine individual intellectual performance? A test in China. *International Journal of Psychology, 50*(1), 81–84. Accessed at https://onlinelibrary.wiley.com/doi/full/10.1002/ijop.12076 on June 15, 2021.

Simon, D., Colesberry, R. F., & Noble, N. K. (Executive Producers). (2002–2008). *The wire* [Television series]. New York: Home Box Office.

Sorkin, A., Rudin, S., Poul, A., Liberstein, P., & Biggs, D. (Executive Producers). (2012). *The newsroom* [Television series]. London: Home Box Office & Warner Home Video.

Sullivan, B. (2019). *Why we like what we like: A scientist's surprising findings.* Accessed at www.nationalgeographic.com/science/2019 /08/why-we-like-what-we-like-a-scientists-surprising-findings on June 15, 2021.

Swann, W. B., Jr., Gomez, A., Seyle, D. C., Morales, J. F., & Huici, C. (2009). Identity fusion: The interplay of personal and social identities in extreme group behavior. *Journal of Personality and Social Psychology, 96*(5), 995–1011.

Taleb, N. N. (2008). *What is a "black swan?" [Video file].* Accessed at www.youtube.com/watch?v=BDbuJtAiABA on June 15, 2021.

Taylor, T. (Director). (2011). *The help* [Motion picture]. United States: DreamWorks.

Telg, B., Jones, J., & Barnes, C. (2016). *Break your invisible chains: Own the power of your story.* Gainesville, FL: Self Narrate.

Thaler, R. H., & Sunstein, C. R. (2008). *Nudge: Improving decisions about health, wealth, and happiness.* New Haven, CT: Yale University Press.

Thoma, M. V., La Marca, R., Brönnimann, R., Finkel, L., Ehlert, U., & Nater, U. M. (2013). The effect of music on the human stress response. *PLoS One, 8*(8), e70156. Accessed at https://journals.plos.org/plosone/article?id=10.1371/journal.pone.0070156 on August 6, 2021.

Tillmann, B., & Dowling, W. J. (2007). Memory decreases for prose, but not for poetry. *Memory & Cognition, 35*, 628–639. Accessed at https://doi.org/10.3758/BF03193301 on June 16, 2021.

Todorov, A. (2017). *Face value: The irresistible influence of first impressions.* Princeton, NJ: Princeton University Press.

Trevorrow, C. (Director). (2015). *Jurassic world* [Motion picture]. United States: Universal Pictures.

Twenge, J. M. (2017). *iGEN: Why today's super-connected kids are growing up less rebellious, more tolerant, less happy—and completely unprepared for adulthood—and what that means for the rest of us.* New York: Atria Books.

U.S. Departments of Education, Health and Human Services, Housing and Urban Development, & Justice. (2015). *Every student, every day: A community toolkit to address and eliminate chronic absenteeism.* Accessed at www2.ed.gov/about/inits/ed/chronic absenteeism/toolkit.pdf on August 4, 2021.

Van Zant, A. B., & Berger, J. (2019). How the voice persuades. *Journal of Personality and Social Psychology, 118*(4). Accessed at https://faculty.wharton.upenn.edu/wp-content/uploads/2019/01/Voice-Persuades.pdf on June 16, 2021.

Vecchi, G. M., Van Hasselt, V. B., & Romano, S. J. (2005). Crisis (hostage) negotiation: Current strategies and issues in high-risk conflict resolution. *Aggression and Violent Behavior, 10*(5), 533–551.

Vernon, J. L. (2017). Understanding the butterfly effect. *American Scientist, 105*(3), 130. Accessed at www.americanscientist.org /article/understanding-the-butterfly-effect on June 16, 2021.

Villeneuve, D. (Director). (2017). *Blade runner 2049* [Motion picture]. United States: Columbia Pictures.

von Neumann, J., & Morgenstern, O. (2004). *Theory of games and economic behavior* (60th anniversary ed.). Princeton, NJ: Princeton University Press. (Original work published 1944)

Visible Learning. (n.d.). *John Hattie: "Think of feedback that is received not given."* Accessed at https://visible-learning.org/2013/01/john-hattie-visible-learning-interview on September 30, 2021.

Voss, C. (2016). *Never split the difference: Negotiating as if your life depended on it.* New York: HarperCollins.

Voss, C. (2018). *Mastering the art of negotiation* [Video file]. Accessed at https://londonreal.tv/e/chris-voss on June 16, 2021.

Voss, C. (2019). *An FBI negotiator's secret to winning any exchange* [Video file]. Accessed at www.youtube.com/watch?v=llctqNJr2IU on June 16, 2021.

WD-40 Company. (n.d.). *Take a trip through WD-40 Company history.* Accessed at www.wd40company.com/our-company/our-history on August 24, 2021.

Weaver, A., Scherer, P., Hengen, S., & Shriver, M. D. (2020). An exploratory investigation of proximity control in a large-group unstructured setting. *Preventing School Failure: Alternative Education for Children and Youth, 64*(3), 261–270.

Weger, U. W., & Loughnan, S. (2013). Mobilizing unused resources: Using the placebo concept to enhance cognitive performance. *Quarterly Journal of Experimental Psychology, 66*(1), 23–28.

Wehby, J. H., & Lane, K. L. (2009). Proactive instructional strategies for classroom management. In A. Akin-Little, S. G. Little, M. A. Bray, & T. J. Kehle (Eds.), *Behavioral interventions in schools: Evidence-based positive strategies* (pp. 141–156). Washington, DC: American Psychological Association.

Weiss, J., Donigian, A., & Hughes, J. (2018). Extreme negotiations. In *On mental toughness: Harvard Business Review's 10 must reads.* Cambridge, MA: Harvard Business Publishing.

Wisniewski, B., Zierer, K., & Hattie, J. (2020). The power of feedback revisited: A meta-analysis of educational feedback research. *Frontiers in Psychology, 10*(3087). Accessed at www.ncbi.nlm.nih.gov/pmc/articles/PMC6987456 on August 28, 2021.

Willis, J., & Todorov, A. (2006). First impressions: Making up your mind after a 100-ms exposure to a face. *Psychological Science, 17*(7), 592–598.

Wooden, J. (1997). *Wooden: A lifetime of observations and reflections on and off the court.* Lincolnwood, IL: Contemporary Books.

Wright, R. (1995). *The moral animal: Why we are the way we are—The new science of evolutionary psychology.* New York: Vintage Books.

Young, J. W. (1944). *The diary of an ad man: The war years June 1, 1942-December 31, 1943.* Chicago: Advertising Publications.

Zhong, C.-B., Bohns, V., & Gino, F. (2010). Good lamps are the best police. *Psychological Science, 2*(3), 311–314.

INDEX

Motivating Students Who Don't Care, Second Edition
Allen N. Mendler
In the second edition of this valuable resource, Allen Mendler offers specific, practical strategies on how to reignite enthusiasm in even the most unmotivated students. Learn classroom and behavior management strategies that will help support struggling students and build positive teacher-student relationships.
BKF970

Every Student, Every Day
Kristyn Klei Borrero
No-Nonsense Nurturers® are educators who build life-altering relationships with students and hold themselves and their students accountable for achievement. *Every Student, Every Day* details the lessons, mindsets, beliefs, and strategies these high-performing teachers use daily to support the needs of every student.
BKF843

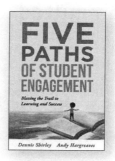

Five Paths of Student Engagement
Dennis Shirley and Andy Hargreaves
Join the authors on a profound educational quest that will take you through exciting and challenging terrain. *Five Paths of Student Engagement* will open your eyes, heart, and mind and empower you to implement practices that lead directly to your students' well-being, learning, and success.
BKF707

Owning It
Alex Kajitani
Today's fast-changing culture presents a great challenge—and a great opportunity—in schools and in the teaching profession. With *Owning It*, you will discover an array of easy-to-implement strategies designed to help you excel in your classroom, at your school, and in your community.
BKF835

Behavior Solutions
John Hannigan, Jessica Djabrayan Hannigan, Mike Mattos, and Austin Buffum
Take strategic action to close the systemic behavior gap with *Behavior Solutions*. This user-friendly resource outlines how to utilize the PLC at Work® and RTI at Work™ processes to create a three-tiered system of supports that is collaborative, research-based, and practical.
BKF891

Solution Tree | Press   *a division of* Solution Tree

Visit SolutionTree.com or call 800.733.6786 to order.

Wait! Your professional development journey doesn't have to end with the last pages of this book.

We realize improving student learning doesn't happen overnight. And your school or district shouldn't be left to puzzle out all the details of this process alone.

No matter where you are on the journey, we're committed to helping you get to the next stage.

Take advantage of everything from **custom workshops** to **keynote presentations** and **interactive web and video conferencing**. We can even help you develop an action plan tailored to fit your specific needs.

Let's get the conversation started.

Call 888.763.9045 today.

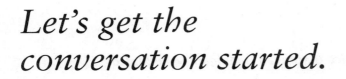

SolutionTree.com